THE HEGEMONY OF INTERNATIONAL BUSINESS 1945–1970

Other titles in the series, *The Rise of International Business*

The Emergence of International Business 1200–1800
Selected and with a new introduction by Mark Casson

The Evolution of International Business 1800–1945
Selected and with a new introduction by Mark Casson

THE HEGEMONY OF INTERNATIONAL BUSINESS 1945–1970

Volume 7

Mark Casson

American Direct Investment in
the Netherlands Industry

Frank Stubenitsky

London and New York

First published 1970 by Rotterdam University Press
Reprinted 2001
by Routledge
11 New Fetter Lane, London EC4P 4EE

Simultaneously published in the USA and Canada
by Routledge
29 West 35th Street, New York, NY 10001

Routledge is an imprint of the Taylor & Francis Group

© 1970 Universitaire Pers Rotterdam

Typeset in Times by Keystroke, Jacaranda Lodge, Wolverhampton
Printed and bound in Great Britain by
Antony Rowe Ltd, Chippenham, Wiltshire

British Library Cataloguing in Publication Data
A catalogue record for this book is available from the British Library

Library of Congress Cataloging in Publication Data
A catalog record for this book has been requested

ISBN 0–415–19038–X (set)
ISBN 0–415–19045–2 (volume 7)

Publisher's Note
The publisher has gone to great lengths to ensure the quality of these
reprints, but wishes to point out that certain characteristics of the
original copies will, of necessity, be apparent in reprints thereof.

Disclaimer
The publishers have made every effort to contact the copyright
holders of works reprinted in *The Hegemony of International Business
1945–1970*. This has not been possible in every case, however, and
we would welcome correspondence from those individuals we have
been unable to trace.

American direct investment in the Netherlands industry

A survey of the year 1966

Frank Stubenitsky

Rotterdam University Press/1970

Contents

Preface

My interest in direct investment dates from the second year at Berkeley when I was attending courses in the theory of international trade by Professors Tibor Scitovsky and John M. Letiche. Subsequent seminars by Professors Letiche and Bo Sodersten were decisive for my choice of the dissertation topic.

Strangely enough the present study is the result of difficulties I encountered in obtaining adequate data for my first subject choice. An attempt to construct a model of US direct investments in the EEC countries stranded on the inaccessability of data collected by the US Department of Commerce on these investments. I subsequently discovered that the Commerce Department is the only source of information on these direct investments. Virtually no country collects data on American investments in their respective economies, and where information is gathered it is incomplete.

Following the example of John H. Dunning for the UK and Donald R. Brash for Australia I decided to conduct a survey of US direct investment in the Netherlands. Questionnaires were sent to subsidiaries of American companies operating in the Netherlands by the end of 1966. Thanks to the gratifying cooperation of these subsidiaries much useful data is now available concerning the American investments in manufacturing and petroleum sectors in the Netherlands.

Although the information contained in the returned questionnaires allows one to assess the magnitude of US direct investment in the Netherlands, a word of caution is in order. The response to the survey, though quite good, is not 100 percent. Furthermore, the type of data collected cannot be used in a test of investment models. The analysis therefore is of a qualitative nature, supported by evidence from the questionnaires and data published by the US Department of Commerce.

In view of the private nature of the survey I did not attempt to collect information on profits, pricing policies and determinants for investment overseas. A formal inquiry, supported for example by the Netherlands

Bureau of Statistics, might well be able to fill these data gaps, at the same time achieving a more complete coverage.

Acknowledgment

In growing up I incurred a debt to many, and the happy ending of my enjoyable and interesting study years, both in Amsterdam and Berkeley, presents itself as an excellent opportunity to show gratitude.

Most of all I want to thank my wife Ellen, my parents, and my longtime comrade Edy Bonsel. A study friend of Amsterdam days, Henk Demper, kept me informed of Dutch developments.

Economically speaking I am indebted to my professors of the University of Amsterdam and the University of California, at Berkeley. In particular I want to mention Professors John M. Letiche, Richard H. Holton and Ralph Miller for advice and support at all stages of the dissertation.

A Ford International Fellowship brought me to Berkeley, and the Institute of International Studies acted as the generous provider during the time of dissertation research and writing.

In the final analysis, procuring adequate typing services presented itself as an almost insurmountable problem, until our friend Marion Hixon decided enough time has been wasted, and simply took over.

All these, and many others unnamed, I thank. To her who is dearest to me, and our son Jaap, I dedicate this study.

WASHINGTON, DC, *September 1969*   F.S.

Summary

The contribution of this publication lies in (1) formulation of the theory of direct investment, and (2) collection by questionnaire of data on American manufacturing enterprises in the Netherlands.

The theory of international capital movements fails to explain direct investments, although it is useful for the analysis of portfolio investments. The theory of direct investment developed here uses the concept of a *multinational corporation*, guided in its actions at home and abroad, by the objective of *sales maximization*, subject to a *profit constraint*. Within this framework two types of direct investment can be distinguished, 'positive' and 'defensive'. Positive investments are investments in response to higher sales and/or profit opportunities abroad, based on, e.g., new product lines, superior technology or better management. Defensive investments result from threats to existing sales and/or profit positions of the enterprise. Such threats are embodied in, e.g., formation of a common market, government policy towards import substitution, or trade restrictions generally. A special case exists where oligopolistic interdependencies in home markets force oligopoly members into 'follow-the-leader' reactions abroad.

Explicit formulation of the theory leads to a number of characteristics of direct investments. These relate to overseas operations of multinational corporations, such as degree of control, financing of the investment, size of the entity, effects on competition, and establishment of R & D programs. Evidence collected by questionnaire on US enterprises in the Netherlands is used to check the validity of these characteristics (or hypotheses). Information from other studies and publications is presented as well. Main conclusion of this exercise is that indeed foreign direct investments demonstrate many of these characteristics. An exhaustive test, however, would require more quantitative data.

The survey of US direct investment enterprises in the Netherlands constitutes the core of the dissertation. Thanks to the gratifying cooperation of American subsidiaries much new information was collected. This data is used extensively to analyze the magnitude of US direct investments. Criteria used are (1) annual investment expenditures, (2) employment and scale of operations, (3) production, imports and exports. On all counts the US investments have contributed significantly to the economic growth of the Netherlands in the post-war period, with every indication that they will continue in the future. This conclusion augurs well for developed countries with American direct investments, although one cannot generalize for underdeveloped countries. Nor is there only reason for optimism: it seems necessary to further strengthen the Dutch ability to compete effectively in the future. This could best be achieved by improvements in education and greater emphasis on applied research and development.

The dissertation also deals with effects of direct investments on home, as well as on foreign (host) countries. It is argued that the conventional analysis of the 'home-versus-foreign investment' controversy does not apply to direct, but to portfolio investments. This analysis concludes that too much capital is invested abroad due to a divergence between private and social cost-benefit calculations, which consequently does not apply to direct investment. Some effects of direct investments in host countries are discussed, with emphasis on underdeveloped economies. A number of recommendations are made whereby governments may be able to significantly reduce the cost of these investments to their countries, while possibly increasing the benefits. Recommendations pertain, e.g., to participation by local investors, financing with equity or bond capital, type of product to be manufactured, and subcontracting.

Finally, Netherlands direct investments in the United States are analyzed. These investments are mostly undertaken by companies that are equal to top American multinational corporations, and their value exceeds that of US operations in Holland. Many similarities exist in the respective foreign operations, but a striking difference is that Dutch companies established their American subsidiaries before 1940, and that growth after the war has been modest.

1. Setting the stage: theory and effects of direct investment

INTRODUCTION

Although the international movements of capital have a very long history, the increased channeling of these investments through private enterprises is a more recent phenomenon. And the widespread interest generated by this development dates only from the late 1950's, after the rapid growth of US direct investments in Canada and Western Europe. Thus, direct investments were only recently rediscovered as an important phenomenon and this explains why no formal theory has as yet been established.[1] In my attempt to formalize the theory of direct investments I have drawn on the contributions of many economists.

The US Department of Commerce definition of a direct investment covers 'Foreign business enterprises in which the US resident person, organization or affiliated group, owned a 25 percent interest (or more), either in the voting stock of a foreign corporation, or an equivalent ownership in a nonincorporated foreign enterprise'.[2] Recently the share ownership has been lowered to 10 percent; the broader definition was adopted in the context of the US Government program to limit the capital outflow connected with the American direct investments abroad.[3]

In the October 1968 issue of the Survey of Current Business, direct investments by American companies were subsequently defined as the 'US ownership interest in foreign enterprises of at least 10 percent'.[4] Thus the statistical concept has been adjusted to the control definition of January 1, 1968. In my dissertation this definition of a direct investment will be used not only in connection with American, but also with Dutch direct investments abroad.

Direct investments abroad are undertaken by domestic business enterprises. Vernon has introduced the term multinational corporation: 'Groups of enterprises whose foreign subsidiaries make up the great bulk of international enterprise today. Each of these groups is linked together by

1

a common parent and a common sense of purpose. Each maintains an interrelated network of facilities, shares a common pool of management, maintains a joint reserve of financial resources, and draws on a collective body of technology. Yet each group is made up of entities of diverse nationality, created under the laws of many governments, responsive to the will of many sovereigns.'[5] Although the entities of a multinational corporation may be responsive to many sovereigns, they are in fact controlled and directed by the parent company. Though *multi*national in appearance, the center of decision making is invariably linked to the nationality of the parent company. With this minor qualification the term multinational corporation will be used.

The plan of this chapter is as follows. First I discuss the reasons for developing a separate theory of direct investments rather than using the accepted theory of international capital movements. Then an attempt is made to formalize the theory of direct investments, and in concluding, the effects of overseas investments in both home and host country are analysed.

I. NEED FOR A THEORY OF DIRECT INVESTMENT

Rather than work within the context of the theory of international capital movements, I will try to develop a distinct theory of direct investments.[6] The justification for this approach rests on several grounds. The theory of international capital movements was developed at a time when portfolio investments accounted for the major share of international capital transfers. Direct investments were undertaken on a very small scale only. As a result, a number of inconsistencies arise when the explanatory framework of portfolio capital movements is applied to direct investments. In addition, there are differences in the macro-economic relationships as between portfolio and direct investments. These points will be discussed in turn.

a. Emphasis in the theory of international capital movements on portfolio investments

The theory of international capital movements was developed in the 1930's by Ragnar Nurkse and Carl Iversen.[7] Classical economists had shown little interest in the problem of capital movements, mainly because of the assumption of international factor immobility. In this manner, movements of capital between countries were conveniently defined away. Furthermore, the classical theory of international trade was based on a labor theory of value.[8] Then, too, whenever transfers of capital were discussed at all, the problem was viewed strictly from the point of *forced* payments between governments. The whole post-World War I tangle of German reparation payments reinforced this emphasis. However, forced transfers have little to do with the free interaction of economic motives. Otherwise these transfers would have taken place earlier of their own accord.[9]

'The immediate cause of profit-oriented capital movements is an interest-rate differential. The main point is to find out how this interest-rate differential can come about.'[10] This quotation from Nurkse shows the central place of interest rates in the theory of international capital movements.[11] Other factors play a role as well, and one can think of, for example, political considerations, and the desire for diversity.

The theory of international capital movements thus tried to explain the flows of portfolio investments between countries. This type of international lending was the dominant one in the years before the first World War, as well as immediately afterwards.[12] And in developing the theory of international capital movements Nurkse, Ohlin and Iversen were consequently most concerned with these portfolio investments. When one tries to apply this 'portfolio-investment' framework of analysis to direct investments, however, a number of inconsistencies arise. These inconsistencies are due to the different nature of the two types of international investment. Hymer discussed these differences in greater detail[13]; a brief listing will suffice for the moment.[14]

1. Cross movements in direct and portfolio investments exist between the US and the rest of the world. American investments are of the direct type, whereas the rest of the world places portfolio investments in the US.

2. Between, for example, Europe and the US, cross movements occur in the field of direct investments itself.

3. The intermediary with portfolio investments is a financial institution. Direct investments, on the contrary, are mostly undertaken by manufacturing enterprises.

4. The activities of direct investors abroad are closely linked to their domestic operations. This is not necessarily the case with portfolio investments.

5. With portfolio investments the capital transfer is equal to the amount of the nominal investment. The establishment or expansion of overseas subsidiaries does not, however, invariably result in capital flows. Other sources of funds may be used, such as locally raised funds, retained earnings abroad and depreciation/depletion allowances.

The above inconsistencies suggest that a difference exists between portfolio and direct investments.[15] This difference is stated rather well in the following quotation:

Direct investment is a financial transaction in the sense that it involves

3

the transformation of savings into investment. But it transcends the purely financial sphere and belongs more to the real world of production: direct investment is the construction or enlargement of a plant, the opening or enlargement of a mine, the cultivation of a new field or the intensification of its cultivation. Direct investment is an act of entrepreneurship; it brings together the factors of production in order to produce additional goods and services. Portfolio and contractual investments, on the other hand, are purely financial phenomena: they are transfers of claims to resources from savers to investors, direct or through financial intermediaries.[16]

To sum up the discussion one can define portfolio investment, such as the flotation of stock or bond issues, as the result of the *demand for capital by foreigners* to finance their *own activities* in their *own countries. Capital flows* connected with *direct investments*, however, are the result of *demand for capital, by a domestic firm* to finance part of its *operations abroad.*[17] This capital outflow serves mainly to acquire or to maintain control of the foreign based operation.

b. *Macro relationships with respect to portfolio and direct investment*

The basic argument for international investment of capital is that under normal conditions it results in the movement of capital from countries in which its marginal productivity is high, and that it thus tends toward an equalization of marginal value productivity of capital throughout the world and consequently toward a maximum contribution of the world's capital resources to world production and income.[18]

This statement by Viner deals with the economic variable, the marginal efficiency of capital, that determines whether or not a country can afford to borrow on the international capital market. Only when the productivity of capital lies above the rate of interest will capital be attracted. Cairncross, Letiche and Thomas among other authors have pointed out that fluctuations in the marginal efficiency of capital between the UK and the outside world resulted in fluctuations in the flow of English portfolio investment.[19] As Professor Letiche states:

Given (such) relatively high capital-output ratios, coupled with Britain's unbalanced resource structure and limited resource base on the one hand, and the consistently high marginal efficiency of capital in the regions of recent settlement on the other, Britain's investors were nearly always able to find profitable outlets for their savings whenever the marginal efficiency of capital at home tended to decline.

4

It was fortuitous historical circumstance that Britain was able to invest much of her excess savings abroad whenever plans to invest at home declined relative to the level of total savings.[20]

The explanation of portfolio investments made by the UK in the rest of the world is thus cast in a macro-economic context, as it properly should be. The relationships between savings and planned investment at home, as functions of real income, employment and production opportunities resulted in either an excess or scarcity of domestic savings. As the marginal efficiency of capital at home and abroad fluctuated, profitable investment opportunities abroad periodically opened up. Thus the fluctuations in Britain's foreign lending were tied to the business cycle fluctuations at home: 'Britain's foreign investment and home investment moved in opposite directions over the long period. Recurring declines in the marginal efficiency of capital schedule at home impelled investors to seek better opportunities for the supply of savings abroad.'[21]

In my opinion it is correct to regard portfolio investment in a macro-economic context, and to view the supply of domestic savings as being either invested abroad or at home in varying proportions, as determined by marginal efficiency of capital schedules. However, there is much doubt as to the validity and usefulness of this approach when one considers direct investments.

On the empirical plane, the accelerated pace of US direct investments abroad in the early 1960's coincided with a business cycle upswing domestically. Rates of return on manufacturing investments in the US during this period were consistently higher than those realized on overseas direct investments.

A more basic argument, however, can be found in the fact that a direct investment does not invariably cause capital to leave the home country. Multinational companies do not depend on the domestic supply of savings to finance their operations abroad. These firms use a variety of sources, such as retained earnings abroad, capital borrowed overseas, and depreciation and depletion allowances, in addition to capital supplied by the parent company to its subsidiaries. Therefore, the macro-economic frame of reference that in the case of portfolio investments allocates available domestic savings among home and foreign investments breaks down when, for direct investments, many other sources of finance are available and actively used.

Again, in the theoretical framework that explains international portfolio investments the rate of interest plays a crucial role. As it reflects the marginal efficiency of capital in individual countries, it determines the

5

direction of the capital flow.[22] The importance of interest rates on direct investment decisions of multinational corporations, however, must be rated as minor, just as is the case for home investment by business firms. The arguments are familiar and among them one can list:

1. interest costs are often very small relative to total costs;
2. interest costs are often tax-deductible; and
3. considerations such as long-term marketing prospects are much more important than interest rates.

Summing up, one can conclude that portfolio and direct investments are very different types of international investment. Whereas portfolio investments can be adequately explained by the existing theory of international capital movements (in a macro-economic framework of analysis), one must turn to micro-economic theories of the firm to properly analyse overseas direct investments by multinational corporations.

2. THEORY OF DIRECT INVESTMENT

a. Goals of the multinational corporation[23]

Direct investments abroad often give rise to movements of capital between countries. There is usually an initial outflow from the country making the investment, although this is by no means necessary, nor the only source of funds available to multinational corporations. In later years the expansion of overseas establishments may require additional domestic funds. Flows of capital into the home country occur when profits are remitted, when the investments are liquidated or when short-term liquid balances abroad are reduced. Presumably because of these international capital transfers, attempts have been made to explain direct investments through the theory of international capital movements. It was argued that this procedure could not be very helpful because of a number of basic differences between portfolio and direct investments.

It was noted that portfolio investment results from the demand for capital by foreigners to finance their own activities in their own countries.[24] Capital flows that result from direct investments, however, are caused by the demand for capital by a domestic company to finance part of its operations overseas. This capital flow serves mainly to acquire or to maintain control over the foreign enterprise. An international capital movement connected with a direct investment is just *one* of the many aspects of the establishment of an overseas operation. It results from a decision by a firm to make a direct investment abroad. Consequently, one has to focus attention on the conditions that will lead the firm to such a decision.

The *overseas operations* of multinational corporations are *extensions of their domestic activities*. The goals of the enterprise and the behavior patterns consistent with those goals are analysed by the theory of the firm. Once the objectives of the firm are made explicit, one is faced with the familiar maximization problem. The solution to the maximization problem provides the entrepreneur with a set of directives or guidelines which, if implemented, will result in the desired outcome. The investment plan is one of these guidelines: it shows how much the entrepreneur has to invest in the period over which the maximization of goals is desired.[25] For a multinational corporation the problem is one of maximization on a world wide basis, rather than for the domestic market alone. And so the investment plan would have to distinguish between the international and domestic *location* of the investment, rather than indicate only the absolute capital requirements. On the whole, however, one would expect that many of the variables that determine domestic investments also play a role in the allocation of capital abroad.[26]

Concerning the *goals* of the enterprise, they will not, in my opinion, be greatly affected by the internationalization of the market. The standard neo-classical analysis of the firm assumes profit maximization to be the prime objective. Applied to direct investments, this assumption would lead one to expect higher rates of return abroad than at home in the same industrial activities. Profit maximization would leave the domestic company with no other reason to start operations overseas.[27] Fortunately there exists empirical evidence to test the validity of this view. Stevens has found that a profit-maximization model adequately explains the fixed investment expenditures of US companies abroad.[28] Morley also tested the neo-classical model on direct investments, and concluded, after rejecting alternative models, that the direct international capital transfers of US companies are consistent with the assumption of profit maximization.[29] Surveys of US direct investments abroad, conducted by the University of Oregon in 1959 and the Economics Department of the McGraw-Hill Company in 1960 showed that for 30, respectively 20 percent of the respondents, profits were at least one of the main considerations.[30] Only 8 percent of the University of Oregon respondents indicated, however, that profits were the *only* motivation. Other evidence against the profit maximization assumption was presented by Johns for overseas investments in Australia. He claims that: 'It would seem that in each year from 1961–62 to 1964–65 inclusive, the rate of profit on direct overseas investments was actually below that obtained by Australian-owned companies engaged in the same broad area of activity. This pattern also continued in 1965–66

7

as far as one can judge from the preliminary figures.'[31] Lastly, Dunning and Rowan have shown that the rate of return on British direct investments abroad is much lower than that realized domestically.[32] This seems to be particularly true for Canada, but Brash has presented evidence to indicate that a similar situation exists for Australia as well.[33] With empirical evidence that both supports and violates the profit maximization assumption in foreign direct investments, it is rather difficult to draw a conclusion as to the validity of this assumption.[34]

In recent years, however, it has been suggested that the behaviour of the modern industrial corporation can be explained more satisfactorily when *sales*, too, are made an objective of the firm. John Maurice Clark was the first to introduce the concept of sales maximization subject to a profit constraint.[35] Many years later, Baumol formalized the idea, and applied it specifically to oligopolistic market structures.[36] Most recently, Galbraith has developed the concept of a technostructure.[37] Like any other organization the natural objective for the technostructure is its own survival. Survival requires, at least for the industrial corporation, the preservation of its autonomy, which depends on 'a secure minimum of earnings'.[38] Once survival of the technostructure (read: multinational corporation) is insured through the minimum profit level, there is a choice from among many other goals. 'However, there is little doubt as to how, overwhelmingly, this choice is exercised: It is to achieve the greatest possible rate of corporate growth as measured in sales.'[39] The objective of the enterprise can thus be formulated as sales maximization subject to a profit constraint.[40]

Many other considerations may play a role in the decision to establish direct investment operations abroad. Chakravarty, for example, has found that factors as cultural affinity and language provide a better explanation for international capital movements in the 1920's than the economic variables.[41] And Kreinin has suggested that American anti-trust legislation may well be the main reason for us direct investments abroad; expansion at home becomes impossible beyond a certain degree and the purchase of foreign firms or the establishment of new operations abroad then serves as an important avenue for growth of the firm.[42] The previously mentioned surveys by the University of Oregon and the McGraw-Hill Economics Department also throw light on the variety of motivations behind foreign investments.

b. Formulation of the theory

To sum up, it will be assumed that the multinational corporation has the objective of sales maximization subject to a profit constraint. The safe,

8

minimum level of profits may vary considerably and will thus depend on the particular enterprise. Given this basic assumption, one can, in my opinion, distinguish between two cases:

1. The domestic company perceives sales and/or profit opportunities in the foreign market, which local entrepreneurs either do not recognize, or for the exploitation of which they lack the appropriate resources.

2. The domestic company is faced with the loss of an export market which threatens the profit and/or sales position. Alternatively, oligopoly interdependencies may result in a follow-the-leader reaction to maintain (worldwide) market shares.

The first type of direct investment, which will be termed 'positive', is undertaken because a one-dollar investment has a higher expected return to the foreign than to the local entrepreneur (in the same, local market). Some of the factors that account for this situation lie in the field of management, marketing, technological skills, or new and improved products. The important consideration is that to the local entrepreneur these factors are *outside* his horizon; he is, in other words, obtaining only a local maximum. This happens because either his perspective is limited and he is unable to have an overall view of the entire range of production possibilities. Or the local entrepreneur does in fact perceive the opportunities for larger sales and/or higher profits, but he simply lacks the resources needed for an appropriate exploitation. Of these resources, the availability of capital (or the capacity to raise it in large enough quantities) may well be the most important, since there are markets for technological breakthroughs (licensing agreements) and management skills (consulting bureaus).[43]

All in all, for the foreign manufacturing company with better product, market and management perspectives, good opportunities are available abroad. Either an existing company is bought up, where the offer exceeds what the company itself considers to be its net worth, or a new establishment is set up in an industry where local competition did not think expansion was feasible or economically warranted.[44]

In the second case, to be called 'defensive' direct investments, the assumption is that the multinational corporation was exporting its products, manufactured at home or elsewhere, to the overseas market.[45] This may be taken as an indication that production in that particular foreign market was not regarded – at that time – as profitable and/or important to the sales volume. A number of new developments may now threaten the export position of the company, such as actual or potential local competition, imposition of tariffs or other barriers to international trade (e.g., the creation of a Common Market), government efforts toward import substitution or the establishment in the foreign country of a competitor in the home market. Whichever the actual factor, the threatened export position will affect the sales volume and profits of the whole enterprise. The direct investment then, is undertaken to maintain the sales volume and/or the rate of return or to prevent it from falling as much as it would in the absence of such action.[46]

Alternatively, if an oligopolistic structure prevails in the home market, and one member undertakes a direct investment, the other oligopolists may very well follow suit. The risk factor in such a situation is asymmetrical, and encourages a leader-follower reaction. If the leader is successful in his foreign venture, and the other oligopolists have not followed, the status quo has changed in favor of the leader. By following the leader other members of the club can assure to themselves a share in the new market. In case the foreign investment is a failure, all oligopolists lose a little, but the status quo at home is unchanged and no one is worse off vis-à-vis the competition.

c. Qualification of the argument

The distinction made above between 'positive' and 'defensive' types of direct investments is in all probability not a watertight one, in the sense that some direct investments may be undertaken for other reasons. In my opinion, however, the categorization is useful in that it differentiates between two distinct economic situations.

A second qualification is called for, because often the multinational corporation already has facilities abroad, and the investment decision relates to the maintenance or the expansion of that foreign-based subsidiary. Under conditions where a *new* direct investment would not be undertaken, the company may well be forced, in the economic sense of the word, to invest in the *existing* facility. When rates of return and/or sales volume of such a facility fall below acceptable levels, the high cost of foreclosure often results in a 'lock-in' effect of foreign operations.

d. Conclusion

The preceding observations on the theory of direct investments can be summarized as follows. It is assumed that multinational corporations, operating in the world market, have as their goal the maximization of sales, subject to a minimum profit level. The establishment of an operation abroad by a multinational corporation, a direct investment, can be classified as positive or defensive, depending on the circumstances that led to its creation. In the case of positive investments the company perceived higher sales and/or rates of return abroad, an opportunity that local entrepreneurs failed to notice. Defensive investments are triggered by developments abroad that endanger the export position of a company; to defend existing profit rates and/or sales volume a foreign operation is established.

In a later chapter a number of characteristics of direct investment will be stated, and empirical evidence to test their validity will be presented.

3. DIRECT INVESTMENT AND THE NATIONAL INTEREST

The analysis of the advantages and drawbacks of direct investments, for the foreign as well as the domestic economy, has an academic interest. But probably more important, it also carries with it policy implications, especially where many countries are actively stimulating direct investments. These investment-attraction programs offer the foreign company many benefits, such as outright grants, subsidies and accelerated depreciation schemes. Often the domestic company is discriminated against in the sense that new local investment does not get the same treatment. On the other hand, in some countries opposition, especially against the American investments, has sprung up, most notably in France and Canada, but also in Germany, the UK and Australia.[47] In what sense are these protests based on economic arguments, real or imagined, and to what extent does nationalism play a role? Of special importance is the role of direct investment in underdeveloped countries. Here contributions to economic growth are greatly magnified, but so are adverse effects. In view of the urgency of development, an analysis of foreign direct investment in these countries is especially needed.

In (a) the conventional arguments pro and con home versus foreign investments will be discussed. Then I will indicate why a different analysis is required (b), and in (c) some effects of direct investments are presented. The impact of direct investments in foreign countries occupies most of the discussion.

a. Conventional arguments

The argument whether or not the national interest is best served by investments at home or abroad arises from a divergence between private and social cost-benefit calculations. The accepted way to discuss the problem is from the lender's point of view.[48] Some of the factors that cause the aforementioned divergence include the following:

1. The risk evaluation. With a foreign investment the risk for individual and nation is the same, but this is obviously not so with a domestic investment. For example, where a bankruptcy involves a domestic investment, the nation itself does not lose the investment, although the individual does. In case of a foreign investment both nation and individual lose, with the foreign host country no better or worse off. The difference in risk evaluation is also quite clear in cases such as nationalisation.

2. The diminishing marginal returns. To the extent that home investment lowers the rate of return on the existing capital stock, it raises the marginal product of other factors. Thus a redistribution of income takes place from domestic investors to owners of other factors of production. Investment abroad will result in a redistribution of income from the domestic investor to foreign owners of other factors.

Another way of looking at this problem is by focusing on the marginal and average productivity of the investment. Where indeed the marginal product is below the average, the investment abroad yields the home country and the investor the marginal product. Of course, this is also what the individual investor would have received by investing at home. But with a foreign investment the difference between marginal and average product accrues to the foreign country, rather than to the home country of the investor.[49]

3. The fiscal effects. The taxes on the foreign income are lost to the nation, since double taxation is not common due to international tax agreements. Again a divergence between individual and nation arises because the investor compares the rate of return after taxes at home and abroad. For the nation, however, the comparison is between returns *after taxes from abroad* and returns *before taxes* at home.

4. The terms of trade. Whereas the three previous effects all lead to an excess of foreign over domestic investments, the terms of trade effects are ambiguous. Foreign investment can be complementary to the domestic economy in ways that home investment is not, e.g. by cheapening imports, by facilitating the marketing of exportables or by perpetuating a primary product orientation of the foreign country.[50] But adverse effects can come from the development of competitive sellers of exportables or from the creation of competitive buyers of imports.

The conclusion from these conventional arguments is that the home country tends to invest abroad more capital than is economically justified.

A quotation from M. C. Kemp is illustrative:

> I shall consider matters from the viewpoint of the lending country and advance reasons for believing that capital rich countries tend to invest too much of their wealth abroad, too little at home.[51]

Thus the home country should curb foreign and encourage domestic investments, for example by a system of taxes and subsidies that will bring social costs and benefits into equality.[52] Many countries however rather like the idea of investing abroad, especially in direct investments.[53] This suggests that either governments do not understand the arguments of the economists, or that the conventional analysis of direct investments fails to present the whole picture.[54] I would argue the latter.

b. A different view

The standard analysis of the 'home versus foreign investment' argument centers on the notion that what is invested abroad could also have been invested at home. In this context the value of foreign direct investments is taken to be a correct measure of the capital transferred from the home to the foreign country.

The conventional analysis is misleading, however, because it suggests that capital flows from the home to the foreign country are the *only* way to finance the direct investment. Were this true, then indeed we would have the alternative of investment at home or abroad, and we could fully accept the argument. But actually, direct investments abroad are only partly financed out of capital flows from the home country.[55] For US investments this share amounts to roughly 20 percent, but it is considerably lower for foreign investments in the United States. If we classify reinvested earnings as a capital flow (because the funds are not remitted to the direct investor) the share of US funds in the financing of American direct investments is higher, at around 35 percent of the total direct investment. Other sources are depreciation and depletion allowances, and locally raised capital. The returns to the multinational corporation of course relate to the full extent of the investment, not only the part financed with home funds. More important, however, the figures for the shares financed by capital from the home country and other sources relate to *total* investments, that is, new investments as well as expansion. There is some evidence to suggest that established direct investment enterprises grow almost completely through reinvested earnings, local borrowing and the use of depletion and depreciation allowances.[56] Miss Penrose wrote about the GM-Holden automobile producer in Australia, where reinvested earnings and local borrowing boosted the total investment, without drawing any additional American capital into the country (aside from the initial outlay to acquire control).[57] Ultimately, such a development results in profit remittances that are exhorbitant in relation to the original capital flow from the investing country.[58] The following quotation describes the growth of a F. W. Woolworth subsidiary in England, while underscoring the fact that direct investments *do* increase *without* capital flows.

The British subsidiary was established as a private company in 1909, with an initial outlay of $ 63,000 and has since expanded from its own profitability, i.e., from reinvested earnings. The subsidiary has since (1939) been made a limited company under English law, the parent company receiving $ 27,000,000 in cash from undistributed earnings and 52 percent of the new ordinary shares. The shares on the London market, ..., are quoted at nearly 60 shillings.

At the end of 1939 the controlling interest was carried on the books of the American company at $ 6,000,000, while the market value was in excess of $ 235,000,000.[59]

Other examples are known, less publicized while still remaining dramatic.[60] As I stated before, the capital flows connected with direct investments are as a rule the minimum needed to acquire control, or start the operations.[61] In some cases when massive injections of money were needed, capital also flowed from the parent to the subsidiary at later stages, as, e.g., when General Electric took over Bull Computer Company. But on the whole, growth of direct investments is financed mostly out of retained earnings, depreciation and depletion allowances, and out of local borrowing.

Consequently, the conventional analysis of 'home versus foreign investment' appears to be restricted to *portfolio* investments, and certainly does not apply to direct investments. The difference between these two types of investments has been recognized rather early as the following quote from the 1931 MacMillan Report illustrates.

... in the realm of foreign investments it is primarily *towards British owned enterprises abroad* that we should wish to see our energies and capital turned rather than merely towards subscribing to foreign government and municipal loans, which *absorb our available balance while doing little for our industry and commerce.*[62]
[my italics]

And in a discussion of Netherlands portfolio investments in the United States, Bosch laments that:

Of these important economic transformations brought about by Dutch capital exports only the US receives the fruits, the Netherlands ... does not take any part in it.[63]

To conclude, one can accept the conventional arguments of the 'home versus foreign investment' analysis as applied to portfolio investments. In case of direct investments, however, one must look for other criteria and conduct a different analysis.

c. Costs and benefits

The effects of direct investments in host countries have been analysed by a number of writers. Their studies concern either specific cases, such as the ones published by the National Planning Association, or deal with individual countries.[64] In the latter category we find a number of publications dealing with Canada, by among others Brecher and Reismann, and Bernard Bonin.[65] For the United Kingdom we have a study by John Dunning, and Donald Brash has written about direct investments in the Australian economy.[66] A theoretical analysis has been presented by MacDougall; his model deals with the Australian experience.[67] Norwegian experience with direct investment has been studied by Stonehill.[68]

In the discussion of the costs and benefits of direct investments one would have to follow the distinction in types of investment that was made in Part 2, namely *positive* and *defensive*. And this would have to apply to both home and foreign country. We will treat the effects of direct investments first, discussing each effect and indicating in a fairly general way how the type of investment, positive or defensive, might lead to differences in the analyzed outcomes. Subsequently, the impact on the home country will be covered briefly.

The whole analysis will be rather selective, pertaining only to those aspects of direct investment that have relevance to this study.[69]

i. Not import on the foreign country

To a very large degree the impact of direct investment in manufacturing industries is measured by the extent to which production is carried out locally,[70] ranging from assembly to full production of parts and semi-finished goods (possibly through subcontracting). The actual stage of production decided upon by the multinational firm will depend, among other things, on the type of product and on the level of economic development of the foreign country. The company may find it desirable to change the way in which the activities are conducted abroad over the years. The logical development seems to be from exports through agents abroad, to trading establishments, then to assembly abroad of components produced in the home country. The final stage is the full-scale manufacturing operation in the overseas country.[71] This process can be affected by one or more of the following: (a) the growth of the local market for the product, (b) the development of the overseas country, economically as well as in other areas such as industrial competence, and (c) any measures of the overseas government to encourage or enforce local production of former imports.[7]

In addition to the stage of production in the direct investment sector the analysis also has to distinguish between the long and the short run although a clear demarcation is not always possible.

Technology and skills

One of the most important results of direct investment, especially the positive type, is the introduction of new products, techniques and skills The production structure is modernized, industrial output diversified, and the labor force trained to handle new machinery. Particularly in the developing nations these contributions are of great value and constitute a real boost to the market economy. Much depends, however, on the *type* of product and the *extent* to which production takes place locally. A standardized product, which requires only assembly of imported parts, will obviously have less impact than a full line of diversified products coupled with local subcontracting. Also, will the technological know-how be disseminated, or does it remain an island in the local economy? Especially if research and development are conducted in the home country of the investor, a superior technology may be confined indefinitely to the foreign sector.[73] Finally, for defensive types of investment, a real danger exists that domestic producers will be forced out of business.

Entrepreneurial talent

In this field possibilities for *benefits* and *costs* exist. The local entrepreneurial talent may be developed, and existing entrepreneurs made aware of new managing and marketing techniques. The actual example set by the foreign firm could offer great attractions to the private enterprising sector. But to the extent that foreign entry is often based on foreign superiority, the existing talent may be destroyed rather than developed. Especially if the direct investment is defensive, or represents a substitute to a locally manufactured product, the impact on entrepreneurial talents can be disastrous. It follows that for existing industries some protection is needed, which Stephen Hymer has called the 'infant entrepreneurship' argument in the case of Canadian industry versus the US investments. Hymer's thinking is reflected by the following:

> The large volume of foreign investment in Canada seems to suggest a shortage of Canadian entrepreneurs. But which is cause and which is effect? We usually think of foreign investment as a consequence of a shortage of domestic entrepreneurs, but perhaps the former has helped create the latter.[74]

n many countries foreign investments seem to be selfsustaining or claiming n increasing share of total industrial activity. Actually, the only cases, known to the writer, where foreign investment has given way to domestic ontrol, short of revolutions, occurred in the United States, where the two World Wars led to the Americanization of German and English subsidiaries. Another way to terminate foreign investments is through nationalization and a good example of this is Mexico.

Market structures[75]

Direct investments may create or preserve oligopolistic market structures, which will lead to a misallocation of resources, reduction in efficiency and a redistribution of income.[76] The first two are detrimental to the nation as well as to the world, whereas the third involves a redistribution of income away from the host country to the lender. In this sense it reduces the local economy's national income on all three counts. Of course there always the question how low the national income would have been without the direct investment. On the positive side, one should allow for the Schumpeterian argument that an oligopoly over time leads to greater output than does a perfectly competitive economy.[77]

In cases where the multinational firm has succeeded in establishing a vertically integrated manufacturing organization, prices can be set in such way that the tax bill is minimized.[78] As is true for many of the aspects discussed here, this behavior makes sense for the firm, but does it also maximize the benefits for the host country? Although the country may gain from lower prices of the final product, it will lose through foregone tax revenue. Worst of all, monopolization of market structures may preempt any domestic production from being established and will thus perpetuate the foreign control of industries. This may be the reason for the self-sustenance or growth of direct investments, as mentioned in the previous section.

We now turn to some short run measures of the contribution that direct investment can make in the receiving country. The only empirical study that I know of is the one by Anthony Y. C. Koo of US direct investment in Latin America.[79] Using four criteria, namely local payments per sales dollar, local sales to total sales, rate of plant replacement and the ratio of inflow to outflow of funds, Koo ranks the investments per sector and country. He finds that for Latin America the ranking in terms of short run economic contribution is (1) public utilities, (2) manufacturing, (3) agriculture, (4) petroleum and (5) mining and smelting.[80] The analysis by Koo is useful, but it would be difficult to generalize his findings to all foreign direct investments. Furthermore, ranking of contributions is not

equivalent to establishing usefulness, and thus we have to look for othe
measures.[81]

Production and employment
With regard to production and employment the extent of the operation
conducted by the foreign company is crucially important.[82] Where onl
assembly takes place, with all parts imported from the parent or othe
affiliated enterprises, the employment generated locally may not be sig
nificant, although this would depend on the type of product as well. Or
the other hand, if most of the parts and semi-finished products are locall
produced, either by the firm itself or by subcontractors, the impact i
considerable. Subcontracting directly stimulates the domestic manufac
turing sector and provides a favorable climate for other manufacturing
operations. The type of operations (assembly or full production) also
determines the value added in the host country, which affects income an
consequently stimulates other sectors of the economy.

Regardless of the type of operation, the type of product to be produce
and marketed by the foreign investor is of great importance. As long a
locally produced substitutes exist, the foreign investment should be regarded
with suspicion, especially in an underdeveloped country. Rather than create
additional employment, the result of the venture might very well be a ne
decrease of employment. If the local industry is outdated there may b
ways to improve the efficiency of the operation, such as licensing agree
ments. However, the country could also be faced with the choice of a
direct investment that will compete vigorously with the backward loca
industry, or letting the efficient new direct investment go into a neigh
bouring country and compete from there with the local products through
exports.

Capital and saving
In many countries, especially the underdeveloped, local capital is in shor
supply and very often acts as a constraint on investment plans. Foreigr
capital can therefore play an important role by increasing the supply o
available funds. As was stated before, however, foreign subsidiaries o
multinational corporations tend to finance their expansion to a large
degree out of local borrowing.[83] To the extent that the parent compan
guarantees the loans, these borrowings carry a premium over local issue
and the foreign subsidiary will thus be able to secure the needed funds. I
this entails only a mobilization of funds that would not have otherwis
been invested, all is well, and the local borrowing may be an incentive fo
the formation of a capital market. But if local borrowing by a foreign firm

is done in competition with domestic producers, the latter may well lose out to the foreign sudsidiary and thus be hampered in their expansion. Protection of the local entrepreneurs would then be necessary, especially in less developed countries.

It was noted earlier that control of equity capital is a typical aspect of direct investments.[84] This means that the natives are virtually excluded from participation in risk-bearing investments which offer a high expected return. In so far as this leaves only investments with lower yields, total savings may be reduced.[85] Forcing foreign owners to sell shares in their operations to local investors, or to divest themselves completely from the investment after a number of years, may be a good way to generate more savings, and thus to finance more investment projects.[86]

Recently Rosenstein-Rodan has drawn attention to yet another aspect of the equity financing of private direct investment.[87] The renumeration of equity investment lies between 15 to 24 percent before taxes and 10 to 15 percent after taxes. Bond credit or portfolio investment costs anywhere from 5 to 6 percent. Thus the price a country pays for a direct investment is from 2 to 3 times higher than for portfolio investment. Of course, to the lower bond rates one has to add the costs for complementary technical assistance, but even so the transfer burden of equity (direct) investment appears to be much higher.[88] The costs of foreign capital can thus be reduced by using more portfolio investments. This point has also been made by Hymer with respect to American investments in Canada.[89]

The balance of payments[90]
For many countries, developed as well as economically backward, equilibrium or a surplus in the balance of payments vis-à-vis the rest of the world constitutes an important goal of economic policy-making. For underdeveloped countries, however, the balance of payments typically is a constraint on the national development effort, and is consequently of a very serious nature.[91] The foreign exchange commodity is always in short supply, and it is interesting to analyse in what ways direct investments can alleviate the problem. To facilitate the discussion one can use the following equation, which holds true for every single foreign investment.

$CF + MS + CE \gtreqless NM + RE$, where on the plus side, either bringing in foreign exchange or helping not to spend it, one finds:

CF = capital inflow for either the initial investment, expansion or replacement
MS = import substitution
CE = created exports

19

and on the negative side foreign exchange outflows as a direct result of the investment:

NM = new imports
RE = remitted earnings.

The capital inflow as a result of the start of the operation, its expansion or the replacement of machinery may vary quite a bit depending on a number of factors. A new establishment probably requires the full amount of the investment in foreign exchange and for the purchase of existing facilities the equity shares have to be paid. In financing expansions and replacement, the direct investment firms rely to a great extent on reinvested earnings, depreciation and depletion allowances, and on local borrowing. For the United States it is maintained, that capital flows actually finance considerably less than 20 percent of the total expenditures of existing direct investments. Stephen Hymer has even gone so far as to state that capital flows connected with direct investment serve only to acquire control of foreign subsidiaries; once this has been accomplished, no more capital from the parent is needed.[92] I personally think that this is an exaggeration, especially in view of the real problems some US companies faced after the limitation on capital outflows of January 2, 1968. The rush on the European dollar market in London as a result of the restrictions on US dollar outflows implies that American capital was also used for expansion and replacement.

Import substitution may be a direct result of the investment, especially if we are dealing with defensive direct investments. This type of investment is the result of either a threatened export position, or government action – the latter especially in underdeveloped countries. In cases where new products are manufactured by the foreign subsidiary, no import substitution takes place; we would expect this mostly from offensive investments.

New export created by the foreign investment can contribute very much to the exchange problem, aside from their impact on economic growth.[93] What is the likelihood that a foreign direct investment will indeed sell part of its production abroad? Again the answer varies depending on the type of product and the development stage of the country. When a multinational company produces a standardized product in many foreign countries, chances are that production is for the local market. I suspect that these conditions hold, for example, in a country like Canada or for products like Coca-Cola or petroleum derivatives. Defensive investments due to government pressure are another example where high costs and small scale prohibit exports (automobiles in Latin America). On the other hand, exploitation of natural resources adds to exports, because such investments are often made to supply the home-based manufacturing establishments with raw materials, such as metal ores and agricultural products. For some countries, e.g. the Netherlands and Belgium, the export performance of. American and other foreign manufacturing direct investments is quite good.[94] For all US direct investments in manufacturing industries, exports accounted for around 17.5 percent of total sales in 1964. While the percentage is 22.8 in Europe it remains much lower for other areas, namely 8.9 percent.[95] One can tentatively conclude from these data that the more developed the country, the better the possibility for exports from direct investment companies.

The establishment of a direct investment can lead to *new imports* needed in the production process. The actual extent of these imports depends on the type of operation, ranging from assembly to full production, and whether or not raw materials and semi-finished products can be purchased locally.[96] In a well-developed industrial country subcontracting will be possible, but it is quite a problem in an underdeveloped economy. In the latter the import content of foreign-produced goods may go up as high as 90 percent. An example given to me of a 'movie-stage' production facility is quite illustrative. This direct investment, producing a 'tankard' per day of, say product X, served as cover-up of the import not only of the bulk of local sales of product X, but also of many other finished products of that company. Thus the newly created imports are not only those needed in the actual production but may very well consist of finished products. In these cases the right to import is purchased by setting up a local production facility that supplies a minor share of the total sales.

Remittance of earnings to the parent company, a normal consequence of successful foreign operations, is of course a real drain on foreign exchange. In the sense that they are the price for imported capital they are not much different from interest payments on a foreign loan. But there are some aspects that create a tremendous difference between direct and portfolio investments. One relates to the return on capital, which is usually quite a bit higher than interest charges on portfolio borrowing.[97] And, of course, with a direct investment no amortization is required. But the main difference lies in the fact that remitted earnings may become very large in relation to the initial capital inflow. This is due to the financing of expansion, where internally generated funds and local borrowing are mostly used and capital inflows seldom. Edith Penrose has been one of the first to draw attention to this aspect of direct investments.[98] The fact that a relatively small capital inflow may expand into sizeable investments, over which profits have to be remitted, raises a question as to the type of foreign capital a country wants to attract for industrialization. With a portfolio investment, the internally-generated funds and growth of the firm financed by them benefits the host country, whereas with a direct investment the foreigner is the main beneficiary. Therefore, it is important for the host country that the direct investment be a joint venture rather than a wholly owned subsidiary, and that some agreement is reached for the ultimate transfer of the foreign equity interest to the native investors.[99] The case of Japan illustrates that insistence on joint ventures does *not* constitute an important deterrent to foreign investment.

Summing up the discussion, one must conclude, not surprisingly, that the balance of payments effect of direct investments differs from one case to another, with the type of product and operation, as well as the development status of a country as the decisive factors. What seems pretty clear, however, is the fact that direct investments cannot be counted on to solve the foreign exchange problems of underdeveloped countries. The total capital inflow may only be a small percentage of the total investment, the transfer of earnings presents a heavy burden, and very often the operation of the establishment may require sizeable imports without always contributing to exports.

The analysis presented above suggests that on the whole foreign countries may not have been critical enough in their acceptance of direct investment establishments. And insofar as these countries have tried to attract direct investments their governments may not have realized the costs involved. A number of recommendations can be made [not necessarily in order of importance], many of them of special interest to underdeveloped countries.

1. Participation by local investors in the equity capital of the foreign direct investment should be made an important requirement. As control is the main characteristic of direct investments there is some question whether a multinational corporation will undertake the investment at all if it is denied absolute or majority control. The case of Japan illustrates that when the venture is attractive enough the control considerations do assume secondary importance.

2. An effort should be made to determine whether and to what extent the proposed project can be financed with a combination of direct (equity) and portfolio (bond) capital. Thus for example, those sectors where a strong dependency exists on the complementary input of know-how would be undertaken with private direct investments. When technological and/or managerial skills can be more easily obtained portfolio financing should be considered.

3. In an underdeveloped country the type of product to be manufactured

should be a major consideration. A simple rule would be necessities first and luxuries last, as a first attempt to rank priorities. I am thinking here of direct investment operations that produce strictly for the local market. There may be cases where the theory of comparative advantage would dictate the production of luxuries rather than necessities; by definition this would entail foreign trade. The South African diamond and gold industries are a good example.

4. With direct investments in extractive industries or in agriculture, an effort should be made to establish processing industries for these raw materials as well. In this way the country is able to build up a manufacturing sector, and appropriate a larger share of the value of the end-product.

5. The possible extent of local production should be considered, with an emphasis on subcontracting, even if such subcontracting would have to be organized or created by the foreign firm itself. (See the experience in the Netherlands after World War II.)

6. Consideration should be given to the balance-of-payments contributions of the direct investment, again with special reference to underdeveloped countries. This includes import substitution, the creation of new exports, as well as the subcontracting aspects mentioned above.

7. Regulation of the foreign investor may be necessary to prevent monopolization of the markets, particularly in those countries where the market economy is not yet well established.

8. Ideally, the direct investment should be made with an understanding, possibly an explicit agreement, to turn the whole investment ultimately over to domestic entrepreneurs. This may not be too realistic a requirement, because many companies may not want to invest at all if they knew their investment had nothing more than, say, a 25 year life. Local participation in direct investment projects, however, is of utmost importance, and if such participation is not possible when the investment is undertaken, provisions should be made for such action at a later date.

Since governments reserve for themselves the right to judge every direct investment the above recommendations could be negotiated with the foreign investor. By implementing these suggestions the host country might be able to acquire the benefits of direct investment at substantially lower cost than seems to be the case now.

ii. *Effects in the home country*
In part I of this chapter it has been established that the main motives behind direct investments are either positive, defensive or a mixture of both. In any case, the investment would either not have been undertaken at home or would have yielded less if the opportunity to invest abroad

would not have existed.[101] By implication, the multinational corporation and the home country thus benefit from these direct investments. The discussion here will be very brief, and touch mostly on two recent studies that deal with the effect of direct investment on the home (investing) country.

The first of these studies concerns the United Kingdom and was undertaken by Reddaway.[102] The analysis concentrates on

(1) The initial effect on exports and the continuing impact such as, (2) the effect on profits, (3) the effect of capital appreciation and (4) the additional exports of goods and services connected with the foreign investment.[103] The initial impact of a £ 100 increase in the net operating assets of British overseas subsidiaries results in a very low rise in British exports of £ 9. The continuing impact of the foreign investment has been estimated as an 'effect in an average year for an average project'.[104] The average profits amount to around 8.7 percent, capital appreciation raises the figure to over 12 percent. The continuing effect upon exports and services of a £ 100 million direct investment are as follows[105]: (a) a gain in UK exports of around £ 1 million per year, (b) total sales abroad by British owned companies up by some £ 143 million, and (c) total sales by British companies up by some 3.6 percent. In addition there are other effects on the national economy, viz. productivity effects, economies of scale, research and know-how.[106] For a detailed discussion of the Reddaway report the reader is referred to a series of articles by Dunning.[107]

In the United States interest in the effects on the economy of American direct investment has centered on the balance of payments.[108] The most dramatic item in this context is the capital outflow connected with these investments, but there are sizeable inflows as well for remitted earnings, royalties and consulting fees. Less clear are the effects on exports and imports; data on trade flows connected with overseas investments are now a regular feature of the Department of Commerce reporting on direct investments. Using these data Hufbauer and Adler have recently calculated the effect of US investments on the balance of payments.[109] The authors test for alternative assumptions and come up with some interesting results; rather than discuss the report here the reader is referred to the aforementioned articles by Dunning, who compares the Reddaway and Hufbauer-Adler studies.

In concluding we present a computation made by Behrman of the effects of a US direct investment in Europe. It gives a rather good impression of the benefits occurring from these foreign ventures and is, appropriately enough, titled: 'How a new direct investment in Europe can pay off in two years.'

If the venture is an entirely new one, the actual US dollar outflow may be as much as 40% of the total investment, with the rest financed through overseas borrowing; if merely an expansion of an existing investment, the outflow is likely to be about 20–25% of total capital expenditures and the remainder will be financed through retained earnings and depreciation allowances, as well as foreign-source borrowing. Thus, at the worst, we get an initial debit item of $ 4 million on the $ 10-million investment. Since company practice indicates that something like 15% of European subsidiary purchases of capital equipment, which normally total about one-half of the overseas investment, are made in the US, there is an offset of about $ 0.8 million (15% of 50% of $ 10 million) even before production abroad actually begins. This reduces the outflow to about $ 3.2 million. According to Commerce figures, annual US exports of materials, parts and finished goods (other than capital goods) to foreign affiliates in Europe average close to 5% of affiliate sales, and these, in turn, are usually about $2\frac{1}{2}$ times total investment. Thus 5% of $ 25 million ($2\frac{1}{2} \times$ $ 10 million) gives us a $ 1.25 million export credit each year. Adding annual repatriated earnings of $ 240,000 (6% of investment, as noted, European investment earns 12% of book value and at least half is remitted home), we get a balance-of-payments return of close to $ 1.5 million of the initial investment.

Within about two years, therefore, the capital outflow will have been paid for in a balance-of-payments sense, even assuming a 40% initial contribution of US funds. Of course, in these calculations we have made no mention of the additional export sales that may be made during the 'start-up' period either because of intensified company efforts to widen the market or because foreign customers become less uneasy about purchasing imports when they know that a domestic source of supply will soon be available. Also, we have not included the indirect export stimulus resulting from the income-generating effects of the affiliate's presence in the host country, although this may amount to about 1% of the affiliate's sales. Nor, have we counted, on the debit side, the effects of imports sent back to the US, since such sales from US-European subsidiaries have not risen significantly, despite expansion of US investment to this area.[110]

NOTES

1. A *rediscovery* in the sense that US and European direct investment in the 1920's attracted considerable attention. See e.g. FRANK A. SOUTHARD, *American Industry in Europe* (Boston and New York: Houghton-Mifflin Company, 1931).

2. US Department of Commerce, *U.S. Business Investments in Foreign Countries*, 1960, p. 76.

3. *Federal Register*, vol. 33, no. 141, Saturday, July 20, 1968, 'Proposed Rule Making', § 1000.305.

4. EMIL L. NELSON and FREDERICK CUTLER, 'The International Investment Position of the United States in 1967', *Survey of Current Business*, October 1968, p. 21.

5. RAYMOND VERNON, 'The Multinational Corporation', *The Atlantic Community Quarterly*, Winter 1967–1968, vol. 5, no. 4, p. 533.

6. See also: CHARLES P. KINDLEBERGER, *American Business Abroad* (New Haven and London: Yale University Press, 1969). My study was completed when Kindleberger's six lectures on direct investment were published.

7. CARL IVERSEN, *Aspects of International Capital Movements* (London, Copenhagen: Levin and Munksgaard, 1935) and RAGNAR NURKSE, *Internationale Kapitalbewegungen* (Wien: Springer Verlag, 1935). Nurkse had published an earlier article dealing with the causes and effects of international capital movements: 'Ursachen und Wirkungen der Kapitalbewegungen', *Zeitschrift für Nationalökonomie*, V (1933), pp. 78–96. This article is translated and reprinted as Chapter 1: 'Causes and Effects of Capital Movements' in: *Equilibrium and Growth in the World Economy: Economic Essays by Ragnar Nurkse*, ed. GOTTFRIED HABERLER and ROBERT M. STERN (Cambridge, Mass.: Harvard University Press, 1961), pp. 1–21. My references are to this chapter.

8. Ohlin emphasized this point: BERTIL OHLIN, 'The Connection between International Trade and International Labor and Capital Movements', *Zeitschrift für Nationalökonomie*, II (1930), p. 162.

9. NURKSE, *op. cit.*, p. 3.

10. *Ibid.*, p. 3.

11. Similarly: BERTIL OHLIN, *Interregional and International Trade*, Revised Edition (Cambridge, Mass.: Harvard University Press, 1967), p. 210: 'To turn now to the circumstances that govern international capital movements, the most important stimulus to export and import of capital is certainly differences in the rate of interest.'

12. Support for this view can be found in: BRINLEY THOMAS, *Capital Movements and Economic Development*, JOHN H. ADLER, ed. (New York: St. Martin's Press, 1967), pp. 3–32. To quote from his contribution 'The Historical Record of International Capital Movements to 1913': 'The great era of British foreign lending had been unique. At the end of the period her capital exports were at the rate of 9 percent of her national income. It had been largely portfolio rather than direct investment, and mainly in securities yielding a fixed return; the plantation type of investment associated with colonies did not occupy a prominent place' (p. 15).

13. Hymer listed most of these inconsistencies in his Ph. D. dissertation. STEPHEN H. HYMER, *The International Operations of National Firms: A Study of Direct Investment* (Cambridge, Mass.: MIT, Ph. D. dissertation, 1960). This publication will be referred to subsequently as: HYMER, *Dissertation*.

14. See Appendix I for a longer statement of these inconsistencies.

15. MARCO FANNO, *Normal and Abnormal International Capital Transfers* (London: H. Milford, 1939). On page 12 he states: 'The capital transfer may be effected ... either as a result of a request for loans from the country with the higher rate of interest, or as a result of the country with the lower rate taking the initiative in granting loans to or *creating new enterprises* in the first country' (my italics). This quotation shows that indeed portfolio and direct investment were regarded as one and the same thing in the theory of international capital movements.

16. FELIPE PAZOS, 'The Role of International Movements of Private Capital in

26

Promoting Development', in: JOHN H. ADLER, ed., *op. cit.*, p. 186.

17. HYMER, *Dissertation*, pointed out this difference.

18. JACOB VINER, 'International Finance in the Post-War World', p. 324 in: *International Economics: Studies by Jacob Viner* (Glencoe, Ill.: The Free Press, 1951).

19. A. K. CAIRNCROSS, *Home and Foreign Investment: 1870–1913 – Studies in Capital Accumulation* (Cambridge: At the University Press, 1953), ch. VII, 'Fluctuations in Home and Foreign Investment, 1870–1913', pp. 250–258.
JOHN M. LETICHE, *Balance of Payments and Economic Growth* (New York: Augustus M. Kelly, 1967), specifically pp. 250–258.
BRINLEY THOMAS, 'The Time-Shape of Capital Movements', in: JOHN H. ADLER, ed., *op. cit.*, pp. 16–30.

20. LETICHE, *op. cit.*, p. 254.

21. *Ibid.*, pp. 256–257.

22. Subject to some other considerations such as diversification, political and cultural motives.

23. My attempt to formalize the theory of direct investments owes much to: BERNARD BONIN, *L'Investissement Etranger à Long Terme au Canada: Ses Caractères et ses Effets sur l'Economie Canadienne* (Paris: Ph. D. Dissertation, Université de Paris, 1966), pp. 146–327.
STEPHEN H. HYMER, *The International Operations of National Firms: A Study of Direct Investment* (Cambridge, Mass.: MIT, Ph. D. Dissertation, 1960). By the same author, 'Direct Foreign Investment and the National Interest', PETER RUSSEL, ed., *Nationalism in Canada* (Toronto: McGraw-Hill, 1966), pp. 191–202.
RAYMOND VERNON, 'International Investment and International Trade in the Product Cycle', *The Quarterly Journal of Economics*, vol. 80, May, 1966, pp. 190–207.

24. Examples are bond flotations by foreign governments and stock issues by foreign companies on the American capital market (see also the many foreign stock quotations on the New York Stock Exchange). Note that this type of portfolio investment covers only new issues. The sale to a US investor of shares in a Dutch enterprise held by a European investor is obviously a different kind of transaction, although also a portfolio investment. In the discussion above we refer only to the flotation of new issues' on a foreign market.

25. Jorgensen has shown how a profit-maximization solution results in an explicit investment function for the company as well. DALE W. JORGENSEN, 'Capital Theory and Investment Behaviour', *American Economic Review*, vol. 53, No. 2, May 1963, pp. 247–259.

26. Guy Stevens has attempted to explain investments in fixed assets by US companies abroad. About his model he remarks that: 'When specified empirically, it uses as explanatory variables for fixed investments many of the variables used in the fitting of domestic investment functions.' GUY V. G. STEVENS, *Fixed Investments Expenditures of Foreign Manufacturing Affiliates of U.S. Firms: Theoretical Models and Empirical Evidence* (Yale University, Ph. D. Dissertation, 1967), p. 3. See also pp. 15–19: 'Lessons from the theory of domestic investment'.

27. It has to be kept in mind that the rates of return as such would not be a good measure unless they are corrected for the risk factor inherent in the foreign investment.

28. STEVENS, *op. cit.*, pp. 23–25.

29. S. A. MORLEY, *American Corporate Investment Abroad Since 1919* (University of California at Berkeley: Ph. D. Dissertation, 1965).

30. RAYMOND F. MIKESELL, ed., *U.S. Private and Government Investment Abroad* (Eugene: University of Oregon Press, 1962); see specifically: JACK N. BEHRMAN, 'Foreign Associates and their Financing'.

McGraw-Hill Economics Department, *Overseas Operations of U.S. Industrial Companies, 1960–1961* (New York: McGraw-Hill, 1961).

31. B. L. JOHNS, 'Private Overseas Investment in Australia: Profitability and Motivations', *The Economic Record*, vol. 43, no. 102, June 1967, p. 233.

32. JOHN H. DUNNING, 'U.K. Capital Exports and Canadian Economic Development', *Moorgate and Wallstreet*, Spring 1962, pp. 3–38.
JOHN H. DUNNING and D. C. ROWAN, 'British Direct Investment in Western Europe', *Banca Nazionale del Lavorno*, June 1962.

33. DONALD T. BRASH, *American Investment in Australian Industry* (Canberra: Australian National University Press, 1966).

34. It must be remembered that even if profit differences today would not justify the direct investment, this may have been the case at the time the investment was made. For an adequate test of the profit maximization assumption one would have to look for the flow of direct investment per period and calculate rates of return *for that period*.

35. JOHN MAURICE CLARK, 'Towards a Concept of Workable Competition,' *American Economic Review*, June 1940. Reprinted in: *Readings in the Social Control of Industry* (Philadelphia: The Blakiston Company, 1949), pp. 452–475. See specifically pp. 460–463.

36. WILLIAM J. BAUMOL, *Business Behaviour, Value and Growth* (Harcourt, Brace & World, Inc., 1967), Revised Edition, specifically chapter 6.

37. JOHN K. GALBRAITH, *The New Industrial State* (Boston: Houghton Mifflin Company, 1967), chapters 6 and 15.

38. *Ibid.*, p. 167.

39. *Ibid.*, p. 171.

40. Galbraith points out that the effects of earnings below and above the constraint are asymmetrical. Low earnings mean loss of autonomy, whereas high returns do not increase the security of the firm. The autonomy is nearly absolute anyway. Since the explicit maximization of revenues increases the risk of loss, the technostructure will try to play it safe. Thus, according to Galbraith, a mature corporation will not want to maximize profits at all. *Ibid.*, pp. 168–169.

41. See footnote 3 on page 53 of chapter 2.

42. M. E. KREININ, *Alternative Commercial Policies – Their Effect on the American Economy* (East Lansing: Michigan State University Press, 1967), p. 89. A discussion on the goals of the firm on pp. 85–89.

43. In cases where a domestic company has an advantage over foreign producers, possibilities exist for licensing agreements to obtain an adequate return. However, when imperfections in the market structure exist, it may not be possible to obtain a satisfactory price for the advantage. In such cases the company would start a direct investment to fully appropriate the returns on the advantage. HYMER, *Ph. D. Dissertation*, p. 24.

44. A high price is obviously not the only reason why owners would sell the enterprise. It is conceivable that the offer is less than the company's net worth, but that considerations as retirement or succession in a family business play a role. See chapter 3, Part 2, sub (f) for the motivations of existing Dutch companies to affiliate with American companies.

45. GETHYN DAVIES writes about the defensive aspects of UK investments in Singapore in: 'Direct Investment in Sterling Area Export Markets', *The Banker's Magazine*, July 1969, pp. 17–21.
See also: S. J. WELLS, *British Export Performance* (Cambridge: At the University Press, 1964), p. 46.

46. Raymond Vernon also refers to the situation where the threat to the established position of an enterprise may force an exporter into making a direct investment.

28

RAYMOND VERNON, 'International Investment and ...', *op. cit.*, p. 200.

47. See for instance: ALLAN W. JOHNSTONE, *United States Direct Investment in France* (An Investigation of the French Charges) (Cambridge: The MIT Press, 1965), p. 106, and HEINZ F. KUBY, *Provokation Europa* (Köln, 1965). The discussions in Australia are briefly covered by W. M. CORDEN, 'Australian Economic Policy Discussion in the Post-War Period: A Survey', *American Economic Review*, Supplement part 2, vol. LVIII, no. 3, June 1968, pp. 89–138. In particular, pp. 113–120; also contains a bibliography on pp. 131–138.
For the European view on these matters the reader is referred to: J. J. SERVAN-SCHREIBER, *Le Défi Américain* (Paris: Denoel, 1967), American edition: *The American Challenge* (New York: Atheneum, 1968).
For another 'laundry list' of complaints about US direct investments, KINDLEBERGER, *op. cit.*, lecture 3, pp. 74–105.

48. These arguments are discussed at much greater length in, among others: J. C. MURPHY, 'International Investment and the National Interest', *The Southern Economic Journal*, vol. XXVII, no. 1, March 1960, pp. 11–17; A. E. JASAY, 'The Social Choice between Home and Overseas Investment', *The Economic Journal*, vol. LXX, no. 277, March 1960, pp. 105–113; M.C. KEMP, 'Foreign Investments and the National Interest', *The Economic Record*, vol. 38, no. 81, March 1962, pp. 56–62; T. BALOGH and P. O. STREETEN, 'Domestic versus Foreign Investment', *Bulletin of the Oxford University Institute of Statistics*, vol. 22, no. 3, August 1960, pp. 213–224. M. FRANKEL, 'Home versus Foreign Investment: A Case against Capital Export', *Kyklos*, no. 3, 1965.

49. Even if the investor would allow for greater uncertainty and risk associated with the foreign investment, and consequently would insist on a higher marginal product abroad than at home, the nation would still lose the difference between marginal and average product. In cases where the marginal product (profits) are reinvested, the foreign country benefits once more from the investment.

50. Singer has pointed out that foreign investments have been traditionally concentrated in the primary product sectors of the underdeveloped countries. These products were exported to the investing countries. H. W. SINGER, 'The Distribution of Gains Between Investing and Borrowing Countries', *American Economic Review*, vol. XL, no. 2, May 1950, pp. 477, 478.

51. M. C. KEMP, *op. cit.*, p. 56.

52. Note that the terms of trade effect are the only ambiguous effect of foreign investment. The actual end result can only be analyzed for each case separately and would depend on factors such as the type of investment, the type of industry (export or import substituting), the patterns of supply and demand, and the methods of correcting imbalances.

53. The US Government at one time actively stimulated the direct investments by American corporations. The same is true for the Netherlands. We refer also to page 14 in this chapter for a quotation from the MacMillan Report, which illustrates the view of the UK Government at that time.
Lastly, we quote from an article by Vernon: 'As far as the US Government is concerned, these multinational enterprises simply extend the reach of the US economy into foreign countries and add to the economic power of the American economy.' RAYMOND VERNON, 'The Multinational Corporation', *op. cit.*, p. 538.

54. Interestingly enough, when direct investments are curbed it is hardly ever for the conventional reasons that were discussed above. Thus, in the case of the United States the controls on direct investments abroad were instituted for balance of payments considerations.

55. Refer to chapter 2 for information on the sources to finance expenditures on property, land and equipment, during the discussion of some facts concerning US direct investments abroad. Also Annex I in the Appendix.

56. EDITH T. PENROSE, 'Foreign Investment and the Growth of the Firm', *The Economic Journal*, Vol. LXVII, No. 262, June, 1956, pp. 220–235.

57. WELLS, *op. cit.*, p. 47, remarks: 'It is by no means necessary that direct investment be financed from the United Kingdom. An alternative is the reinvestment of locally earned profits in the overseas branch or company. In fact, this appears to have been the most important means of financing UK direct investment during the nineteen-fifties.'

58. *Ibid.*, p. 222.

59. C. D. A. VAN LYNDEN, *Directe Investeeringen in het Buitenland* ('s-Gravenhage: Fa. L. J. C. Boucher, 1945), p. 98. [Quoted from F. G. CONOLLY, *The Importance of Business Foreign Investments*, International Capital Movements Project, Document No. 5–4 IV. 1939, Geneva Research Centre, p. 18.]

60. HOWE MARTYN, *International Business, Principles and Problems* (London: Collier-MacMillan Limited, 1964).

61. Another objective of subsequent capital flows from the parent to the subsidiary is often the *maintenance* of control when the equity capital is increased. A recent example is the $ 210,000,000 capital flow from Royal Dutch Petroleum to its American Subsidiary Shell Co. To maintain its degree of control at 69 percent of the equity capital the parent exercised the right to purchase 69 percent of the newly issued shares. See: *Survey of Current Business*, June 1968, p. 21 under the paragraph 'Special Transactions'.

62. The MacMillan Report – *Report of the Committee of Finance and Industry* (London: 1931), p. 165.

63. K. D. BOSCH, *De Nederlandse Beleggingen in de Verenigde Staten* (The Netherlands investments in the United States) (Amsterdam, Brussels: Uitgeversmaatschappij Elsevier, 1949), p. 614.

64. A number of case studies have been published by the National Planning Association, New York: *Sears, Roebuck de Mexico* (1953), *Casa Grace in Peru* (1954), *The Phillipine in Venezuela* (1955), *The Firesone Operations in Liberia, Stanvac in Indonesia* and *The General Electric Company in Brazil* (1961).

65. I. BRECHER and S. S. REISMANN, *Canada – United Economic Relations* (Ottawa: Royal Commission on Canada's Economic Prospects, 1957).
BERNARD BONIN, *op. cit.*

66. DONALD T. BRASH, *op. cit.*
JOHN H. DUNNING, *op. cit.*

67. G. D. A. MACDOUGALL, 'The Benefits and Costs of Private Investment from Abroad – A Theoretical Approach', *The Economic Record*, vol. 38, no. 73, March 1960, pp. 13–35.

68. ARTHUR STONEHILL, *Foreign Ownership in Norwegian Enterprise* (Oslo: Central Bureau of Statistics, 1965).

69. For more detailed discussions the reader is referred to the publications mentioned earlier that deal specifically with the experience of individual countries. KINDLE-BERGER, *op. cit.*, gives a resume of those publications dealing with US direct investment in the dominions, pp. 106–144.

70. As measured by local *value-added*.

71. This development has been termed 'organic' in a study by the National Industrial Conference Board, JUDD POLK, IRENE W. MEISTER and LAWRENCE A. VEIT, *U.S. Production Abroad and the Balance of Payments* (New York: The National Industrial Conference Board, 1966), pp. 132–136.

A similar notion is developed in the so-called Reddaway report on the effects of direct investments by the UK: W. B. REDDAWAY (with others), *Effects of U.K. Direct Investment Overseas – An Interim Report* (Cambridge: At the University Press, 1967), pp. 33–34. Also in the *Final Report*.

72. REDDAWAY, *op. cit.*, p. 34. The final report was published in 1968 under the same title. It does not materially alter the argument of the interim report.

73. There is a danger that the foreign owned sector will not be adequately integrated with the domestic economy. Singer has pointed out that the 'traditional' investments (as he has called them) by developed countries in underdeveloped areas have been concentrated in export producing sectors. There have very often been primary materials or food sectors, which have depended for their development on demand conditions in developed countries and 'have not become a real part of the economies of underdeveloped countries'. SINGER, *op. cit.*, p. 475.

74. STEPHEN H. HYMER, 'Direct Investments and the National Interest', *op. cit.*, p. 198.

75. See also the discussion in chapter 6 on the characteristics of direct investment.

76. STEPHEN H. HYMER claims that direct investments abroad are a vehicle for the elimination of competition, namely by buying up the existing firms. HYMER, *Dissertation*, p. 3. He does not, however, present evidence for this claim.

77. JOSEPH A. SCHUMPETER, *Capitalism, Socialism and Democracy* (New York: Harper and Bros., Publishers, 3rd edition of 1950). A quotation from page 106 reads: 'What we have got to accept is that it (the large scale establishment or unit of control) has come to be the most powerful engine of progress and in particular of the long-run expansion of total output .... In this respect, perfect competition is not only impossible but inferior, and has no title to being set up as a model of ideal efficiency.' See also chapters VII and VIII, 'The Process of Creative Destruction' and 'Monopolistic Practices' on pp. 81–86 and pp. 87–106 respectively.

78. The possibilities for such action through judicious use of transfer prices between subsidiaries have diminished somewhat as a result of measures taken by the US Internal Revenue Service. The 1962 Revenue Act was designed to eliminate tax havens such as Switzerland. For sales from US parents to their subsidiaries the rule on transfer pricing is: 'costs plus 10 percent.' With higher margins the company runs the risk of an investigation by IRS. At the same time that the Revenue Act was enacted, host countries became aware of the potential disadvantages of these transfer pricing policies. A good example of the pricing policies that result in profits at one geographic point in the multinational organization and in losses elsewhere can be found in the petroleum industry. I quote from a recent article in the *Survey of Current Business*: 'But in each of the last 3 years, the European oil industry has shown net losses. This in part reflects accounting practices of the integrated petroleum companies' refining and marketing operations, which are important in Europe, generally do not show significant net earnings.' *Survey of Current Business*, October 1968, p. 26.
The implication is, of course, that the production operations show the profits, presumably because the tax treatment in those countries is better than in Europe.

79. ANTHONY Y. C. KOO, 'A Short-Run Measure of the Relative Economic Contribution of Direct Foreign Investment', *The Review of Economics and Statistics*, vol. XLIII, no. 3, August 1961, pp. 269–276.

80. The information used by KOO resulted from a US Department of Commerce study, published as: *U.S. Investments in Latin America* (Washington, D.C., 1957).

81. I have omitted from this analysis the terms of trade effects of foreign direct investments. For some views on this aspect the reader is referred to JOHN M. LETICHE, *Balance of Payments and Economic Growth* (New York: Harper, 1967 [2nd edition]).

Bo Sodersten, *A Study of Economic Growth and International Trade* (Stockholm: Almquist and Wicksell, 1964).

Also the Proceedings of the Conference of the 'International Economic Association', John H. Adler, ed., *Capital Movements and Economic Development* (New York: St. Martin's Press, 1967).

H. W. Singer, 'The Distribution of Gains Between Investing and Borrowing Countries', *American Economic Review*, vol. XL, no. 2, May, 1950, pp. 477–479.

82. Hirschman has introduced the terminology 'backward' and 'forward' linkages to describe the effect of investments on an underdeveloped economy.

Albert O. Hirschman, *The Strategy of Economic Development* (New Haven: Yale University Press, 1958).

83. Figures to support this contention can be found in Chapter 2.

84. See with respect to this characteristic the discussion in Chapter 6, 'The Characteristics of Direct Investments'.

85. Hymer, *Direct Foreign Investment and the National Interest*, p. 200.

86. *Ibid.*, p. 200.

Mr Homan has suggested that foreign direct investors turn the facilities over to local interests after a number of years. His motivation though is quite different from the one used here: he regards this as an attractive way for the multinational corporation to free the capital and move on to more profitable investment outlets.

A. Gerlof Homan, *Some Measures and Interpretations of the Effects of the Operations of U.S. Foreign Enterprises on the U.S. Balance of Payments* (Menlo Park: Stanford Research Institute, 1962).

87. P. N. Rosenstein-Rodan, 'Philosophy of International Investment in the Second Half of the Twentieth Century', in: John H. Adler, ed., *op. cit.*, pp. 175–185.

88. *Ibid.*, p. 176–177.

89. Hymer, *op. cit.*, pp. 199–200.

90. My discussion here is brief and of a general nature. For a recent and thorough analysis: G. C. Hufbauer, and F. M. Adler, *Overseas Manufacturing Investment and the Balance of Payments* (Washington D. C.: US Treasury Department, 1968). Also: Jack N. Behrman, *Manufacturing Investment and the Balance of Payments* (New York: National Foreign Trade Council, 1969) containing a critique of the Hufbauer-Adler study.

91. Typically the economic growth models dealing with underdeveloped countries deal with 'resource gaps', with the binding constraint more often than not the supply of foreign exchange. There of course the usual exceptions to the rule, e.g. Kuwait and Venezuela.

92. Hymer, *Dissertation*, p. 3.

93. Robert F. Emery, 'The Relation of Exports and Economic Growth', *Kyklos*, vol. XX, fasc. 2, 1967, pp. 470–484.

94. US Department of Commerce, *Survey of Current Business*, November, 1966, p. 9, gives the ratio of exports to total sales for US manufacturing establishments in the EEC for 1965. This ratio is 35 for the Benelux, 27 for Germany, 17 for France, 14 for Italy and almost 24 for the whole Common Market.

95. Source is the *Survey of Current Business*, November, 1966, p. 9. The figures for 1964 are the latest available. Sales in all areas amounted to $ 27,438,000 in 1964, with $ 6,568,000 exported. For Europe total sales were at $ 16,653,000, of which $ 3,810,000 was exported.

96. Reddaway, *Final Report*, discusses the main continuing effects of UK direct investments abroad on the host countries. In the ranking of these effects by the contribution made to the UK exports the underdeveloped countries come in the top half of the

table, with the developed ones in the bottom half. The suggestion is made that the ordering closely matches a ranking by the degree of industrialisation (pp. 215–217).

97. See the remarks made in the preceding section on Capital and Savings with respect to the *costs* of foreign capital and the transfer-burden connected with private investments.

98. EDITH T. PENROSE, *op. cit.*, pp. 220–235.

99. ROSENSTEIN-RODAN, *op. cit.*, pp. 178–179, has suggested an approach along similar lines. To quote: 'In the initial phase foreign investors may hold a higher percentage of equity, but they should offer an option to national investors, or firmly announce their intention to sell some proportion of the shares to them in the future. Other forms of in advance mutually agreed upon 'nationalization' (in the sense of gradual acquisition of a majority holding) should be studied' (p. 178).

100. One can make a very good case against these recommendations on the ground that they all will reduce the economic returns to the multinational enterprise, and possibly in the short run even to the host country. Thus e.g. a system of local subcontracting may be more expensive than to import these products, most certainly so for the company. The host country itself has to weigh the alternatives and decide upon such action that will – over the long pull – maximize the returns from the foreign controlled operation.

101. From the point of view of the domestic country a direct investment abroad can be classified according to *production* and *financial* interdependencies. The former follows the traditional division of entities within the multinational corporation between raw materials or intermediate goods producers and final goods producers. This pattern is most clear in extractive or agricultural direct investments, but also occurs in manufacturing when parts or components are traded between parent and subsidiary. In this sense the foreign investment is *complementary* to the domestic investment. Financial interdependency rests on the imperfections in the credit market, and the enterprise faces a rising supply curve of external finance or refuses to consider external finance at all. The supply of retained earnings then becomes a determinant of investment. In this sense the foreign investment is a *substitute* to the domestic investment. See: STEVENS, *op. cit.*, pp. 10–11.

102. REDDAWAY, *Interim* and *Final Report*.

103. *Ibid.*, pp. 121–126.

104. *Ibid.*, pp. 123; 233–237.

105. *Ibid.*, pp. 212–213.

106. *Ibid.*, pp. 306–331.

107. JOHN H. DUNNING, 'The Foreign Investment Controversy', series of three articles in *The Banker's Magazine*, May, June and July 1969.

108. Among others see: JUDD POLK, IRENE W. MEISTER and LAWRENCE A. VEIT, *U.S. Production Abroad and the Balance of Payments: A Survey of Corporate Investment Experience* (New York: The National Industrial Conference Board, 1966); G. C. HUFBAUER, and F. M. ADLER, *op. cit.*, and JACK N. BEHRMAN, *op. cit.*

109. In a sense Hufbauer-Adler have updated earlier work by PHILIP BELL, 'Private Capital Movements and the Balance of Payments Position', in *Factors Affecting the U.S. Balance of Payments* (US Congress, Joint Economic Committee, 87th Congress, 1962).

110. Quoted from *Business Abroad*, May 30, 1966, p. 11.
This article was adopted from: JACK N. BEHRMAN, 'Foreign Investment Muddle: The Perils of Ad Hoccery', *Columbia Journal of World Business*, vol. 1, Fall 1965.
Hufbauer and Adler however calculate recoupment periods that are typically around 15 years (14.7 for the world), varying from 13.0 for Europe to around 17.5 for Canada and Latin America. These are the recoupment periods for mixed financing, i.e. US capital and local borrowing. When financing is limited only to US capital the recoupment periods are a bit longer. HUFBAUER-ADLER, *op. cit.*, pp. 17–18.

2. Some facts about US direct investments

The role of the United States in the field of direct investments began as recipient when, in the 18th and 19th centuries, capital and know-how were attracted from Europe, mainly from the United Kingdom, France and the Netherlands.[1] These investments contributed in an important way to the economic development of the US and were actively encouraged by, among others, Alexander Hamilton.[2] Their role in such diverse sectors as railways, steel, real estate, and gold mining is described in the aforementioned book by Cleona Lewis (see note 1).

It was not until the turn of this century that the US itself had any sizeable direct investments abroad. After the first World War, the American holdings increased rapidly until the 'great crash' of 1929 put a stop to this development. During the next thirteen years, total US investments abroad grew by less than half a billion dollars, which can be partly attributed to devaluations and bankruptcies, but mainly to the unfavorable political and economic climate. Table 1 illustrates the growth in the value of US investments and also shows that Latin America and Canada attracted most of these funds.

After World War II the American direct investments grew very slowly, again because of political (cold war) and economic factors. But in the mid-fifties the rate of growth picked up considerably, especially after 1957. This increase was stimulated very actively by the US government and the Department of Commerce. As one executive put it, 'If your company did not have at least one foreign operation, you were completely out and some even regarded this as slightly unpatriotic.' Prestige certainly influenced the growth rate of direct investments, as did the 'red-carpet treatment' many businessmen received – and still do receive – abroad. These observations serve to underscore the fact that many non-economic factors greatly affect the extent and direction of foreign investments.[3]

Table 1. Value of U.S. direct investments abroad: selected years and areas (in millions of dollars)

Area	1897	1908	1914	1919	1924	1929	1936	1943
Latin America	308 (49)	754 (46)	1,281 (48)	1,988 (51)	2,819 (52)	3,462 (46)	2,803 (42)	2,721 (35)
Canada	160 (25)	405 (25)	618 (23)	814 (21)	1,081 (30)	2,010 (37)	1,952 (30)	2,378 (30)
Europe	131 (31)	369 (23)	573 (22)	694 (18)	921 (17)	1,353 (18)	1,259 (19)	2,051 (26)
Others	36 (6)	111 (7)	180 (7)	384 (10)	568 (11)	703 (9)	677 (10)	712 (9)
Total value	635	1,639	2,652	3,880	5,389	7,528	6,691	7,862

(Figures in parentheses are the percentage shares)
Source: CLEONA LEWIS, *America's Stake in International Investments* (Washington, D.C.: The Brookings Institution, 1938) p. 606, for the years 1897, 1908, 1914, 1919, and 1924. US Department of Commerce, *U.S. Business Investments in Foreign Countries* (Washington, D.C.: 1960) p. 92, table 4, for the years 1929, 1936, and 1943.

Table 2. Value of U.S. direct investments abroad: post World War II development (in millions of dollars)

Area	1950	1957	1960	1963	1966	1967	1968[p]
Latin America	4,445 (38)	7,434 (30)	8,387 (26)	8,662 (21)	9,826 (18)	10,265 (17)	11,010 (17)
Canada	3,579 (20)	8,769 (35)	11,198 (34)	13,044 (32)	16,999 (31)	18,097 (30)	19,488 (30)
Europe	1,733 (15)	4,151 (16)	6,645 (20)	10,340 (25)	16,209 (30)	17,926 (30)	19,386 (30)
Other countries	2,031 (17)	5,040 (20)	6,535 (20)	8,640 (21)	11,680 (21)	13,198 (22)	14,872 (23)
Total value	11,788	25,394	32,765	40,686	54,711	59,486	64,756

(Figures in parentheses are percentage shares)
p = preliminary
Source: US Department of Commerce, *Balance of Payments: Statistical Supplement* (1962) for the years 1950, 1957, and 1960.
Survey of Current Business, September, 1965 for 1963; October, 1968 for 1966; October 1969 for 1967 and preliminary figures for 1968.

Table 3. *Distribution of U.S. direct investment by major industry: some post World War II years (in millions of dollars)*

Industry	1950	1957	1960	1963	1966	1967	1968^p
Mining & smelting	1,129 (10)	2,361 (9)	3,011 (9)	3,369 (8)	4,315 (8)	4,876 (8)	5,370 (8)
Petroleum	3,390 (29)	9,055 (36)	10,948 (33)	13,652 (34)	16,205 (30)	17,404 (30)	18,835 (29)
Manufacturing	3,831 (32)	8,009 (32)	11,152 (34)	14,937 (37)	22,058 (40)	24,167 (41)	26,354 (41)
Public utilities	1,425 (12)	2,145 (8)	2,548 (8)	2,061 (5)	2,284 (4)	2,393 (4)	2,672 (4)
Trade	762 (6)	1,668 (6)	2,397 (7)	3,307 (8)	4,716 (9)	5,010 (8)	5,266 (8)
Other	1,251 (11)	2,157 (8)	2,709 (8)	3,359 (8)	5,133 (9)	5,636 (9)	6,258 (9)
Total	11,788	25,394	32,765	40,686	54,711	59,486	64,756

(Figures in parentheses are percentage shares)
p = preliminary
Source: US Department of Commerce, *Balance of Payments: Statistical Supplement* (1962) for the years 1950, 1957, and 1960.
Survey of Current Business, September, 1965 for 1963; October, 1968 for 1966; October 1969 for 1967 and preliminary figures for 1968.

Off late we have witnessed an interesting reversal of the government attitude toward direct investments. These investments and the capital outflows connected with them are now regarded as the major cause of US balance of payments deficits. The very high rate of growth of the American direct investments that was set in the early sixties will thus be slowed down, although, of course, not halted.[4]

The growth of US direct investments after 1950 is illustrated with data presented in Table 2, broken down by geographical area. Aside from the rapid growth of these investments, an interesting shift has taken place, both in geographical direction and type of activity. Whereas Latin America initially attracted most of the investments and very little went to Europe, now the reverse is true. As to the type of activity, a growing emphasis lies on the manufacturing sector, away from smelting and mining, and petroleum (Table 3). Similarly, within the manufacturing industries themselves dramatic changes have taken place, as is illustrated in Table 4.

Table 4. Value of U.S. direct investments in manufacturing enterprises abroad by commodity (in millions of dollars)

Industry	1929	1950	1957	1960	1963	1964
Food products	222 (12)	483 (13)	723 (9)	943 (8)	1,234 (8)	1,393 (8)
Paper & allied	279 (16)	378 (10)	722 (9)	861 (8)	1,055 (7)	1,126 (7)
Chemical & allied	138 (7)	512 (13)	1,378 (17)	1,902 (17)	2,605 (17)	3,068 (18)
Rubber	60 (4)	182 (5)	401 (5)	520 (5)	625 (4)	674 (4)
Primary & fabricated metals	150 (8)	385 (10)	941 (12)	1,256 (11)	1,664 (11)	1,830 (11)
Machinery, except electrical	185 (10)	420 (11)	927 (12)	1,333 (12)	1,809 (12)	2,027 (12)
Electrical machinery	259 (15)	387 (10)	731 (9)	918 (8)	1,196 (8)	1,316 (8)
Transportation equipment	184 (10)	485 (13)	1,204 (15)	2,118 (19)	2,946 (20)	3,351 (20)
Other	337 (18)	599 (16)	983 (12)	1,301 (12)	1,803 (12)	2,076 (12)
Manufacturing total	1,813	3,831	8,009	11,152	14,937	16,861

(Figures in parentheses are percentage shares)
Source: US Department of Commerce, *U.S. Business Investments in Foreign Countries* (1960) for 1929.
US Department of Commerce, *Balance of Payments, Statistical Supplement* (1962) for the years 1950, 1957 and 1960.
US Department of Commerce, *Survey of Current Business*, September, 1965 for the years 1963 and 1964. These are the latest available figures.

Finally some data are presented concerning the sources of funds of American direct investment expenditures abroad. Table 5 illustrates that capital flows from the United States finance only 20 percent of these expenditures. The remainder comes from internally generated funds [such as retained earnings plus depreciation and depletion allowances], as well as locally raised capital. The latter category is becoming increasingly important, accounting for almost 32 percent of all sources in 1965. Due to

37

Table 5. Financing of U.S. direct investments abroad: sources of funds in all areas for some selected years (in millions of dollars)

	1957	1960	1963	1964	1965
Capital from the US	2,033 (28)	1,046 (21)	1,393 (18)	1,422 (16)	2,490 (22)
Retained earnings*	1,758 (24)	995 (20)	1,501 (20)	1,390 (16)	1,471 (13)
Depreciation & depletion allowances	1,626 (22)	1,927 (39)	2,590 (34)	3,012 (35)	3,390 (30)
Locally raised capital	1,718 (24)	1,017 (20)	2,056 (27)	2,743 (31)	3,578 (32)
Other	167 (2)	n.a.	96 (1)	154 (2)	318 (3)
Total sources	7,292	4,985	7,636	8,721	11,247
* Net income	3,649	3,255	4,262	4,645	4,985
paid out	1,819	2,260	2,761	3,255	3,514
retained	1,758	995	1,501	1,390	1,471

(Figures in parentheses are percentage shares)
Source: US Department of Commerce, *Survey of Current Business*, September issues. No data available for 1966 and 1967 yet.

the recent measures taken by the US government to correct the balance-of-payments deficit these foreign funds will be relied on even more to finance American investments abroad. If one keeps in mind that large numbers of new American subsidiaries are established every year these figures lend support to the contention that US capital is being primarily used to obtain, and subsequently to maintain, control over foreign operations.[5]

The general discussion of US direct investments will be kept very brief and serves only to set the stage for a slightly longer survey of the picture in Europe. Subsequently, American investments in the Netherlands will be treated rather thoroughly.

WESTERN EUROPE

The total value of US direct investments abroad was quite small until around 1900, and the investments in Western Europe amounted to less than two percent in 1908, an insignificant share. This is not too surprising, as Europe was investing heavily in the United States at that time and held an economic as well as technological superiority over the rest of the world.

After 1918, however, American companies set up many subsidiaries in Western Europe and the value of their direct investments grew from $ 694 million in 1919 to $ 1,353 million ten years later. In the same period, the value of the investments in Canada and Latin America also increased rapidly. Although the American stake in Europe was relatively small, its growth apparently causes an anxiety among Europeans similar to what was recently experienced in the Common Market countries, particularly in Germany and France.

It is amusing to read in Frank A. Southard's book on American industry in Europe the titles of articles and books that cry out against the 'takeover by America of Europe's economy.'[6] This was 1929! It is even more striking to read about the concern caused, just a few years later, by European investments in the United States. One particularly indignant writer urges us '... to consider the value to foreign nations of the power – economic and political – wielded over us by their foreign investments here.' He then proceeds: 'Do not their agents control the stock market? Do not their agents here control our banks?'[7] All of which seems a bit overdone in view of the fact that in 1935 total foreign investments in the US amounted to 1.9 billion dollars as compared to at least $ 7.2 billion in American direct investment abroad. Furthermore, according to Cleona Lewis, there were only 54 branches or agencies of foreign banks operating in the US in 1936; of these only eight were authorized to do regular banking business. Together they held $ 16.8 million in deposits, as compared to $ 50,000 million for all banks in the US.[8] Many of the recent emotional outbursts against the American investments in Europe seem to be similarly founded upon ill-conceived notions about its scope or upon fallacious and irrelevant comparisons with national figures.[9] This is not to say that all the criticism and worries expressed by Europeans would be irrational or ill-founded. A good example of a balanced view on the American presence in Western Europe, and in any country, for that matter, is the recent book by Servan-Schreiber. He discusses not only advantages and drawbacks of US direct investments, but also suggests remedies to change unsatisfactory developments.[10]

The recent spotlight on the American investments in Europe is largely due to the rapid growth in value and scope of these investments. Whereas US direct investments used to be concentrated in Latin America, in Canada, and in all other areas of the world, rather than in Europe, this situation has changed considerably since 1957. The figures presented in Table 2 show clearly that the share in total American direct investment of Western Europe has grown quite rapidly, mostly at the expense of Latin America. Canada managed to maintain its share, and 'other countries' registered an increase from 17 percent in 1950 to 23 percent in 1968. In the eighteen years from 1950 to 1968, Latin America's share dropped from 38 percent to 17 percent of the total of US foreign investments, whereas Europe doubled its share from 15 to 30 percent by 1968.

It is not the aim of this dissertation to analyze the American investments in Europe as a whole, or those in the EEC countries in particular. Consequently, no effort will be made to present detailed figures on such aspects of US operations as concentration in industries, market shares and size of establishments. Much of this material is already published and, on the whole, easily accessible.[11] Furthermore, all these publications draw basically on the US Department of Commerce statistics of US direct investments abroad, and in that sense do not provide new evidence. Some general figures, however, will be presented.

Table 6. Distribution of U.S. direct investment in Europe by major industry (in millions of dollars)

Industry	1950	1957	1960	1963	1966	1967	1968ᵖ
Mining & smelting	31	55	49	55	54	61	61
	(2)	(1)	(.7)	(.5)	(.3)	(.3)	(.3)
Petroleum	426	1,253	1,726	2,776	3,977	4,423	4,640
	(25)	(30)	(26)	(27)	(25)	(24)	(24)
Manufacturing	932	2,195	3,797	5,634	8,879	9,798	10,778
	(54)	(53)	(57)	(54)	(55)	(54)	(56)
Public utilities	27	38	45	44	67	78	94
	(2)	(1)	(.7)	(.4)	(.4)	(.4)	(.5)
Trade	186	433	736	1,237	1,928	2,060	2,126
	(11)	(10)	(11)	(12)	(12)	(12)	(11)
Other	130	177	291	595	1,294	1,507	1,688
	(8)	(4)	(4)	(6)	(8)	(8)	(9)
Total	1,733	4,151	6,645	10,340	16,200	17,926	19,386

(Figures in parentheses are percentage shares). p = preliminary.
Source: US Department of Commerce, *Balance of Payments: Statistical Supplement* (1962) for the years 1950, 1957, and 1960.
Survey of Current Business, September, 1965 for 1963; October, 1968 for 1966; October 1969 for 1967 and preliminary figures for 1968.

Table 6 shows that most of the investments in Western Europe are concentrated in the petroleum and manufacturing sectors, and within manufacturing a few sectors seem the most attractive (Table 7). It is obviously the concentration in some important and rapidly-growing sectors that causes concern, rather than the overall size of the American investments. The chemical, machinery (electronics) and transportation sectors each have attracted sizeable us investments. Each of these industries is expanding rapidly and has enormous growth potential for the future.

Table 7. Value of U.S. manufacturing investments in Europe: by class of industry (in millions of dollars)

Industry	1950	1957	1960	1963	1964[a]
Food	64 (7)	149 (7)	224 (6)	326 (6)	389 (6)
Paper & allied	5 (.5)	42 (2)	63 (1.5)	81 (1.4)	102 (1.5)
Chemicals & allied	74 (8)	319 (15)	537 (14)	855 (15)	1,073 (16)
Rubber	31 (3)	59 (3)	90 (2)	158 (3)	168 (3)
Primary & fabricated metal	111 (12)	178 (8)	324 (9)	488 (9)	544 (8)
Machinery, except electrical	175 (19)	488 (22)	782 (21)	1,060 (19)	1,186 (18)
Electrical machinery	153 (16)	214 (10)	288 (8)	442 (8)	506 (8)
Transportation equipment	192 (11)	475 (22)	1,074 (28)	1,565 (28)	1,783 (27)
Other	128 (14)	272 (12)	415 (11)	659 (12)	796 (12)
Total	932	2,195	3,797	5,634	6,547

a. Latest available figures for 1964. (Figures in parentheses are percentage shares).
Source: us Department of Commerce, Balance of Payments, Statistical Supplement, 1962 for the years 1950, 1957, and 1960.
us Department of Commerce, Survey of Current Business, September, 1965 for 1963 and 1964.

The same holds true for the petroleum industry, where US companies dominate the European market.

With respect to the growth of American investments in Europe, Table 8 is instructive. Western Europe is divided into various country blocs, and the percentage shares as well as growth rates of US direct investments are given for the years 1950–1966, and for the sub-periods 1950–1958 and 1959–1966.[12] The figures indicate that the rate of growth in the UK has been much lower than in the rest of Europe, though appreciably higher than that for total US investments.

Table 8. *Percentage shares and compound growth rates of U.S. direct investments in Western Europe: by country blocs, 1950–1966**

	Percent share in US direct investments			Annual compound growth rates sub-periods		
	1950	1958	1966	1950–1966	1950–1958	1959–1966
United Kingdom	7.2	7.8	10.4	12.5	12.5	13
Non-EEC (including UK)	9.3	9.7	15.8	13.5	12	16
EEC	5.4	7.0	13.9	16.5	14.5	19
Non-EEC (excluding UK)	2.1	1.9	5.4	16.5	9.5	24.5
World				10	11	9

* The table compares 8 years before the formation of the EEC with the 8 years after that event. For this reason the growth rates have not been calculated up to 1968, although the preliminary information for that year is available.
Source: Calculated from US Department of Commerce data, as published annually in the September issue of the *Survey of Current Business.*
Annual compound growth rates are rounded off to nearest half percent.

The Common Market countries appear to have attracted much American investment, with a growth rate of more than double that for all areas in the period 1959–1966, when total US direct investment increased at a rate of nine percent. For the rest of Europe, excluding the UK and the EEC-countries, one finds an even higher rate of growth, which to a large extent may be due to the low initial value of US investments in those countries.

Among the many publications dealing with American direct investments in the EEC-countries, one of the latest is that by Scaperlanda and Maurer; their bibliography lists the extensive literature on this topic.[13] Scaperlanda and Maurer attempt to determine the economic factors that have motivated US direct investors in the years 1952–1966. Of the three hypotheses tested, viz. size of market, economic growth and obstacles to trade, they find only the size of market variable, as measured by gross national product, to be statistically significant. The test for structural change in the relationship as a result of Common Market formation is inconclusive, and the authors conclude that the 'market-size elasticity of EEC demand for US direct foreign investment is rather stable between the sub-periods 1952–58 and 1959–66, although a slight decline may have occurred.[14] It is interesting to note that no statistical support could be found for the factor of trade discrimination, which is generally thought to have a strong positive correlation with the flow of direct investments.[15]

THE NETHERLANDS

1. History and figures

Although the Netherlands has a long history of direct investments in the United States (see Chapter 5), it was not before 1896 that an American company started operations in the Netherlands. The distinction of being the first *producing* establishment goes to Quaker Oats, with the manufacture and sale of food products.[16] Earlier, sales offices had been set up by, among others, the Singer Company (1870), Mobil Oil (1890) and the American Petroleum Company (1891), predecessor of Esso Nederland. Cleona Lewis mentions that the capitalization of the latter company amounted to $ 3,155,700 in 1891.[17] She also notes that Pure Oil operated two storage stations by 1908 which were established by the 1890's and that Sinclair had Dutch operations by 1914.[18] Furthermore, the US had investments in public utilities of 2.8 million dollars in both 1908 and 1914, after which they seem to have been terminated.[19] For manufacturing no early information is available, except the date of establishment as published in the US Department of Commerce trade-list.

Robert Dunn writes in 1926 about '... the $ 25 million American investment in bonds of the Jurgen United Works [predecessor of Unilever] and the Holland-American Line, ..., Standard Oil, the Radio Corporation of America, and various film companies as well as scores of sales agencies from the United States are active in the Dutch market. American money has built electric railways and assisted in other public utilities in Holland.'[20]

By 1929 total American direct investment in the Netherlands was valued at 43.2 million dollars, of which $ 12.1 million were in the petroleum sector (mostly storage and marketing).[21] During the early 1930's the value of the US stake decreased to $ 18.8 million, after which it grew again to a value of $ 59.6 million in 1943.[22]

After the war and the early reconstruction years, the American investments in the Netherlands were valued at $ 84 million in 1950. Around that time the Dutch government put up a determined effort to woo more foreign, and particularly American investors. This effort formed part of an ambitious industrialization program that was to change the Netherlands from a predominantly agricultural to a modern industrial nation. (For a discussion of the investment attraction program, see Part 3.) It is hard to establish clearly the effect of this program on the American direct investments in the Netherlands. As it turned out, even without special attractions US companies decided to set up shop in Western Europe, and part of these investments would have gone to the Netherlands anyway.

The value of the American investments in the Netherlands increased rapidly, especially after 1958, as illustrated in Table 9. But then again, so did US investments in other Western European countries. The petroleum sector has traditionally attracted a huge share of the American direct investments in the Netherlands (in 1929: 12.1 million dollars worth of investments in petroleum out of a total value of 43.2 million dollars). Recently, however, the manufacturing industries have surpassed the petroleum investments as the most important sector in the Netherlands. And after 1964 these manufacturing investments continued to grow at a fast pace, with the preliminary figure for 1968 indicating a doubling in value over the last four years. In this period the value of the US investments in petroleum has hardly increased at all.[23]

Significant growth has also taken place in the 'trade' and 'other activities' sectors. Many companies that do not have production establishments have set up sales outlets for their products, manufactured either in Europe or in the US. 'Other activities' include banking, management and other consulting offices which typically follow the manufacturing investments.

Further evidence of the increased activities of US companies in the Netherlands can be found in the number of American establishments. The following table (Table 10) summarizes the information published by the US Department of Commerce. In the ten years from 1957 to 1966 the number of establishments more than tripled from 195 to 597 by October, 1967, with the total value of the investments going up from 191 million to 859 million dollars. The preliminary value for 1968 was put at $ 1,073 million; no recent data are available on the number of establishments.

2. The Netherlands compared to Common Market countries

It is useful to view the American investments in the Netherlands in the larger perspective of member EEC countries. After all, the investments in

44

Table 9. Value of U.S. direct investments in the Netherlands – total and by sector, 1950–1967 (in millions of dollars)

Year	Total value	Value by sector				
		Petroleum	Manufact-uring	Public utilities	Trade	Other
1950	84	43	23	1	13	5
1951	101	55	24	1	15	6
1952	110	62	25	1	17	6
1953	125	72	29	1	18	6
1954	138	78	34	1	20	7
1955	159	87	38	1	25	8
1956	189	101	45	8	25	10
1957[1]	207	106	50	18	22	12
1957[2]	191	107	38	15	27	5
1958	207	112	48	15	27	5
1959	245	135	59	14	29	8
1960	283	143	80	15	36	9
1961	309	144	95	15	44	10
1962	376	163	119	15	59	14
1963	446	201	155	16	56	19
1964	593	244	216	16	92	25
1965	686	238	270	17	127	33
1966	859	267	372	18	155	47
1967	942	221*	463	18	161	79
1968p	1,073	259	557	18	157	82

p = preliminary

1957[1] value based on 1950 survey, 1957[2] value based on 1957 survey.

* The drop in value of petroleum investments in 1967 is due to the fact that a petro-chemical investment has been re-classified under manufacturing, a result of refinement in data collection by the Commerce Department. Information provided by the Department in a telephone call.

Source: US Department of Commerce, *Survey of Current Business*, annual issues.

Holland are but a very small percentage of total US investments,[24] but in the EEC group the Dutch share amounts to about 11 percent. This percentage has remained approximately the same since 1950, when it stood at 13 percent. (See Table 11.)

Although US investments in Holland grew at a fast pace, especially after 1957, the same development occurred in the other EEC members, and for that matter, in all Western European countries. The explanation for the falling share of France in the total EEC investments can be found in the increasingly hostile reception of US investors, in particular after 1962.[25] Even though the growth of American investments in Holland has not diverged much from that of member EEC countries, the investment-density

Table 10. Number and value of U.S. direct investments in the Netherlands: selected years (in millions of dollars)

Period	Number of establishments	Value of the investment
Prior to 1930 (1)	41	24.8
1931–1945 (additions) (1)	39	10.0
1946–1950 (additions) (1)	34	36.9
1950–1957 (additions) (2)	90	52.0
Total by end of 1950 (2)	195	191.0
Total by end of 1963 (3,5)	223	446.0
Total by end of 1966 (4,5)	597	858.0

Source: 1. US Department of Commerce, *Foreign Investments of the United States*, 1953.
2. US Department of Commerce, *U.S. Business Investments in Foreign Countries*, 1960.
3. For the number of establishments by the end of 1963: *Economische Voorlichting*, No. 7-12, February 1964, p. 6 (Publication of the Economic Information Service of the Ministry of Economic Affairs, 's-Gravenhage).
4. For the number of establishments by the end of 1966: US Department of Commerce, *American Firms, Subsidiaries and Affiliates in the Netherlands*, October, 1967.
5. For the value of the investments: US Department of Commerce, *Survey of Current Business*, September, 1964 and 1967.

Table 11. Value of U.S. direct investments in Europe and E.E.C.: selected years (in millions of dollars)

	1950	1957	1960	1963	1966	1967	1968p
Europe	1,733	4,151	6,645	10,340	16,209	17,926	19,386
EEC	637	1,680	2,644	4,490	7,584	8,444	8,992
BLEU*	69	192	231	356	742	867	963
	(11)	(11)	(9)	(8)	(10)	(10)	(11)
France	217	464	741	1,240	1,758	1,904	1,910
	(34)	(28)	(28)	(28)	(23)	(23)	(21)
Germany	204	581	1,006	1,780	3,077	3,486	3,774
	(32)	(35)	(38)	(39)	(41)	(41)	(42)
Italy	63	252	384	668	1,148	1,246	1,272
	(10)	(15)	(14)	(15)	(15)	(15)	(14)
Netherlands	84	191	283	446	859	942	1,073
	(13)	(11)	(11)	(10)	(11)	(11)	(12)

(Figures in ( ) are country percentage of total EEC investment.) p = preliminary.
* BLEU stands for the Belgium-Luxembourg Economic Union.
Source: US Department of Commerce, *Survey of Current Business*, 1962. Various issues for the years 1963, 1966, 1967 and 1968p.
US Department of Commerce, *Balance of Payments, Statistical Supplement*, 1962, for the years 1950, 1957, and 1960.

(i.e., the amount of US investment per capita) is second highest for the Netherlands. In first place are Belgium and Luxemburg Economic Union (BLEU), with Italy in last place (Table 12).

Table 12. Density of U.S. Direct Investment in E.E.C. countries – 1968

	US investments		Population		Investment density in US dollars
	Value in millions of $	% Share	In thousands	%Share	
BLEU	963	11	10,023	5	96
Netherlands	1,073	12	12,781	7	84
Germany	3,774	42	61,073	33	62
France	1,910	21	50,493	27	38
Italy	1,272	14	52,902	28	24
EEC	8,992	100	187,272	100	48

Note: Population figures for 1968 were projected using 1966 UN data and 1963–1966 average annual population growth rates.
The 1968 direct investment figures are preliminary. All percentages and amounts are rounded off.
Source: US Department of Commerce, Survey of Current Business, October, 1969: for direct investment data.
U.N. Statistical Yearbook, 1967, Table 17: for population data.

According to a Chase Manhattan Bank publication of 1965, the number of US establishments in the EEC countries during 1958–1964 amounted to 2,290. France leads with 616 new establishments and the Netherlands is last with 291.[26]

Lastly, a look at the industry distribution of American investments. For the Common Market as a whole, the manufacturing sector is the most important, followed by the petroleum industry (Table 13). The pattern of industrial distribution for the Netherlands used to be quite different from that of the other EEC countries. Only in 1964 did manufacturing overtake petroleum as the most important sector. For all EEC countries, manufacturing accounts for almost 60 percent of the total value of American investments, to about 50 percent for the Netherlands in 1967, the highest share in any year for which data are available.[27] (See Table 14). The trade sector in the Netherlands has the largest share in the US investment of all EEC countries with 17 percent, as compared to the Common Market average of 10 percent.

Table 13. Distribution of U.S. direct investment in the E.E.C. countries by industrial activity: selected years (in millions of dollars)

	1950	1957	1960	1963	1966	1967	1968p
Manufacturing	317	831	1,436	2,538	4,401	4,976	5,373
Petroleum	210	606	827	1,330	1,980	2,086	2,149
Trade	49	149	254	438	779	853	848
Public utilities	10	22	29	34	47	49	54
Mining & smelting	3	9	9	10	17	19	19
Other	48	63	90	150	360	461	549
Total	637	1,680	2,644	4,490	7,584	8,444	8,992

p = preliminary
Source: US Department of Commerce, *Survey of Current Business*, 1962.
Various issues for the years 1963, 1966, 1967 and 1968p.
US Department of Commerce, *Balance of Payments, Statistical Supplement*, 1962, for the years 1950, 1957, and 1960.

Table 14. Percentage distribution of U.S. direct investments by industry in E.E.C. countries – 1967

	Total value of US investment (in millions of dollars)	Percentage shares			
		Manufacturing	Petroleum	Trade	All other
BLEU	867	63	3	16	18
France	1,904	69	16	10	5
Germany	3,486	60	30	7	3
Italy	1,246	48	39	8	5
Netherlands	942	49	23	17	11
EEC	8,444	59	25	10	6

Source: Calculated from data published by US Department of Commerce, *Survey of Current Business*, October, 1969.
For 1968 only preliminary figures are available.

3. Program to attract foreign industry[28]

Shortly after the end of World War II the Netherlands government initiated a program aimed at encouraging foreign enterprises to establish manufacturing operations in the Netherlands.[29] This program was part of an ambitious effort to bring about an industrial revolution.[30] In the first industrial Note of 1949 it is stated that:

Among the most important economic problems with which the Netherlands is faced, now and in the years to come, industrialization holds a prominent position. The future standard of living of the Dutch nation, as well as the stability of its economic and social structure, is largely dependent on the way our problems (*of balance of payments, increasing population* and *employment opportunities*) are solved. A satisfactory solution is only conceivable if it is based, in an important if not predominant degree, on a vigorous further development of Dutch industry.[31]

It is clear from this quotation that industrialization was regarded as the solution for some of the most pressing problems with which the Netherlands was confronted after the war. Most important among these was the creation of jobs for the rapidly growing population and for the absorption of displaced farm workers. Also urgent was the need to increase exports, through diversification, in order to continue to meet the import requirements, roughly 40 percent of the national product. These sizeable imports are largely due to the disparity between population and natural resources.[32] Foreign industry was expected to contribute significantly in the solution of those pressing problems. The emphasis, however, was not so much on capital brought in or on simply *more* industry. What was needed was diversification and broadening of the industrial base, as well as technological know-how and skills. In addition, the need to export was and is still emphasized. In a recent publication the foreign investor is warned that

... the domestic market alone would not justify the establishment of manufacturing operations ... Exports to other European and non-European markets should therefore be a major objective of the project.[33]

This, briefly, was the rationale behind the program to attract the foreign investment, an effort described as 'the most aggressive and intelligent in operation anywhere'.[34] It certainly was the first of its kind, followed later by other Western European countries.

The Netherlands industrial climate for foreign as well as domestic investors was made more favorable through a combination of investment subsidies and grants, accelerated depreciation schemes and fiscal stimuli. In the early stages of the program these benefits applied to all investments independent of their location in the Netherlands. Also, the main emphasis was on the creation of employment. As a result of the vigorous expansion of Dutch trade and industry and the resulting full employment, more importance is now put on the raising of qualitative standards of industry. In addition, the special benefits are restricted to investments in the

49

so-called 'development areas,' in particular the northeast and southern parts of the Netherlands. For specifically designated 'industrialization centers,' the investor may claim an investment grant of 25 percent of the total investments in fixed assets (with a maximum of around $ 830,000). In the 'development areas' extra facilities have been made available, in addition to the investment grant. These include interest subsidies on loans from third parties, government guaranteed loans and special assistance with the financing of the investment.[35] The most favorable opportunities for new investments exist in the southern province of Limburg, where Dutch and Common Market subsidies are aimed at the creation of jobs for mine workers. In this area, as well as in Belgium, coal mining is being phased out, and the economic structure has to be transformed. In addition to the previously mentioned Netherlands government incentives, readaptation aid is granted by the European Coal and Steel Community. These subsidies are contingent upon employment of former miners.[36] It should be pointed out that all investment attraction programs in the Netherlands apply to foreign as well as domestic investors. There is no discrimination among investors on the basis of the nationality of the parent company.

In the early 1960's it was thought that the opportunities for investing in the Netherlands were sufficiently well known in American business circles. In addition, the tight labor market resulted in much pressure on wages and prices, and less, rather than more, employment seemed necessary. As a result, the Institute of Dutch-American Industrial Cooperation was closed down on January 1, 1964, followed by the Commissariat for Industry on May 1, 1964. Although the open-door policy with respect to foreign industry was maintained and their establishment in development areas encouraged, the closing down of the offices in New York created the impression that US investors were no longer welcome in Holland.[37] This impression was strengthened as the Dutch action came in a period when strong French and German objections were raised against American direct investments. The opening of the new promotion office in New York on February 1, 1968, will undoubtedly help to eradicate the unfavorable impression made earlier.

Aside from government incentives, the general investment climate in the Netherlands is quite attractive. Some of the reasons why so many foreign companies choose the Netherlands to establish their subsidiaries are as follows:

1. The country has an ideal geographical location, on the North Sea, and with ready access to the key European inland waters. Rotterdam and Amsterdam harbors are situated at the two branches of the Rhine, the main

freight artery of Western Europe. Two other important rivers flow through Holland, the Meuse and the Scheldt.

2. An excellent communication network exists which allows Holland the claim of being the 'Gateway to Europe.' In addition to the rivers, the country boasts the world's largest port, Rotterdam, expected to handle some 155 million tons of freight in 1969.[38] A well developed highway and railroad network completes the excellent communication with the German, Swiss and Belgian hinterland.

3. A favorable international climate exists due in part to long history in trading, as well as to the presence of a number of multinational enterprises, Royal Dutch, Unilever, AKU and Philips.

4. The country has a good record of labor peace and management-labor relations are excellent, as illustrated by figures on lost time due to strikes. In the period 1953–1962 the average loss of working days each year per 1,000 inhabitants stood at 8.9 for the Netherlands, 15.9 for West Germany, 64.6 for France, 76.0 for the UK, and 94.5 for Belgium.[39] For the years 1963–1967 pretty much the same picture holds, as indicated by ILO statistics.[40]

5. Many Dutchmen speak one or several foreign tongues and thus there are language advantages in management as well as other positions.

6. The wage and salary level used to be low in comparison with other European countries, but since 1966 such is no longer the case.

Some of the disadvantages to investment in the Netherlands have to be mentioned as well.

1. Especially in the early years, there was a serious problem with subcontracting, because most Dutch companies used to produce everything themselves. Now that the industrial base has been broadened, this disadvantage has been eliminated.

2. A problem that seems to be getting worse is that of housing. A foreign investor (as well as a domestic employer) must in general be prepared to supply housing facilities to attract personnel, and due to the short supply he is often forced to build himself. As construction is still rationed, and this applies to industrial structures as well, long delays are standard. In Belgium the housing situation is better, which has probably resulted in a loss of many prospective investors for the Netherlands.

3. A bottleneck in the last four or five years has been the tight labor market; except in the 'development areas' it has been difficult to hire employees.

4. A rather serious complaint concerns the 'red tape' at the governmental level. Not only in building but in other fields as well, permits are required, resulting in much paper work and long delays.

I will now briefly examine some of the results of the incentive programs. In Part 2 we have seen that the growth of American investments in the Netherlands has been about equal to that in other EEC countries. As the Netherlands was the first country to actively woo foreign investors, one can only conclude that either the program was a failure or else that without the incentives, growth would have been lower. As to the effectiveness of the program, the general view seems to be that it has been a success. In the Sixth Industrial Note of 1959 it was put as follows:

> Both quantitatively and qualitatively these foreign establishments contribute considerably to the industrial development of the Netherlands and also to the strengthening of the Dutch industrial export position ... Their total annual turnover is about Fl. 600,000,000 ($ 165 million), excluding the oil industry, and about three-fifths of their production is exported. The increase in employment may be put at around 20,000 jobs.[41]

An article, 'Foreign Industrial Establishments,' of 1964 concludes that foreign industries had created extra sales of around $ 400 million and that the value added in the Netherlands was very high.[42] The author, unfortunately, does not indicate how he arrived at these estimates, which are lower than the government figures calculated in 1959. De Smidt argues that foreign establishments are characterized by a strong propensity to export and by high qualitative standards of production.[43] This, he continues, 'has led to a wider range and an improvement of the quality of domestic exports.' Again there is no indication as to the source of his information. De Smidt does, however, mention the introduction of new products manufactured on a large scale by foreign investors, such as the electronics, petro-chemicals and instruments industries. Lastly, reference is made to the role of foreign industry in the Netherlands in the foreword to the *Guide to Establishing Industrial Operations in the Netherlands*. Here Dr. L. de Block, then Minister of Economic Affairs, states:

> We realize, of course, that foreign entrepreneurs come here to do business, profitable business. But we also realize that in so doing *they render a service to the Dutch economy and strengthen the industrial structure of our country* [my italics].[44]

Summing up these statements, it is indeed the consensus that foreign investment has been beneficial to the Netherlands and that the incentive program has been a success.

NOTES

1. A good and highly interesting account of these early investments can be found in CLEONA LEWIS, *America's Stake in International Investments* (Washington, D.C.: The Brookings Institution, 1938).

2. ALEXANDER HAMILTON, 'Rather than be judged a rival, it [foreign investment] ought to be considered an auxiliary all the more precious, because it alone permits an increased amount of productive labour and useful enterprise to be set to work.' Quoted from: JEAN-JACQUES SERVAN-SCHREIBER, *Le Défi Américain* (Paris: Denoel, 1967), p. 21. The English edition has been published under the title: *The American Challenge* (Atheneum).

3. S. CHAKRAVARTY, 'A Structural Study of International Capital Movements', *Economia Internazionale*, August, 1961, Vol. 14, No. 3, pp. 377–403. This study found that international capital movements in the 1920's were best explained by cultural affinity and language, rather than economic variables as the rate of return and the degree of economic development.

4. Expansion of the investments relies heavily on retained earnings and locally-borrowed funds. The investments will only be frustrated insofar as the company relied on capital funds remitted from the US. This source of funds has, in the last few years, only financed about one-fifth of the annual increase in value of investments.

5. For a longer discussion of these aspects of direct investments the reader is referred to Chapter 1, Part 1.

6. FRANK A. SOUTHARD, *American Industry in Europe* (Boston and New York: Houghton Mifflin Company, 1931), bibliography pp. 225–247.

7. F. P. GARVAN, *Hot Money and Frozen Funds* (New York: Chemical Foundation, Inc., 1937), in the foreword.

8. CLEONA LEWIS, *op. cit.*, p. 108.

9. One example of these comparisons is that made by UNICE (Union of Manufacturing Industries of the EEC) in its publication, *Aspects of Scale of European Leading Industries as Compared to their International Competition*, 1965, 'The sales of the 20 largest US company is about equal to the gross national product of West Germany', p. 8.

10. SERVAN-SCHREIBER, *op. cit.*, p. 27.

11. RAINER HELLMANN, *Amerika auf dem Europamarkt* (Baden-Baden: Nomosverlagsgesellschaft, 1966).

G.-Y. BERTIN, *Les Investissements des Firmes Etrangères en France* (Paris: Presses Universitaires de France, 1963).

JACQUES HOLLANDER, *Les Investissements Américains en Belgique* (Bruxelles: Les Editions du Centre Paul Hymans, 1963).

JOHN H. DUNNING, *American Investment in British Manufacturing Industry* (London: George Allen and Unwin Ltd., 1958).

K. H. STANDKE, *Betriebswirtschaftliche Aspekte Amerikanischer Investitionspolitik in der E.W.G.*, (Berlin: R.K.W. Frankfurt, 1965).

EDWARD A. MCCREARY, *The Americanisation of Europe* [The Impact of Americans and American Business on the Uncommon Market], (Garden City, N.J.: Doubleday, 1964).

ALLAN W. JOHNSTONE, *United States Direct Investment in France* (Cambridge, Mass.: The MIT Press, 1965).

ARTHUR I. STONEHILL, *Foreign Ownership in Norwegian Enterprise* (Oslo: Central Bureau of Statistics, 1965).

12. The periods were chosen so as to represent the eight pre- and post-EEC formation years respectively.

13. ANTHONY E. SCAPERLANDA and LAURENCE J. MAURER, 'The Determinants of US Direct Investments in the EEC', *American Economic Review*, September 1969, pp. 558–568.

14. *Ibid.*, p. 566.

15. *Ibid.*, pp. 563, 567. In my opinion, however, this result is of rather dubious value, because of the way in which the trade-obstacle variable was handled. Due to the difficulties of isolating the effects of internal tariff abolition and external tariff imposition, the authors use as a proxy for trade discrimination the ratio of US exports to the EEC over the level of exports of EEC-countries to other EEC-countries (p. 562). Two obvious shortcomings of this proxy are (1) the assumption that trade diversion has been more important than trade creation, a point that has not been, as far as I know, proved conclusively, and (2) the fact that of US exports to the EEC countries agricultural products represent a sizeable share. Discrimination against these products has been very strong, but direct investments are, of course, virtually non-existent in agriculture.

16. The information on US subsidiaries in the Netherlands is contained in a US Department of Commerce publication, *American Firms, Subsidiaries and Affiliates – The Netherlands*, of October, 1967. It would presumably be more precise to say the oldest *surviving* US subsidiary.

17. Lewis, *op. cit.*, p. 580.

18. *Ibid.*, pp. 183, 184–582.

19. *Ibid.*, p. 603.

20. ROBERT W. DUNN, *American Foreign Investments* (New York: B. W. Huebsch and The Viking Press, 1926), p. 159.

21. Value of the total investment in *Foreign Investments of the U.S.*, US Department of Commerce, 1953.

22. Value of the petroleum sector in LEWIS, *op.cit.*, p. 188.

23. For an explanation for the drop in value of the petroleum, see the note in Table 9.

24. For 1966: $ 858 million represents 1.57 percent of US total investments of $ 54,562 million. For 1967: $ 917 million represents 1.55 percent of US total investments of $ 59,267 million. *Survey of Current Business*, October, 1968, p. 24.

25. For a discussion of the French charges and attitudes see especially ALLAN W. JOHNSTONE, *op. cit.*, and RAINER HELLMANN, *op. cit.*, pp. 25–32.

26. Chase Manhattan Bank, *Report on Western Europe*, March-April, 1965.

27. A readjustment of the figures for the petroleum and manufacturing sectors resulted in a percentage distribution not much different from that of other EEC countries. The readjustment caused a drop in the value of the petroleum investments of $ 46 million, from $ 267 million in 1966 to $221 million in 1967. Before this readjustment (involving a petro-chemical plant included in the petroleum sector till 1966) the Dutch manufacturing sector showed the lowest percentage share of all EEC countries.

28. For a discussion of the Canadian efforts in this respect, see BERNARD BONIN, *L'Investissement Etranger à Long Terme au Canada: Ses Caractères et Ses Effets sur L'Economie Canadienne* (Paris: Dissertation at the University of Paris, 1966).

29. In 1946 private Dutch capital established the Netherlands Industrial Institute (later renamed the Institute for Dutch-American Industrial Cooperation), a body that helped US companies to study plant sites, labor supply, financing and staff procurement, all gratis. The government Commissariat for Industry in New York was established in 1950.

30. American companies received better treatment than local investors, as can be judged from the following quotation: 'The days are now past when committees from Western European countries queued up at the doors of huge American corporations to

invite them to establish factories in their cities or district, and when governments one after another – secretly or not – offered attractive fiscal advantages.' DR. C.F. KARSTEN, 'Should Europe Restrict US Investments', *Harvard Business Review*, Sept.-Oct., 1965, p. 53.

31. H. GEORGE FRANKS, *Holland's Industries Stride Ahead – The New Netherlands of the 1960's* (Federation of Netherlands Industries, 1961), p. 6. He quotes from the first of seven industrial notes, published in 1949.

32. Even in 1966 the population growth continues to be fairly high, around 1.1 per thousand, which is three times the rate of West Germany and double that of the UK. It is also slightly higher than in the US.

33. *Guide to Establishing Industrial Operations in the Netherlands*, Netherlands Ministry of Economic Affairs, December, 1967, p. 64.

34. HERBERT SOLOW, 'The Dutch Get Private Dollars', *Fortune*, September, 1954, pp. 120–31.

35. For more specific information, see pp. 26–27 of the previously mentioned *Guide to Establishing Industrial Operations in the Netherlands*, under the heading: Regional Industrialization Incentives.

36. 'EEC Ace: Opportunity in Limburg', *Knicherbocker International*, July, 1968, pp. 17–23.

37. In my conversations with American businessmen, this feeling was expressed quite often.

38. *Journal of Commerce*, March 24, 1969, 'Rotterdam: City and Port Gear for New Growth'.

39. M. DE SMIDT, 'Foreign Industrial Establishments Located in the Netherlands', *Tijdschrift voor Economische en Sociale Geografie*, 57ste Jaargang, No. 1, januari/februari 1968, p. 4.

40. International Labour Organisation, *Yearbook 1968*, tables on working days lost due to strikes and lock-outs.

41. *Sixth Industrial Note, 1959*, as quoted by FRANKS, *op. cit.*, p. 12.

42. 'Foreign Industrial Establishments' (Buitenlandse Industrievestiging) *E.T.I.-Kwartaalbericht*, 2e Kwartaal 1964, pp. 2–10.

43. DE SMIDT, *op. cit.*, pp. 1–19.

44. *Guide, op. cit.*, p. 3.

3. Survey of U.S. companies in the Netherlands: manufacturing and petroleum sectors in 1966[1]

INTRODUCTION

The population of the US affiliated or associated companies operating in the Netherlands by the end of 1966 was conveniently defined by the US Department of Commerce.[2] The so-called 'Trade List' published by the Department gives an exhaustive tabulation of all the direct investments by US companies in the Netherlands as of October, 1967. It provides information on the name and address of the affiliate, nationality and name of the managing director, as well as the name and address of the parent company. In addition, the list contains the year of establishment, relation between parent and affiliate or associate, as well as the nature of the business.[3]

The last year of establishment included in the survey is 1966; as it turned out, quite a few companies had not yet begun to operate by the end of 1966, and some were not yet fully in operation. Table 15 gives us a breakdown of all the US affiliates in the Netherlands as of October, 1967 by main activity, as specified by the US Department of Commerce. Thus, the total population, defined as all US affiliated and associated companies

Table 15. *U.S. affiliated or associated companies in the Netherlands, established by October, 1967*

Activity	Established in or before 1966	Established in 1967	Total
Manufacturing	249	2	251
Petroleum	18	0	18
Trading	168	1	169
Services (finance, travel, insurance)	152	4	156
No activities yet	3	–	3
Total	590	7	597

Source: US Department of Commerce, *Trade List for the Netherlands*, October, 1967.

manufacturing in the Netherlands by the end of 1966, amounted to 267 companies out of a total of 597 direct investment enterprises.

As a partial check on the information contained in the US Department of Commerce trade list, I used a publication of the Netherlands Ministry of Economic Affairs, concerning foreign industrial establishments, in the

Table 16. *Foreign post-war industrial establishments in the Netherlands: by January, 1967*

Country	Type of investment				
	Wholly owned establishment		Participation or cooperation with Dutch industry		Total
United States		200		119	319
EEC countries		91		104	195
Belgium	27		25		52
France	8		13		21
Germany	56		66		122
United Kingdom		74		86	160
Switzerland		34		40	74
Sweden		36		11	47
Others		22		30	52
Total		457		390	847

Source: *Foreign Industrial Establishments, Participations and Joint Ventures in the Netherlands*, Ministry of Economic Affairs, Directorate General for Industry and Trade, January, 1967.

Table 17. *Distribution according to branch of industry: foreign post-war industrial establishments in the Netherlands by January, 1967*

Industry	Type of investment		
	Wholly owned establishment	Participation or cooperation with Dutch industry	Total
Metal working	189	135	324
Chemical	92	82	174
Textiles	24	37	61
Food	30	20	50
Electrical	35	10	45
Rubber	7	10	17
Miscellaneous	80	96	176
Total	457	390	847

Source: *Foreign Industrial Establishments, Participations and Joint Ventures in the Netherlands*, Ministry of Economic Affairs, Directorate General for Industry and Trade, January, 1967.

Table 18. Relationship between U.S. parent and Dutch affiliate or associate

Relationship	Definition	Manufacturing	Petroleum	Other activities such as trade, services	Total
Branch office	A local office of an American firm, having no independent or corporate status	5	2	69	76
Subsidiary	A Dutch firm established independently, under Dutch law, whose capital stock is 50% or more controlled by an American firm	39	1	22	62
Wholly owned subsidiary	Capital stock controlled for 100%	133	10	158	301
Joint company	A Dutch firm in which the American and Dutch financial interests are usually, though not always, evenly divided	48	1	29	78
Affiliate	A Dutch company in which the financial interest of the participating American firm is < 50%	19	4	20	43
Sub-subsidiary	A subsidiary not established directly by the American parent company, but by another subsidiary or affiliate of the latter	3	–	4	7
Wholly owned sub-subsidiary		2	–	4	6
Other		–	–	14	14
		249	18	320	587
Firms established in 1967		2	–	5	7
No activities yet		–	–	3	3
		251	18	328	597

Source: US Department of Commerce, Trade List for the Netherlands, October, 1967, p. 3.

Netherlands, by January, 1967.[4] This listing includes all foreign investments, and because it was published earlier than the US trade list, it is not as complete. In addition, the Netherlands publication does not mention the year of establishment.

An interesting piece of information from the Dutch listing is reproduced in Table 16, which shows the industrial establishments by foreigners in the Netherlands since World War II, by country of origin and industrial classification (table 17). Many purely trading companies are included in the list of the Dutch Ministry, which explains the higher number of establishments as compared with the US trade list.

Before proceeding to the survey itself, Table 18 summarizes the type of relationship between the US parent company and the Dutch affiliate or associate, by industrial classification.

I. POPULATION AND RESPONSE

The companies selected for the survey numbered 267 and were defined as: *U.S. affiliated or associated companies in manufacturing industries, operating in the Netherlands by the end of 1966*. Only producing establishments in the manufacturing and petroleum sectors were included. The description of the business activity given in the US Department of Commerce trade list served as a guide in distinguishing between the purely trading and the producing establishments.

Subsequently some 52 firms had to be eliminated from the survey population. These companies had either terminated their activities or sold the US interest to Dutch or other (non-US) foreign enterprises. Some did not classify as manufacturing units, reselling imported finished goods or subcontracting the whole production to Dutch companies. Table 19 summarizes corrections made in the original survey population and shows the overall response.

In all 111 questionnaires were returned of which 16, unfortunately, were only partially completed. These incomplete questionnaires have been tabulated separately and the results presented in the Appendix. As far as possible, the information contained in these partially answered surveys will be used together with the data in the completed questionnaires.

The 95 fully completed questionnaires represent better than 44 percent of the corrected sample size of 215 firms, covering 91 manufacturing and four petroleum establishments. Including the partially completed question-naires, the cooperation rate is almost 52 percent. A mere seven percent of the firms refused to cooperate in the survey for various reasons, mostly as a

Table 19. Summary of survey population of U.S. affiliated or associated companies in the Netherlands – 1966: corrections and responses

Original survey population		267 companies
Not applicable:		
Sales or services only	18	
US share sold	7	
No activities yet	6	
Exploration only	4	
Subcontracting only	7	
Licensing	3	
Holding company, financial interest only, etc.	6	52
Corrected survey population		215 companies
Responses		131 companies
Fully completed questionnaires	95	
Partially completed questionnaires	16	
No cooperation	20	
No reaction		84
Corrected survey population		215 companies

matter of company policy. One questionnaire was returned because of a wrong address in the trade list, and five subsidiaries forwarded the questionnaire to their parents for completion. These five firms notified me of their action, but no word was received from the parent companies. Consequently, these replies are categorized as refusals to cooperate. In terms of the total original sample the response rate amounts to more than 68 percent, with only 84 companies not reacting at all (some 31 percent of the total population). A copy of the questionnaire is presented in the Appendix.

2. INDUSTRIAL CLASSIFICATION

The role that US direct investment enterprises play in the Netherlands and in any host country, for that matter, cannot be properly analyzed without a knowledge of the industrial distribution of those investments. It has been generally noted that the American direct investments are concentrated in relatively few industries, which, as a rule, are the most important or the fastest growing ones.[5] Such a breakdown by industrial activity was made possible by using the information in the US Department of Commerce trade list for the Netherlands. In addition, the survey presents data on the value of the investments and the sales volume by industrial category.

Table 20 gives a rough industrial classification of the information contained in both the trade list of US investments in the Netherlands and the Dutch Ministry of Economic Affairs' publication on all foreign industrial establishments in the Netherlands since 1945.[6] These data show that the concentration of direct investments in a few industries is not typical only of US investments, but holds true for all foreign direct investments, at least those in the Netherlands. If one assumes that businessmen everywhere are guided by the same motives and have similar objectives, there is indeed no a priori reason to expect a different pattern.

Table 20. Comparison of the survey population with all foreign establishments in the Netherlands by major industrial category: by January, 1967

Industrial sector	US establishments in the Netherlands		All foreign establishments
	Original sample	Corrected sample	
Metal working	86	75	324
Chemical	63	52	174
Textiles	13	12	61
Food	18	14	50
Electrical	17	14	45
Rubber	4	3	17
Miscellaneous	66	45	176
Total	267	215	847

Note: The survey of US investments concerns 215 enterprises; the Dutch statistics use the term establishment, which may relate to production units rather than to the decision unit, the company.

Industrial breakdown of US establishments from the trade list: metal working includes metal products and machinery (ISIC 35 and 36). Excluded are transportation (ISIC 38) and scientific and control instruments (ISIC 391). These categories, together with footwear (ISIC 24), paper (ISIC 27), printing (ISIC 28), petroleum (ISIC 32), leather (ISIC 29), glass (ISIC 33), and photographic (ISIC 392) are included in the miscellaneous category, as is the ISIC 399, other manufactured products.

There is no indication in the list of the Dutch Ministry of Economic Affairs as to the respective industries included in their classification.

Source: Foreign Industrial Establishments, Participation and Joint Ventures in the Netherlands, Ministry of Economic Affairs, Directorate General for Industry and Trade, January, 1967.

US Department of Commerce, *Trade List for the Netherlands,* October, 1967.

Table 21 summarizes the pertinent information with respect to the survey of US direct investment companies in the Netherlands, by industrial

Table 21. Population and responses by industrial category: survey of U.S. companies in the Netherlands in 1966

Industrial sector	ISIC Code	Original Survey	N.A.	Corrected Survey	Questionnaires Comp.	Inc.	No cooperation	Total responses	No reaction
Food, tobacco, beverage	20 21 22	18	4	14	5	2	1	8	6
Textiles and wearing apparel	23 24	16	1	15	11	–	1	13	2
Paper and printing	27 28	5	2	3	1	–	1	2	1
Leather, photography, glass	29 392 33	6	–	6	1	1	1	3	3
Rubber	30	4	1	3	1	–	–	1	2
Chemicals	31	64	11	53	24	5	5	34	19
Petroleum	32	18	14	4	4	–	–	4	–
Metal products	35	36	2	34	13	4	2	19	15
Machinery	36	50	9	41	21	–	7	28	13
Electrical equipment	37	17	3	14	6	2	–	8	6
Transportation	38	3	–	3	2	–	–	2	1
Scientific and control instruments	391	22	1	21	6	1	2	9	12
Other industries	399	8	4	4	3	–	–	–	4
Total		267	52	215	95	16	20	131	84

N.A. = not applicable.
Source: Survey of U.S. affiliated or associated companies operating in the Netherlands by the end of 1966.

category. The industrial classification used is that published by the United Nations Statistical Office, the so-called International Standard Industrial Classification (ISIC).[7] Since 1964, the Netherlands Bureau of Statistics (Centraal Bureau voor de Statistiek) uses the same classification. From this table, and even more so from the detailed breakdown in the Appendix, it is clear that US investments are, indeed, highly concentrated, mostly in the metal and chemical industries.

The ratio of completed questionnaires to the number of companies in the corrected sample ranges from 0 to 100 in the various industrial categories, with the average at 44. It would obviously be wrong to apply the individual industry ratios to the investment and sales data, hoping to arrive in this way at the 'correct' US investment picture per industrial category. For the whole sample, however, it is hoped (and assumed) that this procedure will yield approximately the value of all US investments and sales in the Netherlands in 1966. It will be interesting to compare these figures with the data published by the US Department of Commerce in its monthly 'Survey of Current Business.'

3. SURVEY QUESTIONS AND COLLECTED DATA

In this part I will discuss the various sections of the survey as they relate to aspects of American direct investment in the Netherlands. Some of the collected information will be presented as well. The analysis of the main results will be found in Chapter 4, 'The Magnitude of US Direct Investments in the Netherlands.' The discussion here will be arranged under the following headings: (a) degree of control (b) value of the investment (c) scale of the operations (d) sales, exports and imports (e) research and development (f) motives of Dutch companies (g) some motives of the US parent companies.

a. Degree of control

Control is the distinguishing characteristic of all direct investments. In the discussion of the total population of US controlled enterprises in the Netherlands I presented a breakdown of the relationship between the US parent and the Dutch company, using the qualitative classification of the US Department of Commerce (Table 18). That classification distinguishes between majority, minority, and jointly shared interests, but does not give a more detailed breakdown of the percentage of equity controlled by the US firm. In the survey of US affiliated or associated companies in the Netherlands the American firm was asked to indicate the degree of control, in terms of equity ownership, exercised by the parent company. Rather than request the exact degree of control, a breakdown into six percentage classes was used. A higher response rate was expected when no exact figures were asked concerning this sensitive type of data. Furthermore, by using this particular classification, the results from our survey will be comparable to information on US direct investments in other studies, such as the one by Donald Brash, for Australia.

Table 22 contains the answers of 110 responding companies, with either fully or partially completed questionnaires. Only one company refused to answer this particular question, which could be an indication that these data are not quite as sensitive as was thought initially. Of the 110 cooperating companies some 63 are wholly US owned and nine companies fall in the class from 75–99 percent ownership in share capital. Five other firms indicated that the degree of control varied from 51 to 74 percent, so that in all 77 of the 110 companies have a majority share of their equity capital owned by the American parent company.

Table 22. U.S. ownership in equity capital: survey of U.S. companies in the Netherlands in 1966

Degree of control (percent)	Manufacturing companies		Petroleum companies		All companies
	Questionnaires		Questionnaires		
	Complete	Incomplete	Complete	Incomplete	
100	53	6	4		63
75–99	6	3			9
51–74	4	1			5
50	19	4			23
25–49	6	1			7
Less than 25	3	–			3
Total	91	15	4		110

Source: Information collected in 95 complete and 15 partially complete questionnaires.

Twenty-three companies did establish joint ventures with US enterprises, as measured by the 50–50 share in the equity capital. Note that this definition of a joint venture differs from the one used by the US Department of Commerce, where 'the financial interests are usually but not always evenly divided'. Some 10 companies reported a minority holding, where for seven subsidiaries the degree of control varied from 25 to 49 percent. Three companies indicated that the US share ownership amounted to less than 25 percent. Previously these investments were categorized as 'associated

64

enterprises', but since October, 1968 the definition of a direct investment has been broadened so as to include equity ownerships as low as ten percent.[8]

b. Value of the investment

An estimate of US investments in Dutch industry can be calculated using the degree of US control in equity, and the total value of property, plant and equipment in every American subsidiary. Data on control were presented earlier, but a problem arises concerning the exact degree of ownership in each case, where only percentage ranges of control are available. The solution is to assume that the actual degree of equity ownership is the average in each range. This procedure fortunately results in fairly accurate figures, as can be judged from the high and low values for each range, and comparing them with the average value. Because so many companies are wholly owned, and a sizeable number joint ventures, the deviations from the average amount to less than two percent (Table 23).

As far as the total value of plant, machinery, land and buildings is concerned, the company was asked to provide the approximate amount of the total investment in the Netherlands by the end of 1966. In addition, the firms were requested to indicate whether they were using market value (present prices) or historical value (actually-paid prices) in their valuation of the investment. The purpose of this refinement was to discount the historical values with a price deflator and thus render these values compatible with the investments valued at market prices. However, many companies were already in operation before becoming a US direct investment enterprise, and thus it proved impossible to determine the time period over which the price deflator had to be applied. In addition, there would naturally have been the problem of deciding on the precise extent of price deflation. Consequently, the two investment valuations were not corrected and simply added together. This procedure undoubtedly distorts the picture, although I have been consoled by the knowledge that no two companies arrive at the book value of their investments in quite the same way, so that even with a proper deflating technique, one would be adding up, and comparing with each other, quite different entities. Many of these book values undoubtedly understate the 'true' value of the investment, as was indicated for one firm by a comment in the margin: 'excluding our hidden reserves.'

Regarding the compatibility of the survey results with the data collected by the US Department of Commerce it should be noted that the American figures refer to the book value, as supplied by the parent company, of its

Table 23. Value of U.S. direct investments in the Netherlands: survey of U.S. companies in the Netherlands in 1966

Industrial sector	Corrected population	Completed questionnaires	Value of the investment (000 dollars)			
			Total	US share		
				Average	High	Low
Food, tobacco, beverage	14	5	31,892	26,490	28,146	24,834
Textiles and wearing apparel	15	11	15,746	10,700	11,289	10,110
Paper and printing	3	1	2,127	787	1,042	532
Leather, glass, photography	6	1	4,972	4,972	4,972	4,972
Rubber	3	1	16,989	2,888	4,077	1,699
Chemicals	53	24	134,162	102,588	106,499	98,677
Petroleum	4	4	308,756	308,756	308,756	308,756
Metal products	34	13	7,823	6,022	6,038	6,005
Machinery	41	21	18,864	17,826	18,100	17,550
Electrical equipment	14	6	9,127	7,970	8,100	7,841
Transportation	3	2	6,133	5,479	6,082	4,876
Scientific and control instruments	21	6	5,088	5,036	5,084	4,991
Other industries	4	–	–	–	–	–
Total	215	95	561,679	499,516	508,185	490,843
Difference from the average					+8,669	—8,673

Source: Survey responses from 95 companies.

share in the foreign-based company (plant, machinery, land and buildings). No allowance is made for different methods of calculation, depreciation, and/or valuation. Thus, the aggregate figures published by the Commerce Department are also a conglomerate of noncompatible values, and are subject to the same qualifications as the data collected by our survey. Of course, this is no justification for a basically incorrect procedure; it merely shows that the data are subject to measurement errors, which are quite difficult to correct.

Table 23 presents data on the total value of investments and the US share, by main industrial activity. The information is contained in 95 fully completed questionnaires. The value of total investments in property, plant and equipment stood at $ 561,679,000 by the end of 1966, and the US share amounted to some $ 499,516,000. This latter figure is the average share, with a 'high' value of $ 508,185,000 and a 'low' of $ 490,843,000. The US share represents almost 90 percent of the total value of investments, a good indication of the overall degree of control by US parent companies. The total value of the investment can be broken down into the petroleum and manufacturing sectors, showing the importance of petroleum in the US direct investments. In this sector American control is absolute, against about 75 percent for the manufacturing industries.

Table 24. Value of U.S. direct investments in the Netherlands in manufacturing and petroleum industries: survey of U.S. companies in the Netherlands in 1966

Industry	Response ratio (percent)	Total value	US share	Percent US control
		(in 000 dollars)		
Petroleum	100	308,756	308,756	100
Manufacturing	43.1	252,923	190,760	75.4
Total	44.2	561,679	499,516	83.9

Source: Survey responses from 95 companies.

c. Scale of operation

In the section of the survey dealing with the scale of operations of the US direct investment enterprises in the Netherlands, the companies were asked to give the following information: number of factories, total number of employees, employees working on imported finished goods only, and size of factories in terms of employees. A number of preliminary remarks are in order before the survey results are presented.

67

Information on the number of employees was requested for the period at the end of September, or the beginning of October, following the procedure of the Netherlands Bureau of Statistics. Since many of the surveyed companies also import finished products for immediate resale, the number of employees working in this line of activity had to be known in order to arrive at the correct figures for manufacturing employment. Also, to measure the scale of operations by using employment figures makes the separation of manufacturing and trading employment mandatory. Often, however, the distinction may not be easy to make, and the figures are therefore approximations only.

Table 25 contains the data on employment and production units collected in the survey. The information collected by questionnaire pertains to 109 companies, of which 95 returned fully completed and 14 partially answered questionnaires. Two companies failed to give employment data.

d. Sales, imports and exports

The sales aspects of US direct investments in the Netherlands are presented in Table 26; these figures provide useful information concerning the actual contribution of American investments to Dutch national product. And since the investment data are not completely reliable and employment figures obviously do not reflect the capital intensity of the production process, it is necessary to use output as an additional yardstick.

To the extent that a large part of the total sales of US controlled firms were made to foreign customers, and raw materials or semi-finished products imported, the activities of these companies affect the Netherlands' balance of payments position. Also, many products now being produced in the Netherlands by the US affiliated companies were previously imported from the American parent or other companies in the same group. This process of import substitution affects the international trading position of the Netherlands, in addition to the more direct balance of payments items such as capital inflows to finance the investment, and capital outflows in the form of remitted earnings.

Of particular interest to the United States, particularly because of the chronic deficit in its balance of payments position from 1958-1968, are the effects on US imports and exports of direct investments by American companies abroad. To what extent are exports replaced by production abroad, and/or imports generated through cheaper production? Also, how important are the exports generated by these investments because of new supplier relationships between the US parent and the foreign-based subsidiaries? This type of information is extremely useful in the testing

Table 25. *Employment and plants by industrial sector: survey of U.S. companies in the Netherlands in 1966*

Industrial sector	ISIC code	Numbers of enterprises		Number of plants	Numbers of Employees				
		Total population	Questionnaires returned		Total		On imported finished products	On manufacturing	
					Number	%		Number	%
Food beverage tobacco	20 21 22	14	7	17	4,470	16	–	4,470	17
Textiles, wearing apparel	23 24	15	12	16	1,821	7	10	1,811	7
Chemicals	31	53	29	33	4,098	14	142	3,956	14
Petroleum	32	4	4	5	3,320	12	5	3,315	13
Metal products	35	34	17	18	2,071	7	20	2,051	8
Machinery	36	41	21	31	4,849	17	443	4,406	16
Electrical equipment	37	14	7	9	2,208	8	266	1,942	7
Transportation	383	3	2	2	1,650	6	200	1,450	5
Scientific and control instruments	391	21	7	8	1,256	5	73	1,183	4
Other industries	–	16 (a)	3 (b)	3	2,138	8	26	2,112	9
Total		215	109	142	27,881	100	1,185	26,696	100

Note: (a) includes papar (2), leather (1), glass (3), printing (1), rubber (3), photografic equipment (2) and miscellaneoes industries (4). (b) includes printing (1), rubber (1), and photographic equipment (1).
Source: Survey responses from 109 us companies, contained in 95 complete and 14 partially complete questionnaires. Two companies faited to give the required information.

Table 26. Sales, imports and exports: survey of U.S. companies in the Netherlands in 1966 (in millions of dollars)

Industrial sector	Total sales	Imports (finished products)			Exports		
		Total	From parent company	From other affiliates	Total	To EEC	To US
Food, beverage, tobacco	54,964	1,137	–	1,137	29,437	8,035	2,052
Textiles and wearing apparel	35,120	2,025	9	2,016	26,187	21,670	–
Chemicals	156,788	39,069	31,664	7,405	116,106	45,924	757
Petroleum	333,094	45,028	–	45,028	125,000	49,647	3,347
Metal products	19,114	4,162	1,448	2,714	5,987	3,736	180
Machinery	48,289	6,433	3,836	2,597	31,247	14,428	1,182
Electrical equipment	25,885	9,176	433	8,743	7,251	4,506	162
Transportation	108,425	70,994	552	70,442	21,354	21,354	–
Scientific and control instruments	22,604	1,809	1,806	3	15,920	11,572	75
Other industries (a)	22,873	939	939	–	10,072	5,475	77
Total	827,156	180,773	40,688	140,085	388,562	186,347	7,833

Source: Survey responses from 95 companies: (a) includes printing (1), photography (1) and rubber (1).

of models that were constructed to estimate the effects of US direct investment on the balance of payments, such as, for example, the one by
Phillip W. Bell.[9] In a small way the results of this survey throw light on
these problems and may contribute to more reliable estimates.

Total sales of 95 responding US companies amounted to $ 827 million,
of which $ 333 million was accounted for by the petroleum refining sector.
(One petro-chemical plant was included in the total figures of one petroleum company, and could not be excluded for lack of detailed information.)
The 91 companies in the manufacturing industries sold a total of $ 494
million, which testifies to the size of the petroleum enterprises. In Chapter
4 the sales, imports and export data will be further analyzed and compared
with data for the Netherlands as a whole.

e. Research and development

An important aspect of modern industry is the research and development
effort geared to introduction of new products or improvement of existing
ones. Many publications deal with the relation between research and
development and the economic performance of an enterprise.[10] Suffice it to
say here that R & D is regarded by many as the underlying factor that
enables US companies to establish themselves successfully in foreign markets.[11] In the questionnaire coverage of this topic is inversely related to its
importance. One reason for the sketchy treatment is the secrecy with which
many companies surround their R & D programs; another is that careful
coverage of the subject would have resulted in a much longer questionnaire,
and this would undoubtedly have affected the response rate.

The companies were asked if the parent organization did engage in a
program of R & D, and if so whether or not any R & D was being undertaken in Western Europe, and more specifically, in the Netherlands. The
important question in this context is: Has the US parent company an
effective monopoly on the creation of new technologies and new knowledge, or do their subsidiaries abroad also participate in this process? The
mere fact that some R & D is farmed out to other countries does not, in
itself, indicate whether or not the parent company effectively has such a
monopoly. But the existence of such programs outside the US opens an
avenue for possible dispersion of the technological know-how and stimula-
tion of local R & D efforts.

Regarding R & D programs of US affiliated companies in the United
Kingdom it is said that:

... there is good evidence that where US enterprise has subsidiary firms
manufacturing in the United Kingdom, the research intensity there is

much lower than in the United States and in some cases there is no British-based research at all.[12]

The survey results indicate that a similar situation exists in the Netherlands, and in Western Europe as well.

Some 109 companies answered the question, of which 22 indicated that the company had no R & D program (Table 27). This answer is rather suspect and could, in a number of instances, be easily checked when it was found to be incorrect. Of 87 companies with R & D programs in the United States, 31 had no program in either the Netherlands or the rest of Western Europe. In addition 9 companies had no such program in the Netherlands and 30 had none in other countries of Western Europe. No information was available in 9 cases. Where the affiliated companies were conducting

Table 27. *Existence and location of research and development programs: survey of U.S. companies in the Netherlands in 1966*

Companies responding	Questionnaires	
	Complete	Partially complete
Parent company has R & D program	75	12
Parent company has *no* R & D program	20	2
No answer given	–	2
Total number of companies in the survey	95	16

Responses of 87 companies	R and D programs located in		
	Netherlands	Western Europe	Both
Parent has R & D program, but none in the Netherlands or Western Europe	9	30	31
No information available	–	5	4
R & D programs located in the Netherlands or Western Europe	37	11	6
Percentage of parent companies' total program allocated			
No percentage available	3	3	2
Negligible	1	–	1
0– 4 percent	13	2	2
5– 9 percent	6	3	–
10–19 percent	–	1	–
20–29 percent	1	1	–
30–49 percent	5	–	–
50–74 percent	–	1	–
75–99 percent	2	–	–
100 percent	6	–	1

Source: Information from 95 fully completed and 16 partially completed questionnaires.

72

some of the research (37 companies only in the Netherlands, 11 only in other Western European countries and 6 firms in both) the percentage share of the total R&D program was exceedingly small in most cases. Where the percentage shares were higher, joint Dutch–US companies were usually involved. In these cases it would be difficult anyway to determine the research efforts of the parent companies and the information is thus not very relevant.

All in all, the additional insight provided by the survey with respect to R&D programs would seem to be marginal.

f. Motivation of Dutch companies for association or cooperation with American enterprises

Interest in and study of the motives behind foreign direct investments have always been concentrated, at least to my knowledge, on the US companies investing abroad.[13] This survey, instead, has inquired into the reasons for existing Dutch-owned companies to relinquish some or all control to US enterprises.

First we deal with the way in which the US investment came into being, that is, whether a new firm was established or an existing operation bought up. This aspect of the US direct investments is interesting in that the purchase of existing assets does not add to the wealth or production capacity of the nation, whereas a new establishment does. Referring to modern lending patterns, Mrs. Joan Robinson labels them '... largely mere replacement – buying up assets that already exist.'[14] She characterizes direct investment that takes the form of replacement as 'finance [that] can pick out the plums from a bigger pie.'[15]

With respect to the Netherlands, our survey reveals that 29 of the 111 responding companies were already in operation, whereas the other 82 were newly established by the US parent, either as a wholly-owned subsidiary or in conjunction with a Dutch company as a joint venture. Judging from the number of companies only it does not appear that US direct investment in the Netherlands has consisted merely of 'buying up existing assets.'[16] However, for a more complete picture, one has to look at the investment and sales figures to determine the share of these 'replacements' in the total of direct investments. Table 28 gives the relevant figures for the 19 companies with complete questionnaires and compares them to the total manufacturing sector.

The number of companies already in operation amounts to around 20 percent of all manufacturing establishments (19 out of 91) and the total value of the investments, as well as the US share show virtually the same

73

Table 28. *Investment and sales data of U.S. companies already in operation: survey of U.S. companies in the Netherlands in 1966*

	Value of the investment (in thousands of dollars)			Number of factories	Number of employees	Sales data		
	No. of firms	Total	US share			Total	Imports from multi-national group	Exports
Companies already in operation	19	52,154	42,385	33	6,494	124,198	32,526	68,320
Percentage of all companies in manufacturing	20.8	20.6	22.2	27	31.2	25.1	23.9	25.9
All manufacturing companies	91	252,933	190,760	122	20,818	494,060	135,745	263,562
All companies in survey (manufacturing and petroleum)	95	561,679	499,516	127	24,138	827,154	180,773	388,562

Source: Survey responses from 95 companies.

Table 29. Control aspect of U.S. enterprises that were already in operation under Dutch control – survey information

Degree of control (percent)	Companies already in operation			All companies		
	Questionnaires		Total	Questionnaires		Total
	Complete	Incomplete		Complete	Incomplete	
100	11	2	13	57	6	63
75–99	3	3	6	6	3	9
51–74	1	1	2	4	1	5
50	1	3	4	19	4	23
25–49	3	–	3	6	1	7
Less than 25	–	–	–	3	–	3
Total	19	9a	28a	95	15	110

a. One company that returned a partially completed survey refused to give the information regarding control.
Source: Information contained in 95 complete and 15 partially complete questionnaires.

percentage share. The number of factories and employees is 27 and 31 percent, respectively, of the manufacturing excluding petroleum, suggesting that these companies had more factories as well as bigger ones relative to the group as a whole.

The sales, the imports from the multi-national group, and the export figures also indicate a higher percentage of the group totals than the number of companies and the value of investments (sales – 25 percent; imports – 24 percent; exports – 26 percent). On the whole, however, these figures are not too much out of line, suggesting that the companies already in operation do not differ much from the US direct investments as a whole.[17]

The control aspect of these companies (fully and partially answered together) is summarized in Table 29. For a proper perspective, the control distribution of all responding companies is also included. Of the 29 companies under consideration 21 were majority controlled by the US parent, almost 27 percent of the total sample of 78 companies with US majority share. The jointly-owned companies numbered only four, and three companies indicated that the US parent owned a minority share between 25 and 49 percent of equity capital (both represent about two percent of the total number of companies in each control category). One company refused altogether to answer the question concerning control.

Thus the degree of control is higher in those companies already in operation when compared with the whole sample. This result is contrary to what one would expect, because cooperation on a joint-venture basis seems intuitively the most likely solution for companies in operation that want to expand sales or improve their R&D programs. One reason for this contradiction could be the motive that the sole owner (or owning family) wanted to get out of the business. In such cases, joint ventures are obviously not an answer and majority control follows logically.

In answering the question: 'What motives led to the decision to start an affiliation or association with the American company?', many respondents gave more than one reason. The exact wording of each answer is given in the Appendix; a categorization will suffice here.

Motivation of existing Dutch companies to associate with U.S. firms	Number of responses
a. Enhance growth and help in market penetration; face the competition	10
b. Strengthen technological position; add to research and development	6

c. Family ownership; wish to retire; no corporate heirs;
   personal reasons   5
d. Strengthening the financial position   4
e. Developed from long-term relations, usually started
   in trade   3
f. Previous foreign parent bought up by us company   2
g. Various other, such as: passive, takeover by us firm
   (2); American company interested in joining Common
   Market (1); and no response (1)   4

Only the answers of the first four categories can be considered in the sense that these indicate the basis on which the decision to associate or to cooperate was taken. For two companies, the affiliation 'just happened' without initiative or objection from the Dutch firm. In two other cases, the established company already had a foreign parent, and the substitution of control did not in any way involve the Dutch company. In three cases, the present relationship had, in a sense, grown naturally out of a long association that, as a rule, had started with a sales representation. Such an evolution does not reflect the situation where the important decision to relinquish control had to be taken rather distinctly on the basis of important company objectives that could not be attained otherwise.

The most frequently cited reason behind affiliation turned out to be the desire to expand operations, to add to the line of production, or to improve the competitive position (ten answers). In a sense, the strengthening of technological (six answers) and financial (four answers) positions serves the same purpose of growth and expansion and are, therefore, an indication of the specific reason why the Dutch company could not achieve this result by itself.

Of the five family-owned establishments that became us subsidiaries, four indicated that only the personal motives of the owner or owning family had played a role. The fifth also mentioned growth as an objective.

g. *Some motives of U.S. companies for direct investment in the Netherlands*

The questionnaire does not deal with the motives that have led us companies to begin production in the Netherlands. A number of respondents, although theirs was a newly-established operation, volunteered to answer the question pertaining to the motivation of already existing companies (Paragraph f). Thus, the unexpected by-product of the survey is presented below. Obviously, these answers cannot be representative at all for us direct investment in the Netherlands.

1. Sales increase	3
2. Foothold in the Common Market	4
3. Lower general overhead, other cost considerations	2
4. Financial and economic	1
5. Cooperative government attitude	1

Common Market potential played the most important role in four cases, with three firms indicating the sales increases as the main motive. Actually, it would be difficult to differentiate between these two reasons, except that the first category indicates precisely what role the formation of the EEC has played in attracting foreign investments. Cost considerations were mentioned in two cases; general financial and economic reasons in another. The cooperative government attitude was important for only one company.

One interesting answer was given by a chemical operation, though this pertained more to the timing of the investment rather than to the motivation behind it. It was indicated that the chemical production in the Netherlands was started only after the sales volume warranted the switch from import to local manufacturing. Similar views were expressed by an executive of a large oil company. Apparently *cost* considerations play a major role here, as determined by the scale of production abroad and in the US itself.

NOTES

1. A translated version of this chapter has been published in *Economisch-Statistische Berichten*, 3 september 1969, pp. 839–846, 'Amerikaanse Ondernemingen in Nederland in 1966'.

2. US Department of Commerce – Trade List, October, 1967, *American Firms, Subsidiaries and Affiliates, The Netherlands.*

3. The breakdown in relationship is qualitative, and does not give the exact percentage for degree of ownership.

4. Ministry of Economic Affairs, Directorate General for Industry and Trade: *Foreign Industrial Establishments, Participations and Joint Ventures in the Netherlands*, January, 1967.

The most recent listing of direct investments dates from July, 1969, *Foreign Industrial Establishments, Participations and Collaborations in the Netherlands*. It indicates that by July 1, 1969 there were 263 US subsidiaries and 101 US-Dutch participations in the Netherlands, as against 200 and 119 resp. by January 1967.

5. See for example RAINER HELLMANN, *Amerika auf dem Europamarkt* (Baden-Baden: Nomosverlagsgesellschaft, 1966), who classifies the US investments into four broad categories: (1) sectors with a very high dynamic in both the US and Europe, (2) sectors with a higher dynamic in the US and whose structure needs reform in Europe, (3) some disregarded sectors, and (4) the so-called 'follower' sectors. Pp. 61–65.

6. Direct investments are a two-way street, and the Netherlands is a case in point. A recent survey conducted in the Netherlands among almost 500 companies with establishments in the EEC countries resulted in a response of 265 of those firms. Together, these companies owned 853 establishments in the EEC countries alone. 'Communication du côté de "l'Europe-Institut" de l'Université de Leyde', by H. W. DE JONG and E. A. ALKEMA (No. 13.530/IV/67–F). See, also, Chapter 5 on Netherlands' direct investments abroad.

7. 'International Standard Industrial Classification' of the United Nations Statistical Office, published in *Statistical Papers*, Series M, No. 4, revised in 1959.

8. The reader is referred to page 1 for a discussion of these changes.

9. PHILLIP W. BELL, 'Private Capital Movements and the Balance of Payments Position', *Factors Affecting the U.S. Balance of Payments* (US Congress, Joint Economic Committee, 87th Cong., 2d Sess., 1962). Also, see WALTER S. SALANT, et al., *The United States Balance of Payments in 1968* (Washington, D.C.: The Brookings Institution, 1963); and RUDOLF R. RHOMBERG and LORETTE BOISSONNEAULT, 'Effects of Income and Price Changes on the US Balance of Payments', *I.M.F. Staff Papers*, Vol. XI, No. 1, March, 1964, pp. 59–124.

10. Recently the relationship between R and D and the foreign trade of countries has been analysed, most notably by D. B. KEESING, 'The Impact of R and D on US Trade', *Journal of Political Economy*, vol. 75, February 1967, pp. 38–48. And in the same issue: W. GRUBER, D. MEHTA, and R. VERNON, 'The R & D Factor in International Trade and International Investment of United States Industries', pp. 20–37.

11. See e.g. JEAN-JACQUES SERVAN-SCHREIBER, *The American Challenge* (New York: Atheneum, 1968).

12. D. SWANN and D. L. MACLACHLAN, *Concentration and Competition: A European Dilemma?* (London: The Chatham House/P.E.P. Despatch Department, 1967) p. 26.

13. RAYMOND F. MIKESELL (ed.), *U.S. Private and Government Investment Abroad* (Eugene: University of Oregon, 1962) and CHRISTOPHER LAYTON, *Transatlantic Investments* (Boulogne-sur-Seine: The Atlantic Institute, 1962) are among the many studies in this field.

14. Mrs. JOAN ROBINSON, *The New Mercantilism* (Cambridge: The University Press, 1966), p. 16.

15. *Ibid.*, p. 16.

16. I am not suggesting that a replacement cannot contribute to production and wealth. On the contrary, many companies already in operation probably improved their performance after the takeover – or would conceivably have done worse without it.

17. Any one company excluded, or a nonrespondent included, could presumably change the percentages a few points either way. Therefore, I regard these differences as inconclusive.

4. The magnitude of American direct investment in the Netherlands

INTRODUCTION

In this chapter the role played by American direct investments in the Dutch economy will be analyzed. The discussion will be limited to the petroleum and manufacturing sectors, which together represent around 75 percent of the total American investment.

The value of US direct investments in the Netherlands for the years 1950–1968 was presented in Table 9 in Chapter 2. However, it is not possible to obtain a proper perspective of the role played by American investments by only considering these book values.

First of all, tremendous valuation problems exist, and some writers maintain that the actual value of American direct investments in Europe is almost double the figures published by the US Department of Commerce. In addition, total figures without further breakdown by industrial activity, can be quite misleading. The US investments are highly concentrated in some industries (chemicals, electronics, transportation) and almost absent in others (steel, cotton, textiles). Then, the impact of an investment lies not so much in its book value, but rather in the number of employees, in expenditures on fixed investment and in production. And direct investments cause changes in imports and exports, with possible displacement of local investment as well.

Given these limitations, a more meaningful discussion of US direct investments in the Netherlands should focus on annual investments (Part 2), scale and employment (Part 3) and production, imports and exports (Part 4).

The data used are those published by the US Department of Commerce (various issues of the Survey of Current Business) and the Netherlands Bureau of Statistics. In addition, the results of the 1966 survey of US direct investment enterprises conducted by the author will be used.

Table 30. Value of U.S. direct investment in the Netherlands – 1966

Industrial activity	Value in millions of dollars		Percentage share	
Manufacturing	372	(557)	44	(52)
Petroleum	267	(259)	31	(24)
Trade	155	(157)	18	(16)
Public utilities	18	(18)	2	(1)
Mining & smelting	less than	$ 500,000	–	(–)
Other	47	(82)	5	(7)
Total	859	(1,073)	100	(100)

(figures in parentheses are preliminary 1968 data)
Source: US Department of Commerce, *Survey of Current Business*, October, 1968.

I. THE VALUE OF THE U.S. INVESTMENT IN THE NETHERLANDS

As was seen in Chapter 2, the value of the direct investment by US companies in the Netherlands was put at $ 859 million by the end of 1966, with the preliminary 1968 figure at $ 1,073 million. The division over the various sectors (Table 30) shows that petroleum and manufacturing together account for 75 percent of the total value in 1966. These two sectors are the object of this study, and consequently a major share of all US investments in the Netherlands is covered.

The value of the American direct investment reflects the 'ownership interest of the reporter' (i.e. the parent company)[1]. It has been recognized that the valuation of American direct investments by the US Department of Commerce may be subject to error. Thus, in a recent article Walther Lederer and Frederick Cutler point out that the value figures represent cumulative amounts invested minus losses and liquidations and that they are neither capitalized earnings nor current market values.[2] There is no easy way to estimate market values, which would obviously depend on the desires and financial resources of prospective buyers and the urgency of liquidation of the owners.

Rainer Hellmann argues that the value of American investments in Europe, as published by the US Department of Commerce, does not reflect the magnitude of the actual investment at all.[3] First, the value refers to the 'ownership interest of the reporter' in the foreign enterprise; only for wholly-owned subsidiaries would we obtain a correct figure. Furthermore, the figures are book values, which usually understate the true or market value. Hellmann also claims that only capital flows from the US and reinvested earnings are regarded as additions to the American investments, excluding locally borrowed funds. This, however, is decidedly not true, as

Lederer and Cutler stated recently in the article referred to above. Anyway, for 1964, when the book value of US investments in the Common Market countries was put at 5.4 billion dollars by the Commerce Department, Hellmann suggests that the actual value of the investments would be around eight to nine billion dollars.[4] He claims that this amount was calculated from unofficial value estimates of the American investment in each EEC country. Being unofficial, no source reference has been provided.

Of course, it should be kept in mind that the accepted practice of *all* business firms is to state their investments at book value, which often implies the existence of hidden reserves. There is no easy way to estimate these reserves.

The survey of US companies operating in the Netherlands provides additional information on the value of these investments. Some 95 companies out of a corrected sample of 215 establishments in manufacturing and petroleum returned fully completed questionnaires. The value of the investment gives the US share in the total value of plant, machinery, land and buildings; the response rate in the petroleum sector is 100, that for manufacturing, 43.13, and for the whole survey the figure is 44.19. By projecting these rates on the value of the cooperating companies, one arrives at a measure of the total value of the American investments (Table 31). Of course, it has to be kept in mind that this projection for the manufacturing sector can result in grossly erroneous figures. One needs to assume for one thing that the responding companies are a perfectly representative sample of the total number of companies operating in Holland (211 enterprises in manufacturing). With these limitations in mind, it is surprising how close the projections on the survey results match the values published by the US Department of Commerce.

For the petroleum sector, the data indicate a value of $ 309 million, versus $ 267 million by the Commerce Department. However, one of the responding petroleum companies included their chemical plant in the total value. Because of insufficient information, these investments could not be separated.[5] The manufacturing sector shows an investment of $ 434 million according to our survey, as compared to $ 372 million calculated by the Commerce Department, a difference of $ 62 million or 16.7 percent. As far as the total value of the investment is concerned, the survey gives a figure of $ 742 million, which is $ 103 million higher than the American figures; the difference amounts to around 16 percent.

The survey results, and their projection to arrive at the total value of the US investment in the Netherlands are therefore substantially in agreement with data published by the US Commerce Department. As long as one remembers that book values are usually understatements of the actual size

Table 31. Value of the U.S. direct investment in the Netherlands in 1966: U.S. Department of Commerce data and survey results (in thousands of dollars)

	US Department of Commerce	Survey results of 95 companies	Response rate	Projected total value of US investments
Manufacturing	372,000	187,031	43.13	433,644
Petroleum	267,000	308,756	100	308,756
Total	639,000	495,787		742,400

Source: US Department of Commerce, *Survey of Current Business*, October, 1968. Results from 95 completed questionnaires.

Table 32. Gross investments in fixed assets: American companies in the Netherlands and total Dutch figures (in millions of dollars)

Year	Investments by American controlled companies in the Netherlands (petroleum & manufacturing sectors)	Total Dutch investments, government and private sectors	Percentage (1) of (2)	Total Dutch investments in: mining, manufacturing, building and public utilities	Total Dutch investments in selected industries where US has at least 1 subsidiary by the end of 1966	Percentage (1) of (5)
	(1)	(2)	(3)	(4)	(5)	(6)
1957	32	2,498	1.28	730	481	6.65
1958	44	2,227	1.98	588	385	11.43
1959	55	2,462	2.23	665	419	13.13
1960	42	2,783	1.51	853	575	7.30
1961	42	3,014	1.39	958	696	6.03
1962	64	3,207	2.00	991	702	9.12
1963	86	3,421	2.66	1,107	779[a]	11.68
1964	110	4,276	2.57	1,425	875	12.57
1965	101	4,704	2.15	1,543	960	10.52
1966	190	5,276	3.60	1,787	1,144	16.59
1967	275	5,833	4.71	1,879	1,215	22.63

a. This figure for selected industries is not available for 1963. An estimate was made by averaging the difference (for the years 1962 and 1964) between all manufacturing investments and the investments in selected industries. The difference amounted to 2½ percent in 1962 and 4½ percent in 1964. The average of these percentages (3½ percent) was subtracted from the 1963 figure for all manufacturing industries to arrive at the (approximate) 1963 investment in selected industries. The error in this estimate cannot be very large.

Source: Column (1) – US Department of Commerce, *Survey of Current Business*, September and October issues for the years 1960–1969. The expected plant and equipment expenditures for the years 1968 and 1969 are $ 229 million and $ 316 million respectively. These estimates were made in June, 1969. *Survey of Current Business*, September, 1969, 'Plant and Equipment Expenditures by Foreign Affiliates of US Corporations, 1968–1970'. Column (2) – Centraal Bureau voor de Statistiek, *Nationale Rekeningen 1966* ('s-Gravenhage: Staatsuitgeverij, 1967), Table 21, p. 88. Column (4) and (5) – Centraal Bureau voor de Statistiek, *Jaarcijfers voor Nederland* (Hilversum: De Haan N.V.), 1957–1966. Data for 1967 from Centraal Bureau voor de Statistiek. *Statistisch zakboek 1968*, Table 19, p. 12.

of the investment, one can accept the American data with reasonable confidence.

2. ANNUAL INVESTMENTS

The role of investments in the economic development of a country is adequately covered in the textbooks. Suffice it to say that at the macro-level investments affect the national income, whereas at the micro-level it changes the supply of products.

On both counts investment by manufacturing industries is important. And the impact of American owned or controlled companies can be measured by their investment outlays in relation to total Dutch expenditures. Table 32 gives the annual outlays of US enterprises on property, plant and equipment, as compared to total Netherlands investments in fixed assets. The figures are gross, as the depreciation data for US direct investments are not available, at least not on a country-by-country basis.[6] In addition, the figures are *not* broken down by industrial activity but show totals for the manufacturing and petroleum sectors.[7] These are the only available data, and they will have to suffice until the European countries collect data on the US and other direct investments.

The figures indicate that US investment expenditures in the Netherlands are very small in relation to total Dutch (private and public) investment outlays; the percentage share increased from 1.28 in 1957 to 3.60 in 1966 and reached 4.71 percent in 1967. (Column 3 in Table 32.) However, one needs to refine the Dutch figures which cover the whole economy, whereas the American data relate only to manufacturing and petroleum industries. The data in column 4 of Table 3 refer to manufacturing, mining and building industries plus the public utilities (gas, water and electricity).[8] These are gross investments by the private sector; industries included fall under categories 1–5 of the International Standard Industrial Classification. Relative to these figures, the American investments are much larger, amounting to more than 10 percent for both 1966 and 1967.[9] However, the Dutch figures can be further refined (Column 5 of Table 32); included are industries with at least 1 American subsidiary or affiliate by the end of 1966.[10]

The US percentage share in the realized total investments of selected industries in the Netherlands, as defined above, has fluctuated from a low of 6.03 percent in 1961 to a high of 16.59 percent in 1966. American investment outlays for 1967 have increased very much to a high of $ 275 million, some 22.6 percent of Dutch investments in selected industries; the 1957–1967 average is well over 11 percent.

A number of qualifications to these results are necessary. First of all, the American investment figures do not distinguish between acquisitions of existing enterprises and other investments (e.g. for expansion or the establishment of a new operation).[11] This distinction is rather important since the buying up of existing assets does not really add to the production capacity, although the new management may increase the efficiency of its use. (The Dutch statistics exclude this type of investment.) There are indications that the acquisition of existing companies by Americans is rather small when compared to total investment expenditures. For Europe the figures indicate that these acquisitions account for almost 11 percent of total investments in the six-year period 1963-1968 (Table 33). For the manufacturing and petroleum sectors the annual percentage ranges from a low of 6.4 in 1967 to a high of 12.8 in 1966, with the six-year average at around 10 percent. Another item included in American data, and excluded in the Dutch figures, is leaseholds. No further information on this aspect is available.

The survey of US direct investment companies in the Netherlands also throws light on the extent of acquisitions of existing enterprises. In section (f) of Part 3, Chapter 3, the information with respect to companies already in operation was presented. Of the 111 responding companies, only 29 were already in operation, of which 19 returned fully completed questionnaires. The value of the investment in these 19 companies amounted to roughly 23 percent of the total US investment in 95 fully cooperating companies (Table 28). This could be a significant figure, except that we do not know whether this represents the actual acquisition investment or whether the value in 1966 was the result of acquisition *and* expansion.

Consequently, one must conclude that the US figures are most certainly an overstatement of the *new* investment outlay and that acquisitions could take up as much as 15 percent of the annual expenditures for plant, property and equipment in the Netherlands. In view of the figures for Europe (presented in Table 33) this percentage seems on the high side.

Another problem concerns the compatibility of statistical data published by the US Department of Commerce and the Netherlands Central Bureau of Statistics. It occurs in general when different agencies, in different countries, each using different definitions, collect statistical information. The economist who works with these figures will try to adjust them in order to increase the compatibility. Usually there is no easy way out, and he has no choice but to make do with the available information.

In this case, however, the discrepancies between the two series do not seem very great. I am supported in my belief by an article of Dr. Botzen on the measurement of investments in fixed assets in the Netherlands.[12]

Table 33. Total gross investment expenditures by American firms abroad and net acquisitions of existing foreign companies: 1963–1968 (in millions of dollars)

	1963 Total	1963 Mfg & petrol	1964 Total	1964 Mfg & petrol	1965 Total	1965 Mfg & petrol	1966 Total	1966 Mfg & petrol	1967 Total	1967 Mfg & petrol	1968 Total	1968 Mfg & petrol
All areas												
Total investments in plant, property and equipment	5,068	4,140	6,199	5,080	7,440	6,161	8,640	7,109	9,267	7,525	9,346	7,463
Net acquisitions	176	158	263	241	279	227	562	500	190	252	569	512
Percentage share	3.5	3.8	4.2	4.7	3.8	3.7	6.5	7.0	2.0	3.4	6.1	6.9
Europe												
Total investments in plant, property and equipment	1,903	1,749	2,179	1,973	2,640	2,463	3,253	3,022	3,632	3,377	3,108	2,846
Net acquisitions	140	133	318	251	256	208	429	386	237	215	366	336
Percentage share	7.4	7.6	14.6	12.7	9.7	8.5	13.2	12.8	6.5	6.4	11.5	11.8

Source: US Department of Commerce, *Survey of Current Business*, 'Plant and Equipment Expenditures', September, 1965 for 1963; October, 1967 for 1964–1966; October, 1969 for 1967 and 1968.
US Department of Commerce, *Survey of Current Business*, 'Net Acquisitions', September, 1965 for 1963–1964; October, 1968 for 1965–1966; October, 1969 for 1967 and 1968.

Dr. Botzen explains that the Netherlands Central Bureau of Statistics uses two methods for measuring investments in fixed assets, the direct or expenditure, and the indirect or commodity-flow method. To determine the expenditures by Dutch manufacturing industry on plant, property and equipment, the direct method is used. Data are collected by inquiry, excluding companies with less than ten employees. For the latter group separate estimates are made. The US figures relate also to realized expenditures on fixed assets and are similarly collected by inquiry. Thus, the measurement techniques of the investment data appear to be compatible, and it is assumed that the bias in the information will be of the same sign, and of a comparable magnitude.[13]

To sum up the discussion, one can conclude that expenditures on fixed assets by US controlled companies in the Netherlands represent a sizeable percentage of total Dutch investments in those industries. This share seems to be growing – from 6.65 percent in 1957 to 22.63 percent in 1967 – and reflects the magnitude of American direct investments in the Netherlands. To the extent that expenditures for acquisitions and leaseholds are included in American but not in the Dutch figures, these percentage shares are an overstatement of the true investments undertaken. The error lies in the range of 10 to 15 percent.

3. EMPLOYMENT AND THE SCALE OF OPERATIONS

One of the objectives of the Dutch foreign investment attraction program was the creation of jobs. Population growth was (and still is) relatively high, and the much needed transformation from agriculture to industry required absorption of farm workers. In addition, the industrial base had to be broadened and diversified, especially in sectors such as machinery, electrical, and scientific and control equipment. In all these sectors American investments and know-how could contribute very much.

The scale of manufacturing operations has an important impact on efficiency of production, ability to compete and financial resources to launch new product lines and maintain an adequate research and development effort.[14]

a. Employment

In the period from September, 1950, to 1966, total industrial employment in the Netherlands increased by about 196,400 persons, from 937,300 to 1,133,700.[15] The survey results of 109 US companies in the Netherlands show a total employment of 27,881 persons.[16] Not all of these jobs, however, are in manufacturing proper, as 1,185 persons were employed for the handling of imported finished products. Thus the approximate number of employees in manufacturing is 26,696.

American direct investment, however, sometimes takes the form of acquisition, and employment by these companies is therefore not additional. A measure of the needed correction would be the number of employees of these companies in the survey, 9,639 persons in 30 enterprises (excluded are 154 persons handling imported finished products). Plant expansion and thus increased employment after acquisition is not taken into account, although there is evidence that growth in American companies, especially those established before 1957, has been very vigorous.[17] Secondly, only about 50 percent of the companies in the corrected population of 215 returned questionnaires. One can use response rate and corrected sample employment figures to arrive at the measure of total industrial employment created by American direct investments in the Netherlands, but this is of course a very rough indication. Finally, American companies make use of sub-contracting to a far greater extent than Dutch industrial establishments. A 1954 *Fortune* article points out that most Dutch firms make everything themselves rather than resort to sub-contracting.[18] The impact of sub-contracting by American companies on industrial employment cannot be measured adequately, but many Dutch firms certainly have had to expand their labor force in order to adjust to these changed conditions.

Given these qualifications, a calculation of total employment by American enterprises in the Netherlands (Table 34) results in a figure of around 40,000 persons. The number of persons employed in American firms by September 1950 has been estimated at 1,900.[19] Consequently, the US controlled companies would have created employment for about 38,000 people in the year 1950–1966, roughly 20 percent of the increase in industrial employment in that period.

De Smidt has made a calculation of employment by 'existing, wholly foreign owned industrial establishments which started production in the Netherlands between 1954 and 1964 and which on the first of January, 1964, employed ten or more persons.'[20] Of the total estimated employment in 196 foreign companies (with 199 plants) of 29,500 by the end of 1963, 64.4 percent or 19,000 were working in American enterprises. De Smidt estimates that 3,000 of the total 29,500 persons were employed by 1950, and he thus finds a total job creation by all foreign companies of 26,500 persons. If we assume that the proportion of American companies among all foreign firms in the Netherlands was the same in 1950 as De Smidt found it to be in 1963, then these American companies would have employed around 1,900 persons in 1950.[21] Using De Smidt's estimated 1963 employment figures of US companies in the Netherlands (19,000 persons) one

Employment in 109 responding enterprises		27,881
Persons handling imported finished products		1,185
Employment in manufacturing		26,696 persons
Acquisitions		
Employment in 30 enterprises in existence before American take-over	9,793	
Persons handling imported products	154	9,639
Employment in manufacturing of 79 newly established enterprises (both wholly owned and joint)		17,057 persons
Total sample (corrected)	215	enterprises
Already in operation	30	
Newly established	185	enterprises, of which 79 returned questionnaires. These 79 companies employ 17,057 persons.

Estimate of total employment in 185 enterprises

$$\frac{185}{79} \times 17,057 = 39,944 \text{ persons}$$

Source: Information from 109 returned questionnaires.

arrives at a job creation of some 17,100 by 1963. However, 'this does not take into account the effect on employment of establishments which were founded as a result of cooperation between Dutch and foreign enterprises.'[22] My survey, of course, does include these companies. The analysis by De Smidt covers one hundred American manufacturing establishments, where establishment is used in the sense of a production unit. Judging from my survey, the number of production units (plants) exceeds the number of companies, so that his analysis actually deals with less than one hundred American companies.[23] My study covers the total population of 215 American manufacturing enterprises as of January 1, 1967, and the survey results relate to 109 companies with 142 production units. The broad definition of direct investment, as well as the accelerated growth in manufacturing investments after 1963 would explain the rather sizeable difference in the number of enterprises in contrast to the survey by De Smidt.

One other reference to the creation of jobs by foreign enterprises was found in the Sixth Industrial Note of 1959, where the increase in employment is put at 20,000.[24] This includes American as well as other foreign enterprises, and no breakdown by nationality of parent is given.

Table 35. Establishments[1] and persons employed by class of industry: Dutch data for October 15, 1963: U.S. data for end of September and beginning of October, 1966

Class of industry	Dutch industry 1963		109 US enterprises operating in the Netherlands – 1966	
	Establishments	Persons employed	Establishments	Persons employed
Food, beverage and tobacco	15,635	224,082	17	4,470
Textiles, footwear, wearing apparel	15,429	234,490	16	1,811
Chemicals and chemical products	1,045	77,975	33	3,956
Petroleum and coal products	56	9,743	5	3,315
Metal and machinery	11,739	220,613	49	6,457
Electrical machinery	1,994	116,350	9	1,942
Other[2]	22,265	275,469	13	4,745
Industries for which at least one survey was returned	67,163	1,158,722	142	26,696
All manufacturing industries	81,379	1,377,096		

1. Establishment refers to production unit.
2. Other includes: printing and publishing, rubber, transport equipment and miscellaneous manufacturing industries.
Source: Centraal Bureau voor de Statistiek, Statistical Yearbook of the Netherlands (Hilversum: De Haan N.V.), 1965–1966. Survey results from 109 US companies.

If the above estimates are correct, American direct investment has contributed very significantly to the creation of new job openings. Though the marginal share is quite impressive, as compared to total Dutch manufacturing industry the magnitude of American operations appears very small. A 1963 survey of Dutch industry gives a total of some 81,000 units of production with almost 1.4 million employees. Even if industry classes are excluded for which no surveys were returned, the figures remain very high, some 67,000 establishments and over 1,1 million employees. Our 1966 survey returns covered 142 units of production employing ± 27,000 persons.

b. Industrial concentration

Employment opportunities vary considerably between industry groups, with machinery (ISIC 36), food, beverages and tobacco (ISIC 20, 21 and 22), chemicals (ISIC 31) and petroleum (ISIC 32) each accounting for 17, 16, 14 and 12 percent of total employment respectively (Table 25 in Chapter III). When the persons handling imported finished products are excluded, the percentage shares remain virtually the same.

In the *Food, Beverages and Tobacco Industries* (ISIC 20, 21, 22) fourteen enterprises are included in the sample, of which seven returned questionnaires. These seven companies manufacture soft drinks (one firm), cocoa and chocolate products (two firms) and processed vegetables and grain products (two firms). One tobacco company appears in this group, as well as some specialized food manufacturers (two companies). In several subsectors of this industry no American companies are present, usually because the existing Dutch enterprises had acquired an early strong position – examples are beer, margarine, distilled drinks, groceries and cigars (in the latter sector there is only one affiliation).

The group *Textiles and Wearing Apparel* (ISIC 23 and 24) contains several sectors that are already occupied by Dutch enterprises (with a danger of overcapacity). Fifteen American companies are operating in this industry of which twelve returned the questionnaires. Most of them are in the nylon and synthetic materials branches and one in metallic yarns. Some of the products are cords trapping materials, felts, lace, elastic netting and knitbacks.

A very large sector is the *Chemicals and Chemical Products Industry* (ISIC 31), where 53 US enterprises were established by January 1, 1967. Of these, 29 cooperated in the survey. The petroleum refineries are not included in this sector, as is also true of one petro-chemical plant that could not be separated because of lack of specific data. The large petro-chemical industry that has developed, together with the refineries, is almost exclusively foreign, much of it American. A number of mixed Dutch-American plants have been established, such as Ketjen-Carbon, Cyanamid-Ketjen, Unilever-Emery and AKU-Goodrich. Other companies in the survey produce a variety of chemical products, especially plastics, toiletries and pharmaceuticals. In the sectors of oils, paints, fats, etc., the American contribution remains insignificant.

In the *Petroleum Refining* sector (ISIC 32) American refineries are prominent, although the Dutch-British Shell is still by far the largest. Four US companies own refineries, and all of them cooperated in the survey. The Netherlands has always attracted significant investments in the petroleum sector, presumably because of its favorable geographic location. The trend to build refineries close to the consumer areas has resulted in an enormous expansion of refining operations on the mouth of the Rhine (Rotterdam). Petro-chemical enterprises were attracted in turn, many of them subsidiaries of refining companies. The impact of this basic industry on the chemical processing industries can hardly be exaggerated. These plants create a tremendous amount of employment in the building, metal products, and measuring and controlling equipment industries. In addition, service sectors such as engineering and business consulting are greatly stimulated, which benefit other industries in turn.

The *Metal Products* industry (ISIC 35) includes a number of machine tool factories and producers of heaters, boilers, couplings, joints and tubes. The survey shows a total of 34 enterprises, of which 17 cooperated. Some of the bigger companies, such as Cincinnati Nederland and Nicholson File, however, did not return questionnaires. Finally, in the basic metallurgical industry, the American contribution is small.

A very important industry is *Machinery* (excluding electrical equipment) (ISIC 36), where the American participation is significant. The machine industry is basic to the whole industrialization process and vital for the introduction of improved production techniques. There is no industry which is not linked in some way to the machine industry. In a sense it can be regarded as an infra-structure, necessary for industrial growth and stimulated by it. A completely new line of production was introduced in the Netherlands by American manufacturers of office and data processing equipment. IBM, Monroe and Remington Rand were among the first companies to start production in the Netherlands after the Second World War. Other companies include Honeywell and lately Bull-General Electric. Of this group Friden Nederland and Royal Typewriter remain the only companies to cooperate in the survey. As was mentioned before, Philips Computer Industries entered the electronics market in June, 1968, with a series of medium size computers.

Employment in the office equipment sector was estimated at 6,500 in 1963 by De Smidt. Since that time IBM has greatly expanded operations. It is difficult to assess accurately the impact of this industry on economic growth, but given the widespread use of electronic equipment, it must be quite important. In all, 41 US companies in this sector were operating in the Netherlands as of January 1, 1967, of which 21 filled out questionnaires. Most of them are of small or medium size, with the exception of Friden and Royal Typewriter Company. Some of the products manufactured are material handling equipment, hydraulic products, elevators and escalators, industrial sewing machines and pumps.

In the sector of *Electrical Machinery and Appliances* (ISIC 37) we find 14 US companies, seven of which cooperated in the survey. The presence of the Philips Company is, of course, not unrelated to the small number of US firms in this important sector. Most of the companies are small, producing centrifugal pumps, solenoid valves, fans, blowers and vacuum components. One major American establishment produces communications and signalling equipment.

The manufacture of *Professional, Scientific, Measuring and Controlling Instruments* derives its importance from the large petro-chemical and chemical operations. Many American subsidiaries have been established in the Netherlands following these chemical enterprises. The response rate in this industry has been particularly poor – only seven companies out of a total of twenty-one. Three of the cooperating enterprises have more than 250 employees; the others are much smaller. Some of the products are ultrasonic cleaning equipment, control valves and pressure regulators, electric counters, read-out instruments, electronic instruments and control equipment.

A rather heterogeneous group of industries remains. In *Rubber Products* three American companies continue to operate, one having closed its plant in 1967. The AKU-Goodrich establishment for synthetic rubber products has been mentioned under chemicals. Two enterprises in the *Transportation Equipment Industry* (ISIC 38) responded, both subsidiaries of American car manufacturers. One of these employs more than 1,300 persons. Separate mention should be made of a medium size establishment for photographic equipment.

c. *Scale of operations*

With respect to the size, Table 36 compares American companies in the Netherlands and Dutch industrial enterprises. On the whole, the US companies are better represented (70 percent) in the larger size categories

(50 persons or more), whereas most Dutch enterprises fall in the ten to forty-nine employees class (68 percent of all Dutch enterprises). Only three percent of all Dutch companies employ 500 or more persons, as compared to 15 percent of the American firms in the Netherlands. However, in the United States itself the small-sized companies similarly represent the bulk of all enterprises in the manufacturing sector (Table 37). And this pattern would seem to hold pretty much true for all countries.[25] In connection with direct investments in manufacturing a number of factors lead to a larger scale of operations. The minimum requirements on management efforts and overhead expenditures involved in foreign activities would seem to rule out very small scale operations. Furthermore, a direct investment is usually undertaken with a view to serving a national or even international, rather than a local market. For the us direct investments there is in addition the technological aspect. Production techniques developed in the United States tend to be of rather large scale, and the technological bias may be reflected in the overseas operations.[26] Consequently, one would rather expect to find a larger percentage of us companies (operating in the Netherlands) than Dutch enterprises in the higher employee classes.

As to the average size of the us and Dutch enterprises, however, one finds no remarkable differences except in the highest employee class, 1,000 and more persons (Table 36). In other categories the averages are virtually the same. No ready comparison is possible with the United States manufacturing sector because of different size-classes used in the American statistics. (Table 37.) It appears, however, that categories up to 1,000 persons are quite comparable, but that us companies are of a much larger average size in the higher brackets.

Table 38 summarizes data on the Netherlands and my survey results with regard to the size of the production units. Figures for the Dutch manufacturing industry were collected by inquiry of October 15, 1963, whereas our survey relates to September/October 1966. Consequently, the comparison is between different entities and strictly speaking not valid. But if one hopes to get a general idea of the size distribution, the 1963 data for the Netherlands are the latest available.

Industrial classes included are those with at least one returned questionnaire. The figures show that on average American production units are of a much larger scale than Dutch establishments, with 196 employees for the American plant, against some 17 for a Dutch unit. This difference holds true for all classes of industry. In the distribution according to size (Table 39) some 90 percent of all us controlled plants are concentrated in the middle and large sizes, whereas 80 percent of the Dutch units fall into the one to

Table 36. *Number of persons employed in manufacturing industries: by size of the enterprise – U.S. and Dutch companies in 1966*

| Size by number of employees | All Dutch manufacturing enterprises | | | | | US enterprises in the Netherlands[1] | | | | |
| | Enterprises | | Employment | | Average employment per enterprise | Enterprises | | Employment | | Average employment per enterprise |
	Number	%	Number	%		Number	%	Number	%	
10 – 49	7,062	68	158,324	14	22.4	32	30	894	3	27.9
50 – 99	1,661	16	114,689	10	69.0	15	14	1,034	4	68.9
100 – 199	852	8	117,937	10	138.4	17	16	2,555	9	150.3
200 – 499	534	5	161,345	14	302.1	27	25	8,253	30	305.7
500 – 999	178	2	121,476	11	682.4	8	8	5,356	19	669.5
1,000 up	131	1	465,414	41	3,552.7	7	7	9,768	35	1,395.4
Total	10,418	100	1,139,185	100		106	100	27,860	100	

1. Represents 106 US enterprises.

Source: Netherlands data – Centraal Bureau voor de Statistiek, *Statistical Yearbook of the Netherlands* (Hilversum: Uitgeversmaatschappij W. De Haan N.V.), 1965–1966.

US companies – Survey results from 106 American companies: three firms employed fewer than ten persons. (93 fully and 13 partially completed questionnaires.)

Table 37. *Number of persons employed in manufacturing industries, by size of enterprise: the United States in 1963*

Size by number of employees	Enterprises		The US manufacturing sector			
			Employment			
	Number	Percent	Number	Percent	Average employment per enterprise	
1 – 19	180,126	70.000	1,009,781	6	5.6	
20 – 99	58,068	23.000	2,456,444	13	42.3	
100 – 249	10,892	4.000	1,659,905	9	152.4	
250 – 499	3,476	1.350	1,199,228	6	345.0	
500 – 999	1,596	.620	1,096,627	6	687.1	
1,000 – 2,499	941	.360	1,464,039	8	1,555.8	
2,500 – 4,999	374	.150	1,331,098	7	3,585.8	
5,000 – 9,999	206	.080	1,439,425	8	6,987.5	
10,000 up	219	.085	6,824,713	37	31,163.0	
Total	255,898	99.645	18,571,260	101		

Source: US Bureau of the Census, *Enterprise Statistics: 1963*, Part I – General Report on Industrial Organization (Washington, D.C.: 1968).

97

Table 38. Size of establishments (production units) by number of employees, by industrial sector: U.S. companies in the Netherlands (1966) and Dutch industry (October 15, 1963)

ISIC	Industrial sector	Number of establishments	Number of employees	Size of establishment by number of persons									Average number of employees
				1–9	10–19	20–49	50–99	100–199	200–499	500–999	1000–1999	2000 up	
20, 21, 22	Food, beverage, tobacco	15,754 (17)	226,652 (4,470)	12,853	1,306	856 (4)	360 (2)	212 (4)	121 (4)	33 (3)	11	2	14.4 (262.9)
23, 24	Textiles and wearing apparel	15,519 (16)	235,470 (1,821)	12,703	915 (3)	971 (2)	464 (5)	256 (5)	153 (1)	41	15	1	15.2 (113.8)
31	Chemicals and chemical products	1,113 (33)	83,444 (4,098)	532 (4)	160 (2)	170 (9)	103 (7)	68 (4)	51 (6)	13 (1)	11	5	74.9 (124.0)
32	Petroleum and coal products	63 (5)	10,707 (3,320)	12	14 (1)	20	4	6 (1)	2 (3)	4	–	1	169.9 (664.0)
35	Metal products	9,120 (18)	130,286 (2,071)	7,234	784 (2)	625 (6)	239 (5)	133 (1)	82 (3)	17 (1)	6	–	14.3 (115.0)
36	Machinery	2,695 (31)	91,553 (4,849)	1,517 (6)	429 (3)	413 (8)	180 (2)	87 (6)	46 (2)	18 (4)	2	3	33.9 (156.4)
37	Electrical equipment	2,014 (9)	116,581 (2,208)	1,511	169	126 (2)	77 (2)	51 (3)	47 (2)	13	13	7	57.9 (245.3)
	Other [a]	19,349 (13)	206,411 (5,044)	16,416	1,428 (2)	966 (2)	315 (2)	131 (2)	51 (5)	25	10 (2)	7	10.6 (388.0)
	Total	65,627 (142)	1,101,104 (27,881)	52,778 (10)	5,205 (13)	4,147 (33)	1,742 (23)	944 (26)	553 (26)	164 (9)	68 (2)	26 (–)	16.8 (196.4)

a. Includes rubber products, transportation equipment, scientific and control instruments.

Figures in parentheses refer to 109 US manufacturing industries in the Netherlands, with 142 production establishments.

Note: Dutch industries included are those where at least one US company returned a questionnaire.

Source: Centraal Bureau voor de Statistiek, *Statistical Yearbook of the Netherlands* (Hilversum: Uitg. W. de Haan N.V.). Information contained in 109 questionnaires from US companies in the Netherlands.

Table 39. Percentage distribution of manufacturing establishments by size of establishment: the Netherlands (1966), U.S. companies in the Netherlands (1963) and the De Smidt study (1963)

Establishment by size	Percentage distribution, including Class 1–9 persons		Percentage distribution, excluding Class 1–9 persons		Percentage distribution, excluding Class 1–9 persons		
	The Netherlands	Survey data	The Netherlands	Survey data	The Netherlands	Survey data	Data by De Smidt
1 – 9	80	7					
10 – 19	8	9	40	10 ⎫	72	35	39
20 – 49	6	23	32	25 ⎭			
50 – 99	3	16	14	17	14	17	25
100 – 199	1.5	19	7	20	7	20	15
200 – 499	1.0	18	4	20	4	20	8
500 – 999	.25	6	1.3	7			
1000 – 1999	.10	1	.5	1.5	2	8.5	13
2000 and up	.04	–	.2	–			
Total percentage	99.89	99	99.0	100.5	99	100.5	100

Source: Adapted from the source material given in Table 38. In addition, M. DE SMIDT, 'Foreign Industrial Establishments Located in the Netherlands', *Tijdschrift voor Economische en Sociale Geografie*, Jan./Feb. 1966, 57ste Jaargang, No. 1, page 12.

Table 40. Percentage distribution of manufacturing establishments, by size of establishment – the Netherlands, U.S. companies in the Netherlands and all U.S. manufacturing establishments

Establishments size by number of employees	Netherlands data (1963) (percentages)	Survey of US plants in the Netherlands (1966) (percentages)	Establishments size by number of employees	US establishments (1963) (percentages)
1 – 9	80	7	1 – 9	52
10 – 19	8	9	10 – 19	15
20 – 49	6	23	20 – 49	16
50 – 99	3	16	50 – 99	8
100 – 199	1.5	19	100 – 249	6
200 – 499	1.0	18	250 – 499	2
500 – 999	.25	6	500 – 999	.95
1000 – 1999	.10	1	1000 – 2499	.44
2000 and up	.04	–	2500 and up	.17
Total percentage	99.89	99		100.56

Source: Adapted from Table 38 for Netherlands and survey data. Data for the United States, adapted from Table I, p. 2–8 in: US Bureau of the Census, *Census of Manufactures, 1963. Vol. I, Summary and Subject Statistics* (Washington, D.C., 1966).

nine persons category. Production units with 500 or more employees amount to 2 percent for the Dutch versus 8.5 percent for the US controlled units in the Netherlands. These results testify rather forcefully of the smallness of Dutch manufacturing operations. Even if we exclude the size class of one to nine persons, the percentage distribution still shows Dutch factories concentrated in the lower sizes, 86 percent in the classes from 10 to 99 employees, against only 52 percent of the American establishments. Establishments with 500 or more employees amount to 2 percent for the Netherlands versus 8.5 for the American establishments. These results are largely confirmed by the figures for 1964 published in the earlier mentioned article by M. de Smidt. The differences in the 1966 survey data and De Smidt's figures are probably due to several big American subsidiaries not cooperating in our survey, whereas they are included in his study.[27]

Finally we compare the size of production units of the US and Dutch manufacturing sector. Table 40 shows that American direct investment operations in the Netherlands are better represented in the larger size categories, not only in comparison to the whole Dutch sector, but to all US manufacturing establishments as well.

In the foregoing some evidence was presented to show that on the whole American controlled *enterprises* in the Netherlands are of a scale comparable to their Dutch counterparts. The one exception is the class of large companies (1,000 or more employees) where the average size of the Dutch enterprise is about two-and-a-half times larger than the US enterprise. With respect to the size of *production units* (establishments) the evidence indicates that here the US operations are (with one exception) of a much larger scale than the Dutch manufacturing sector. A comparison with scale-statistics of the manufacturing sector in the United States reveals two interesting aspects. The first that the US enterprises are of a much larger scale than the Netherlands or Dutch-based American companies. And furthermore that *percentage-wise* there are more large-scale US production units in the Netherlands than in the United States.[28]

4. PRODUCTION, IMPORTS AND EXPORTS

a. Production[29]

The important aspects of American direct investments in the Netherlands discussed above, such as book values, annual expenditures on fixed assets and the number of employees are, in a sense, *inputs* into the production process. Measurement of such inputs is subject to error, and therefore,

Table 41. *Total sales and imports of finished products: 95 U.S. companies in the Netherlands, 1966*

Industrial sector	Sales figures (in thousands of dollars)		
	Total sales	Imported finished products from both US parent and other affiliates	Measure of actual production in the Netherlands
Food, beverages, tobacco	54,964	1,137	53,827
Textiles, wearing apparel	35,120	2,025	33,095
Chemicals	156,788	39,069	117,719
Petroleum	333,094	45,028	288,066
Metal products	19,114	4,162	14,952
Machinery	48,289	6,433	41,856
Electrical equipment	25,885	9,176	16,709
Transportation equipment	108,425	70,994	37,431
Scientific, control instruments	22,604	1,809	20,795
Other industries [a]	22,873	939	21,934
Total	827,156	180,772	646,384

a. Includes: printing (1), rubber (1), and photography (1).
Source: Information from 95 fully completed questionnaires.

al es figures, the *output* of the production process, will be used to further evaluate the magnitude of American investments in the Netherlands.

Table 41 contains the information concerning sales of 95 US companies that cooperated in the survey and returned completed questionnaires.[30] Total sales amounted to around $ 827 million, with $ 333 million in the petroleum sector and $ 494 million in manufacturing. Unfortunately there is no way in which these figures can be double-checked. The US Department of Commerce publishes sales figures of American direct investments abroad, but lumps the Netherlands and Belgium together. Only for 1957, the first year that sales figures were collected, are separate data for both countries available; since 1957, however, only sales of manufacturing industries, excluding petroleum, have been published.

In 1957 sales of US manufacturing units in the Netherlands amounted to $ 162 million, with some $ 307 million in petroleum products. These figures reflect the heavy investment emphasis in the petroleum sector. Since 1964, however, manufacturing industries represent the major share of American investments in the Netherlands. (See Chapter 2.)

Sales data for the Netherlands and Belgium will be presented in section (c) in which the exports of American direct investment enterprises (**Table 44**) will be discussed.

b. Imports

Of the total sales of $ 827 million, slightly less than 22 percent consisted of finished goods, imported from either the US parent company or from another member of the same multinational group. The extent to which finished goods were imported varies widely from one industry to another, with the transportation sector in the lead (around 65 percent of total sales). Of the 95 responding companies, 56 did import finished products from a company in the same group, with fourteen importing from both the US parent and other affiliates or subsidiaries.

The extent to which foreign companies import finished products serves as a measure of the actual production taking place locally and thus of the impact on national income and employment. By subtracting the value of imported finished products from total sales one arrives at a rather crude measure of actual production in the Netherlands. The figure thus calculated amounts to some $ 646 million (Table 41).

Tables 42A and 42B contain survey information on imports of semi-finished products and raw materials, expressed as a percentage of total sales. Here, as with the finished products, purchases from the parent company or other members of the same multinational group are covered. Some 67

Table 42A. Semi-finished goods and raw materials content of total sales of U.S. direct investment firms operating in the Netherlands – 1966 (000 U.S. dollars)

Percentage range	Total sales	Imported raw materials and semi-finished goods		
		Average	High	Low
Less than 5	5,468	164	273	55
5–10	8,024	602	802	401
10–15	8,339	1,042	1,251	834
15–20	46,485	8,135	9,297	6,973
20–30	55,163	13,791	16,549	11,033
30–40	26,990	9,447	10,796	8,097
40–50	20,767	10,384	12,460	8,307
50–60	21,295	12,712	14,777	10,648
60–75	1,754	1,184	1,316	1,052
75 and over	468,398	386,428	421,558	351,299
Total	662,683	443,889	489,079	398,699

Table 42B. By main sector of industry

Industry	Total sales	Imported raw materials and semi-finished goods		
		Average	High	Low
Petroleum	333,094	274,802	299,785	249,820
Manufacturing	329,589	169,087	189,294	148,879

Note: In the percentage class 'less than 5' I have used 1 percent as the lower and 5 percent as the upper boundary. In the class '75 and over' I have used 90 percent as the upper boundary, assuming that at least 10 percent of sales represents value added in the Netherlands.

Source: Information contained in 67 questionnaires of US direct investment firms that imported raw materials or semi-finished products in 1966. The remaining 28 companies did *not* import these types of products, at least not from the multinational corporation.

companies imported such inputs from either parent or affiliated company in 1966. Their total sales amounted to almost $ 663 million, of which an average of $ 444 million was imported, roughly 67%. The import content of total sales varied considerably for each industry, with the whole petroleum sector in the 75% and higher range. An interesting aspect of these imports is not so much their existence per se, but rather that they originate from within the multinational structure.[31] This has implications regarding the effect of US direct investments abroad on the position of the US balance of payments, and the way international competition is affected by direct investments. These aspects have been mentioned in the literature, but will not be further pursued here.[32]

The figures for petroleum and manufacturing sectors separately revea that the import-sales percentage for manufacturing is much lower than for petroleum, 51 percent and 83 percent respectively. The figures on imported raw materials and semi-finished products relate only to the American controlled enterprises, and a comparison with the absolute data on the Netherlands would therefore not make much sense. However, it may be useful to keep in mind that in 1966 about 70 percent of total Dutch imports were raw materials, semi-finished products and fuels.[33] We can conclude that there is nothing unusual about the high raw material and semi-finished product imports of US establishments, at least not in the case of Holland.

Finally, some information was collected on import substitution. A total of 56 companies indicated that products now manufactured in the Netherlands were previously imported from either the US parent or another company in the multinational group. For these companies local sales in the Netherlands, that is total sales minus exports, are used as a measure of the maximum extent of import substitution. This is a maximum, because most of the 56 US companies started production before 1960 so that such imports could have been replaced through Dutch production. Also, availability of a locally manufactured good will probably increase its sales. The data presented in Table 43 show that roughly $ 246 million can be regarded as replaced imports, equivalent to almost 40 percent of the $ 513 million sales. Even if the figure would be off by 50 percent, the magnitude of import substitution remains impressive. It is very high for the petroleum sector while much lower for manufacturing, $\pm$ 65% and 25% resp.[34]

c. Exports

With respect to exports from American affiliated companies, some figures collected by the US Department of Commerce will be presented first. Although no data are available for the Netherlands individually, the information for the Benelux and other EEC countries in Table 44 will be suggestive. For 1965 the ratio of exports to total sales amounted to 23.7 for the whole Common Market, with a high of 35.1 for the Benelux and a low of 14.5 for Italy. Figures for Western Europe, from 1962 to 1965, indicate that the share of exports in total sales has been maintained at around 23 percent, whereas for the Common Market it increased from 15.0 in 1957 to 23.7 in 1965.[35] The ratio of exports to total sales in US manufacturing industries for all areas is quite a bit lower than for Europe; it amounted to 15.9 in 1957, and increased from 17.6 to 18.1 percentage points for the years 1962-65. Thus, growth of this export to sales figure seems to be restricted to the EEC countries.

Table 43. Sales, replaced imports, and exports of U.S. firms in the Netherlands – 1966

| Industrial activity | No. of firms | Number of firms previously importing products from: | | | 000 US dollars | | |
		US parent	Affiliated firms	Both	Total sales	Total exports	Maximum extent of import substitution
Petroleum	3	2	2	1	270,718	93,232	177,486
Manufacturing	53	48	12	7	242,712	173,861	68,851
Total	56	50	14	8	513,430	267,093	246,337

Source: Information contained in 56 questionnaires.

Table 44. Sales and exports of U.S. direct investment enterprises in E.E.C. countries – 1965: manufacturing sector only (in millions of dollars)

Country	US manufacturing enterprises in the respective countries			Totals for each individual country	
	Total sales	Exports	Ratio	Exports	Ratio of total to US exports
Benelux	1,589	557	35.1	8,860	6.3
Germany	4,356	1,160	26.6	15,920	7.3
France	2,665	440	16.5	7,330	6.0
Italy	1,272	184	14.5	5,610	3.3
Total EEC	9,882	2,341	23.7	37,720	6.2

Source: US Department of Commerce, *Survey of Current Business*, November, 1966.

Table 45. Sales and exports of U.S. direct investment enterprises – 1957 (in millions of dollars)

Country	All industries			Manufacturing			Petroleum		
	Total sales	Exports	Ratio	Total sales	Exports	Ratio	Total sales	Exports	Ratio
All areas	38,154	10,459	27.4	18,331	2,912	15.9	14,501	4,980	34.3
Europe	11,181	1,800	16.1	6,313	1,363	21.6	4,449	373	8.4
EEC	5,110	670	13.1	2,524	378	14.9	2,463	291	11.8
Benelux	910	197	21.6	416	89	21.4	477	108	22.6
Belgium	432	86	19.9	254	62	24.4	170	24	14.1
Netherlands	478	111	23.2	162	27	16.6	307	84	27.3

Source: US Department of Commerce, *U.S. Business Investments Abroad*, 1960.

Table 46. Sales and exports of 95 U.S. companies in the Netherlands – 1966 (in thousands of U.S. dollars)

Industrial sector	Number of companies	Total sales	Total exports	Local sales in the Netherlands	Export destination		
					EEC	US	Other
Food, beverage, tobacco	5	54,964	29,437	25,527	8,035	2,052	19,350
Textiles, wearing apparel	11	35,120	26,187	8,933	21,670	–	4,517
Chemicals	24	156,788	116,106	40,682	45,924	757	69,978
Petroleum	4	333,094	125,000	208,094	49,647	3,347	72,006
Metal products	13	19,114	5,987	13,127	3,736	180	2,071
Machinery	21	48,289	31,247	17,042	14,428	1,182	15,637
Electrical equipment	6	25,885	7,251	18,634	4,506	162	2,583
Transportation equipment	2	108,425	21,354	87,071	21,354	–	–
Scientific, control instruments	6	22,604	15,920	6,684	11,572	75	4,273
Other industries [a]	3	22,873	10,072	12,081	5,475	77	4,520
	95	827,156	388,561	438,595	186,347	7,832	194,382
Manufacturing	91	494,060	263,561	230,501	136,700	4,485	122,376
Petroleum	4	333,096	125,000	208,094	49,647	3,347	72,006

a. Includes: printing (1), rubber (1), and photography (1).
Source: Survey responses from 95 companies.

For 1957 export data for the Netherlands individually are available, in petroleum as well as manufacturing sectors. Exports of manufacturing products amounted to only 16.7 percent of total sales for the Netherlands and to 21.6 for the Benelux (Table 45), but the share of exports in total sales has increased to a high of 35.1 in 1965 for the Benelux.

The survey of US enterprises in the Netherlands provides data on exports, with a breakdown in sales to Common Market countries and the United States. Table 46 contains sales and export figures for 95 companies that returned fully completed questionnaires. Of $ 827 million total sales, around $ 389 million or 47 percent was sold abroad in 1966. Exports of petroleum companies were in the order of $ 125 million, 37 percent of their $ 333 million sales. For manufacturing the ratio of exports to sales was quite a bit higher at 53. In view of the trend to establish refineries close to the consumption areas, the high export ratio of the petroleum sector is actually surprising.

For each industrial class the export-sales ratio varies, with highs of 74 for textiles and 73 for chemicals to lows of 27 for electrical equipment and less than 20 for transportation equipment. The survey results indicate that the 1965 figure for the export-sales ratio of the Benelux countries (35.1 in 1965) understates the ratio for the Netherlands (53 in 1966). The information contained in 12 incomplete questionnaires also points to a high exports to sales ratio.[36]

How do these results compare with the export performance of the Netherlands manufacturing industry? Table 47 gives sales and export data of Dutch companies with more than 10 employees for some years between 1957 and 1966. The figures show that the export performance of American companies in the Netherlands is superior to that of Dutch industry; for selected industries (where at least one US-controlled company was in operation by the end of 1966) the export-sales ratio remained virtually the same, 30 in 1957 and 32.3 in 1966. For all industries the percentages were slightly lower.

The survey results indicate that American direct investment enterprises have contributed to a strengthening the Netherlands export position. The significance of a country's exports to its economic growth has recently been emphasized by Robert F. Emery: 'There are grounds for believing ... that exports are a key factor in promoting economic growth and that it is generally a rise in exports that stimulates an increase in aggregate economic growth, rather than vice versa.'[37] To the extent that American companies have exported a significant share of their total production, they have contributed substantially to economic growth in the Netherlands.

As to the *destination* of exports, roughly 48 percent was shipped to mem-

Table 47. Sales and export data of Netherlands manufacturing industries: 1957–1966 (companies with more than 10 employees) (in millions of guilders)

Year	All industries[a]			Selected industries[b]		
	Total sales	Exports	Ratio	Total sales	Exports	Ratio
1957	30,118	8,436	28.0	27,156	8,024	29.5
1959	32,371	9,803	30.2	29,350	9,302	31.6
1961	36,900	11,265	30.5	33,274	10,629	31.9
1963	43,490	13,032	29.9	39,498	12,338	31.2
1965	53,920	16,417	30.4	49,076	15,583	31.7
1966	57,556	17,825	30.9	52,504	16,999	32.3

(1 Hfl = .28 us dollar)

a. All industries, except building sector and public utilities.
b. Included are industries where at least one us company was operating by the end of 1966.

Source: Adapted from: Centraal Bureau voor de Statistiek, Statistical Yearbook of the Netherlands (Hilversum: Uitgeversmaat-schappij W. de Haan), 1957–1966, tables for the turnover in industry, per class of industry.

III

ber EEC countries, and slightly more than two percent in the United States. The high percentage of exports going to Common Market partners reflects the importance of intra-EEC trade; about 56 percent of Dutch exports in 1966 went to EEC members.[38] US destined exports are limited, and a number of industries such as textiles, wearing apparel, printing, rubber and transportation, did not sell any of their products to the United States. For the Netherlands as a whole some 5 percent of 1966 exports were made to the US. One would, of course, expect subsidiaries of multinational companies abroad not to compete with the parent firm in the domestic market.

SUMMARY

Many aspects of American direct investments in the Netherlands have been discussed, and it may be useful to present a brief summary. The objective was to analyze the magnitude of US business operations in the Netherlands and to assess their impact on the Dutch economy, using published data as well as the results of my survey for the year 1966.

A first, and rather crude measure of US investments is *the value of property, plant and equipment*. These book values may well understate the size of the American investment: there is, however, no easy way to correct the downward bias. Investment data contained in the returned questionnaires and adjusted to reflect the whole survey population were higher than the figures published by the US Department of Commerce.

A more useful yardstick are the *annual investment outlays* of American enterprises in the Netherlands. Purchases of existing facilities, however, are included in the Department of Commerce figures and there are differences in the methods of a data collection. Consequently, the results of the analysis have to be qualified. Even so, fixed investments by American controlled companies amount to a sizeable percentage of annual Dutch investment expenditures, especially when the comparison is made between Dutch investments in selected industries where a US company controls at least one subsidiary. In these selected industries the American share in Dutch fixed investments ranges from 6.65% in 1957 to 16.59% in 1966.

With respect to *employment* it is estimated that in the years 1950-66 US controlled enterprises provided 38,000 jobs, or roughly 20 percent of the total increase in the industrial employment in that period. Due to the very tight labor market conditions in the Netherlands in the last five to six years the aspect of job creation by US enterprises has lost most of its significance to the Dutch economy. However, diversification and strengthening of the industrial sector in the Netherlands continues to be an important aspect of US direct investments.

The *scale of operations* of US companies in the Netherlands is compared to that of the Dutch manufacturing industry. In addition, figures are presented for the manufacturing sectors in the United States itself. Not much difference can be found in the *scale of the enterprise* of the American controlled and the Dutch companies, except in the highest employee category. Here, the Dutch companies are almost three times the size of the average US firm in the Netherlands. But the *scale of the production unit* of US controlled plants in the Netherlands is much bigger than Dutch establishments, with differences ranging from almost double the size to a factor eighteen. The percentage distribution of manufacturing establishments by size category confirms the foregoing conclusion.

Subsequently the output of US companies in the Netherlands is analyzed as well as import requirements and export performance. Following the practice of the US Commerce Department, sales figures are assumed to represent *production*. A measure of the actual production of American firms in the Netherlands is found by subtracting from total sales the value of finished products imported from either US parent or other affiliated companies. The survey also deals with *imports* of the US enterprises, ranging from finished goods to semi-finished products and raw materials. When compared to import requirements of the Dutch industry as a whole, imports by US companies fall substantially below the high Dutch percentages; the survey reveals that a very high percentage is purchased from either the US parent company or other subsidiaries within the same multinational organization. Regarding *exports* by American companies, a substantial share of total sales is made to foreigners, and the export-sales ratio ranges from over 70 for textiles and chemicals, to around 20 for electrical and transportation equipment. In view of the role of exports in the economic growth of a country, these high ratios are significant. Other EEC countries are the best customers and attract about 48 percent of all foreign sales, which reflects the trade pattern of the whole Dutch manufacturing industry. Sales to the United States are far below the national figures.

To conclude one can state that the US controlled manufacturing sector in the Netherlands has contributed much to the economic growth of the country, and will continue to do so. Aside from other considerations, the open-door policy of the Netherlands Governments towards foreign investments, American as well as other, is thus firmly based on the economic benefits of these investments. In my opinion, however, the Government should take measures to strengthen the basic technological foundation of the Dutch industry. Servan-Schreiber's comments regarding education, applied research and product development are particularly relevant in this respect.

NOTES

1. US Department of Commerce, *U.S. Business Investments in Foreign Countries* (Washington, D.C.: 1960), pp. 76–77.
2. WALTHER LEDERER and FREDERICK CUTLER, 'National Investments of the United States in 1966', *Survey of Current Business*, September, 1967, p. 41.
3. RAINER HELLMANN, *Amerika auf dem Europamarkt* (Baden-Baden: Nomos-verlagsgesellschaft, 1966), p. 46.
4. *Ibid.*, p. 46.
5. As was indicated before, the US Department of Commerce recently (in 1968) has been able to separate this petro-chemical plant from the total petroleum sector. This procedure resulted in a drop in the value of petroleum investments from $ 267 million in 1966 to $ 197 million in 1967.
6. Only for 1957 did the Department of Commerce publish data by country. US Department of Commerce, *U.S. Business Investments in Foreign Countries* (Washington, D.C.: 1966), p. 141.
7. Total expenditures on plant and equipment by US subsidiaries are much higher than those presented in Table 5–3, which are for manufacturing and petroleum. Only for 1957 is a complete breakdown of these expenditures available for all sectors. The total figures for the Netherlands were $ 44 million in that year, $ 25 million for petroleum, $ 7 million for manufacturing and $ 12 million for public utilities and trade. If this trend continued for other years, the *total* expenditures would be about 25 to 30 percent higher than the figures presented here. (US Department of Commerce, *U.S. Business Investments in Foreign Countries* (Washington, D.C.: 1960), Table 53, p. 142.)
8. From the total investment figures we have excluded the following sectors: (a) agriculture, forestry and fishing; (b) trade; (c) exploitation of houses; (d) moving and transportation services; and (e) other services.
9. Hellmann was presumably writing about this comparison when he stated that: '...the share of US investments in the investments of the Netherlands manufacturing industry, including the petroleum sector, is the highest in the Common Market. For the years 1957 to 1963 it was around 8 percent. HELLMANN, *op. cit.*, p. 52 (translation mine).
10. The US Department of Commerce trade list of October, 1967, and the International Standard Industrial Classification were used to classify the American enterprises.
11. US Department of Commerce, *U.S. Business Investments in Foreign Countries*, 1960, p. 63.
12. Dr. F. W. BOTZEN, 'Investeringen in Vaste Activa' ('Investments in Fixed Assets'), *Economische Voorlichting*, No. 7, 12 februari 1964, pp. 4–6.
13. For a more extensive discussion of the problems involved in a comparison of the Dutch and American investment data, see Dr. F. W. BOTZEN, 'De Positie van Nederland in de Stroom van Amerikaans Investerings Kapitaal naar West Europa', *Economisch-Statistische Berichten*, 1 mei 1968, 53e Jaargang, No. 2642, pp. 423–26; and FRANK STUBENITSKY, 'Annual American Investment Outlays in the Netherlands – A Comment', *Economisch-Statistische Berichten*, 21 augustus 1968, 53e Jaargang, No. 2658, pp. 771–774. Also Dr. F. W. BOTZEN, 'De Amerikaanse Investeringen in Nederland', *Economisch-Statistische Berichten*, 28 augustus 1968, 53e Jaargang, No. 2659, pp. 794–795.

14. For an extensive discussion of the relation between scale of production and such aspects as efficiency, ability to compete and R & D programs, see: D. SWANN and D. L. MCLACHLAN, *Concentration and Competition: A European Dilemma* (London: The Chatham House/P.E.P. Despatch Department, 1967).

15. Centraal Bureau voor de Statistiek, *Maandstatistiek van de Industrie.* Employment in both 1964 and 1965 was higher than in 1966, reflecting the minor recession in the Netherlands during 1966 and 1967. For 1964 1,141,500, and for 1965 1,143,500 persons employed in manufacturing industries.

16. Two companies did not answer the employment question, and thus we have 109 useful answers from 111 cooperating companies (95 with fully and 16 with partially completed questionnaires).

17. M. DE SMIDT, 'Foreign Industrial Establishments Located in the Netherlands', *Tijdschrift voor Economische en Sociale Geografie,* 57e Jaargang, No. 1, januari-februari 1966, pp. 1-19.

18. HERBERT SOLOW, 'The Dutch Get Private Dollars', *Fortune,* September, 1954, pp. 120-131. Some of the problems created by the absence of general sub-contracting are reflected by the following quotation from page 131: 'IBM has had to line up about 120 sub-contractors, many of them Dutchly obstinate. Giving them engineering, training and inspection guidance has been a task that might have killed IBM's manager, except that he is Dutch too.'

19. DE SMIDT, *op. cit.,* p. 1.

20. The aforementioned article.

21. Calculation: 64.4 percent of estimated total employment in foreign companies of 3,000 in 1950 results in a figure of around 1,900 persons employed in American companies.

22. *Ibid.,* p. 6.

23. There is only one indication of the number of companies in his survey: a table, relating to the total results of 196 firms with 199 establishments. No country-by-country breakdown is provided. (*Ibid.,* Table 9, p. 12.)

24. H. GEORGE FRANKS, *Holland's Industries Stride Ahead* (Federation of Netherlands Industries, 1961), p. 12.

25. See for instance the evidence published by Professor JOE S. BAIN in his *International Differences in Industrial Structure: Eight Countries in the 1950's* (New Haven and London: Yale University Press, 1966).

26. BAIN, *op. cit.,* has shown that indeed US manufacturing industry works on a scale that is larger than used elsewhere. The countries included in the study represent the whole range of economic development, including the United Kingdom, Sweden, Japan and India.

27. DE SMIDT also conducted a survey, but rather than send questionnaires to individual companies, he requested and obtained the cooperation of regional Economic-Technological Institutes. His interest was restricted to location and size of the companies in terms of number of employees. My survey is thus more ambitious and had to be routed to the enterprises themselves.

28. Note that this observation refers to the *percentage* shares and does not claim anything with regard to the average size of production units.

29. Following the US Commerce Department, I regard all sales as actual production, with a correction for imported finished goods. (Question 5b pertains to this aspect.) I realize that this is an overstatement of the actual 'value added' in production. However, there was no easy way out of this dilemma without a lengthy statement in the questionnaire on definitional matters. There is doubt that this procedure would have improved the response to the survey.

30. The sales figures are for the whole company and do *not* reflect the American share. Since *control* is the main criterion, and since control can be exercised with substantially less than 100 percent ownership, the total sales are a good measure of the influence of US direct investments.

31. To quote from the Hufbauer-Adler study: 'European companies with interlocking financial ties evidently buy from themselves, while American subsidiaries buy from their parents', p. 27.
G. C. HUFBAUER and F. M. ADLER, *Overseas Manufacturing Investment and the Balance of Payments* (Washington, D.C.: US Treasury Department, 1968), p. 27.

32. Some authors dealing with balance of payments effects of direct investments are: W. PHILLIP BELL, 'Private Capital Movements and the Balance of Payments Position', *Factors Affecting the U.S. Balance of Payments* (US Congress, Joint Economic Committee, 87th Congress, 2nd Session, 1962); W. B. REDDAWAY et al., *Effects of U.K. Direct Investment Overseas*, Interim and Final Reports (Cambridge: University of Cambridge Press, 1967/68); HUFBAUER and ADLER, *op. cit.*, and JACK N. BEHRMAN, *Manufacturing Investment and the Balance of Payments* (New York: National Foreign Trade Council, 1969).

33. From the Foreign Trade Statistics, *Statistical Yearbook of the Netherlands*, 1964–1966, we present the following figures for 1963–1966 in millions of Dutch guilders.

Year	Total imports	Raw materials and semi-finished goods	Fuels	Consumer goods	Investment goods
1963	21,601	14,742	1,031	2,402	3,162
1964	25,548	17,669	1,031	2,991	3,545
1965	27,010	18,239	958	3,585	4,008
1966	29,024	19,393	923	4,173	4,324

34. Of the sixteen companies that returned incomplete questionnaires, nine indicated that finished products now produced in the Netherlands were previously imported. In seven cases these imports came from the US parent and in two cases from other affiliated companies. In no instance did imports originate from both parent and affiliate.

35. The export share amounted to 22 percent in 1962, 23.1 in 1963, 22.9 in 1964 and 23.5 in 1965. (*Survey of Current Business*, November, 1965, p. 19, and November, 1966, p. 9.)

36. Of the fourteen incomplete questionnaires, two did not give *any* sales or export information. Most of the others listed only the *percentage* of total sales exported, without stating sales figures. The distribution of the export to sales percentages is as follows: sales-export ratio higher than 90 – three companies; 70–89 – two companies; 50–69 – three companies; 30–49 – none; 10–29 – three; and less than 9 – only one company.

37. ROBERT F. EMERY, 'The Relation of Exports and Economic Growth', *Kyklos*, Vol. XX, 1967, Fasc. 2, pp. 470–484.

38. Since 1958 the share of Dutch exports to EEC-countries has grown from 41.6 in 1958 to 59.3 for the period June 1968-June 1969 (Source: IMF *Direction of Trade*).

5. Netherlands direct investments in the United States

INTRODUCTION AND HISTORY

International investment is a two-way street, as illustrated by the United States and Europe. In the early history of America, the Europeans provided much of the capital that was needed for economic development. British, Dutch, Germans, French and Swiss all furnished, at one time or another, funds for mines, canals, railways and oil. Foreign land, mortgage and cattle companies were established, as well as ventures in mining and petroleum. Breweries and liquor, banks and insurance were other fields that attracted foreign capital. Cleona Lewis has written an excellent account of foreign investment in the United States covering the eighteenth and nineteenth centuries.[1]

The value estimates of all foreign investments in the United States from 1837 to 1936 are given in Table 48. After a continuous build-up of both portfolio and direct investments until 1914, many of the foreign holdings were liquidated during and after the First World War. The British sold about 70 percent of the $ 3.7 billion in American stocks and bonds, but most of the direct investment was retained (valued at $ 600 million in 1914). During the war the French sold about $ 250 to $ 275 million in securities and disposed of most direct investments in the post-war years. German interests were liquidated either by outright sale or through the office of the Alien Property Commission, with about $ 550 million remaining by 1919 out of a total of $ 950 million invested before the war. The Dutch sold some securities, but the interests of the Royal Dutch-Shell group were greatly increased.[2]

Estimates are that during the First World War foreigners liquidated some $ 3.0 billion in claims on the United States, reducing their holdings from $ 7.2 to about $ 4.0 billion (all classes of indebtedness are included). Portfolio holdings fell from $ 5.4 billion to $ 1.6 billion, and direct investments decreased by $ 300 million; these investments were valued at $ 900 million in 1919.[3]

Table 48. Estimates of the value of foreign investments in the United States 1837–1936

Year	Value Millions of dollars	Comments
1837	200	All American securities
1869	1,406	All types of investments, excluding commercial credits
1883	2,000	All types of investments
1890	3,000	All types of investments
1895	2,500	All types of investments
1908	6,500	All types of investments
1914	7,000	All types of investments
1919	2,523	All investments, short term excluded
1924	2,858	All investments, short term excluded
1929	5,704	All investments, short term excluded
1933	4,083	All investments, short term excluded
1934	4,357	All investments, short term excluded
1935	5,109	All investments, short term excluded
1936	6,108	All investments, short term excluded

Source: CLEONA LEWIS, *America's Stake in Foreign Investments* (Washington, D.C.: The Brookings Institution, 1938), pp. 518–519.

During the 1920's many new direct investments were undertaken, mainly in artificial fibres and chemicals. Some of these companies were Dunlop Tires and Rolls-Royce Ltd., Brown, Boveri and Co., the American Bemberg Corporation and American Enka. By the end of 1936 the value of all foreign direct investments had increased to $ 1,640 million, and in 1941 they were valued at 2,312 million dollars.[4]

After 1945 European and other investments in the US continued to grow, with the emphasis, however, on portfolio investment. (See Table 49.) The increase in direct investments, which is quite modest as compared to US investments of this type, was financed primarily out of retained earnings and locally (in the US) raised capital. Funds from abroad accounted for a minor share of total expenditures. This pattern is similar to that which characterizes the financing of US investments abroad, where roughly 20 percent of all expenditures on plant, property and equipment is financed with capital from the United States. No figures are available for plant and property expenditures of foreign companies in the United States, but the increase in the value of the investment can be used as an indication. The total growth amounted to $ 7,424 million from 1950 to 1968, with capital flows and the foreign share of retained earnings during that period totaling $ 2,552 million and $ 4,532 million respectively (Table 50).

A breakdown of foreign investments by period of establishment shows that pre-war subsidiaries account for roughly 80 percent of the total value

Table 49. Foreign assets and investments in the U.S.: selected years (in millions of dollars)

	1919	1930	1939	1946	1950	1957	1960	1963	1965	1966	1967	1968p
Direct	900	1,400	2,000	2,503	3,391	5,710	6,910	7,944	8,797	9,054	9,923	10,815
Portfolio	2,300	4,300	4,300	4,482	4,606	8,052	11,507	14,847	17,577	17,952	22,088	29,452
Long term	3,200	5,700	6,300	6,985	7,997	13,762	18,417	22,791	26,374	27,006	32,011	40,267
Short term & government obligations	800	2,700	3,300	8,895	11,715	18,593	26,244	28,695	32,365	33,404	37,709	41,054
Total	4,000	8,400	9,600	15,880	19,712	32,355	44,661	51,486	58,739	60,410	69,720	81,121

p = preliminary.
Source: US Department of Commerce, Balance of Payments: Statistical Supplement – 1961, for 1919–1960.
US Department of Commerce, Survey of Current Business, September, 1965 for 1963; September, 1967 for 1965; October, 1968 for 1966 and October 1969 for 1967 and 1968.

Table 50. Foreign direct investments in the United States: 1950–1968 (in millions of dollars)

Year	Value of the investment	Increase per year	Foreign share of undistributed profits	Capital flows
1950	3,391		190	80
1951	3,658	267	169	90
1952	3,945	287	134	131
1953	4,251	306	163	158
1954	4,633	382	162	124
1955	5,076	443	187	197
1956	5,459	383	167	232
1957	5,710	251	157	155
1958	6,115	405	156	98
1959	6,604	489	233	238
1960	6,910	306	174	141
1961	7,392	482	238	73
1962	7,612	220	214	132
1963	7,944	332	236	–5
1964	8,363	419	327	–5
1965	8,797	434	358	57
1966	9,054	257	339	86
1967	9,923	869	440	251
1968p	10,815	892	488	319
Total: 1950–1968		7,424	4,532	2,552

p = preliminary
Source: US Department of Commerce, *Balance of Payments – Statistical Supplement*, 1963 for 1950–1960.
US Department of Commerce, *Survey of Current Business*, August, 1963 for 1961–1962; August, 1964 for 1963; September, 1965 for 1964; September, 1967 for 1965; October, 1968 for 1966, and October 1969 for 1967 and 1968.

by 1959 (Table 51). Quite naturally, the period 1941–1949 saw a relatively small number of new establishments; and though the *number* increased in the years 1950–1959, the total *value* of these investments remained quite small. We have to conclude that the important foreign investments in the United States were all established before the Second World War and that this constitutes the main difference from the American direct investments abroad.[5]

The total value of foreign direct investments was put at $ 10,815 million by the end of 1968. The American government has tried to increase foreign direct investments by providing more equitable tax treatment of non-resident aliens and foreign corporations. These measures are incorporated in the Foreign Investors Tax Act, which took effect January 1, 1967.[6] In addition, Commerce Department representatives abroad have the mission

Table 51. Value of foreign direct investments in the United States: by period of establishment and number of establishments

Area and industry	All periods		Up to 1941		1941 – 1949		1950 – 1959	
	Number	Value	Number	Value	Number	Value	Number	Value
All areas	1,170	6,604	529	5,170	174	464	467	971
Petroleum	58	1,184	13	1,009	5	108	40	67
Manufacturing	251	2,471	128	2,024	32	46	91	400
Transportation & utilities	66	402	39	286	14	88	13	29
Trade	442	614	155	275	87	131	200	209
Finance & insurance	250	1,734	160	1,485	27	85	63	163
Miscellaneous	103	199	34	91	9	6	60	103
Food products	35	931	26	911	4	6	5	13
Chemical & allied products	63	465	32	404	5	5	26	56
Primary & fabricated materials	19	125	8	92	4	21	7	12
Machinery, except electrical	24	275	14	256	6	7	4	11
Electrical machinery	16	83	5	16	3	1	8	65
Other manufacturing*	94	592	43	344	10	6	41	243
Total manufacturing	251	2,471	128	2,024	32	46	91	401

* includes paper and allied products, rubber products, transportation equipment and miscellaneous products.
Source: US Department of Commerce, Foreign Business Investments in the United States, 1962, pp. 40, 41.

to interest European corporations in setting up operations in the US. Assistance is provided in the form of market surveys, advice on plant locations and loan possibilities, a program very similar to that of many European countries. Some individual states also have representatives abroad, e.g. New York and Ohio in Brussels, California in Tokyo, and New York again with offices in Tokyo and Montreal. In some cases a representative has been able to lure a foreign investor to his particular state.[7]

A number of obstacles to foreign investors still exist, however, and the effect of the tax measures will therefore be limited. One of the main problems for the foreign businessman is the unsatisfactory legal and administrative system, with different investment laws and residence requirements in all fifty states.[8] US immigration laws make it difficult for foreigners to execute their business themselves or have personnel from the parent company on temporary assignments. American anti-trust legislation represents another obstacle, as well as the lack of adequate guidelines for business. With regard to the anti-trust legislation, 'a foreign parent corporation will be held by the American courts to be engaged in doing business in the US if it exercises domination or too great a control over its US subsidiary.'[9] The fact that the European parent would be engaged in doing business in the United States gives the US tax collector the right to tax profits of the parent *wherever these profits are made*. International business will therefore be careful not to dominate their American subsidiaries, and it is claimed that, 'they have in fact only very loose ties with their American subsidiaries.'[10] As *control* is one of the main objectives of direct investment, this aspect of American anti-trust law represents a real obstacle. Closely connected is the interpretation by US courts of 'competition' and of acts that would 'limit competition.' An American company can acquire a subsidiary in one Common Market country and then proceed to buy a comparable business in one of the other member states. This pattern of acquisition would most likely be prohibited in the United States because it would eliminate 'potential competition.'[11] A third obstacle mentioned in a NICB study is discriminatory legislation, where low interest funds for settlement in depressed areas are available for US but not for foreign investors. Other problems include high US labor costs, subcontracting with metric unit specifications, and the sheer size of the American market, which scares away many smaller European companies.[12]

Despite the many unfavorable factors, foreign direct investment in the US continues to grow, although the rate has been much lower than of American direct investments.[13] Among the European direct investors in the US Britain remains the leader, followed by the Netherlands and then

Table 52. *Foreign direct investments in the United States: selected years (in millions of dollars).*

					1968p				
	1950	1960	1966	1967	Total	Manufac- turing	Petroleum	Finance & insurance	Other
All areas	3,391	6,910	9,054	9,923	10,815	4,475	2,261	2,305	1,774
Canada	1,029	1,934	2,439	2,575	2,659	1,413	100	376	770
Europe	2,228	4,707	6,274	7,004	7,750	2,941	2,146	1,855	808
United Kingdom	1,168	2,248	2,864	3,156	3,409	1,076	749	1,239	345
Netherlands	334	947	1,402	1,508	1,750	426	1,215	54	55
Switzerland	377	773	949	1,096	1,238	863	—	331	44
Other	349	739	1,058	1,244	1,353	576	182	231	364
Other areas	134	269	341	343	406	121	15	74	196

p = preliminary.
Source: us Department of Commerce, *Balance of Payments, Statistical Supplement*, for 1950, 1960.
us Department of Commerce, *Survey of Current Business*, November, 1968 for 1966; October 1969 for 1967 and 1968.

Switzerland (Table 52). Manufacturing, finance and insurance, and petroleum have attracted the major shares, accounting for $ 4.5, $ 2.3 and $ 2.3 billion respectively in 1968. The Netherlands, with total direct investments of $ 1,750 million in 1968 accounts for more than 16 percent of total foreign direct investments.

I. NETHERLANDS DIRECT INVESTMENTS ABROAD

a. History of Dutch investments

'The Dutch have an investment history that antedates that of the United Kingdom. By the year 1700 they numbered England, France, Russia and many other European countries among their debtors and had made advances to colonial enterprises in various parts of the world.'[14] This quotation actually understates the importance of Dutch direct investment in the seventeenth century. The economies of the Scandinavian countries were literally honeycombed by Dutch enterprises. In 1619 a number of Amsterdam merchants, among them De Besche and De Geer, started the development of iron and copper mines in Sweden. Smelteries and foundries were established and Sweden thus became a first rank producer of munitions.[15] In Russia, Dutch activities included iron and copper mining, metallurgy and manufacture of munitions. 'The first saw-mill, first papermill, first powder-mill, and first glass furnace in Russia were Dutch enterprises; so was the first postal service.'[16] In France, Netherlands direct investment was engaged in the manufacture of pottery, fine cloth, serge and linen; in dyeing, distilling, sugar refining, paper-making, glass and instrument making, and shipbuilding. In Scotland and Ireland there were also industrial ventures linked to Holland. Only in England were the efforts of Dutchmen to establish industries brusquely extinguished.[17] In the seventeenth century it was true that 'where Dutch capital went, there swamps were drained, mines opened, forests exploited, canals constructed, ships built, new industries established, mills turned and trading companies were organized'.[18]

The first Netherlands direct investment in the North American continent dates from 1626, when the Dutch West India Company bought Manhattan to establish a trading post. Not much other information is available concerning the early investments, but it appears that on the whole these were portfolio rather than direct investments.[19] Some notable examples of Dutch portfolio investments are the financing of the *total* foreign debt of the US in 1803 ($ 8.7 million) and $ 13.7 million of the internal government debt. Later, Dutch capital helped to build railroads, not only in the United States but also in Europe and Latin America as well. At the turn of the century large blocks of shares in US Steel were traded in Amsterdam.[20] In the United States the Dutch also ventured into the field of direct investments and established land, mortgage, cattle, mining and petroleum companies.[21] There were establishments in banking and insurance as well.

In 1938 Cleona Lewis estimated the total value of all Dutch investments abroad at $ 4.8 billion, against roughly 500 million in liabilities.[22] Around 42 percent of all Dutch holdings were placed in Indonesia, some two billion dollars, most of which was in the form of direct investments. Tin mines, rubber plantations and petroleum refineries were the favored investment targets, but many other industrial and trading enterprises were established as well.[23] The value of all Dutch investments in the US has been estimated at almost one billion dollars by 1938.[24] A year earlier the value of direct investments was put at $ 179 million, so that indeed the major share of the Dutch holdings were of the portfolio type.[25]

The foregoing discussion, though rather brief, indicates that direct investments abroad are not new to the Dutch. Justice has hardly been done to the long and interesting history of the Netherlands investments in the United States, but here the reader is again referred to the publications of Cleona Lewis and K. D. Bosch mentioned earlier.

b. *Netherlands direct investments in Europe and the United States*

After 1945 the Netherlands faced the problem of reconstruction. Much had been destroyed or hauled away in the war, and the economic infrastructure and industrial base had to be rebuilt. Generous aid from the US and austerity programs of the Dutch government helped to put the country back on its feet, so that by 1950 industrial production had again reached the 1939 level. In those early post-war years, the emphasis was on domestic economic problems; not much attention was paid to investments abroad. But gradually the capital outflows connected with direct investment increased and have as a rule exceeded the capital inflows. Unfortunately, little is known about the *total value* of Dutch direct investments abroad, but an indication of its importance are the capital outflows related to these investments. Table 53 shows that from 1954 to 1967 such outflows amounted to around $ 1.7 billion against inflows of some $ 550 million, thus resulting in a net capital outflow of almost $ 1.2 billion. In the case of US direct investments such capital outflows finance roughly 20 percent of all overseas plant, property and equipment expenditures. If one assumes that a

Table 53. *Capital flows connected with direct investments and private short term capital movements: the Netherlands, 1954 – 1967 (in millions of guilders) (1 Hfl = .28 U.S. dollar)*

	Capital flows connected with direct investments			Private short term capital movements		
Year	Netherlands direct investment abroad	Foreign direct investment in the Netherlands	Balance	Netherlands investment abroad	Foreign investment in the Netherlands	Balance
1954	-100	24	-76	-147	13	-134
1955	-249	93	-156	-116	-53	-169
1956	-168	25	-143	-153	15	-138
1957	-97	39	-58	-169	181	12
1958	-914	88	-826	-36	136	100
1959	-911	131	-780	-151	-84	-235
1960	-354	100	-254	-146	126	-20
1961	-340	86	-254	-433	388	-45
1962	-385	201	-184	-246	46	-200
1963	-489	259	-230	-320	212	-108
1964	-537	324	-213	-49	371	322
1965	-453	242	-211	-391	432	41
1966	-493	214	-279	-700	716	16
1967	-756	162	-594	-799	1,140	341
Total: 1954-1967	-6,248 ($1,725 million)	2,004 ($554 million)	-4,244 ($1,171 million)	-3,856 ($1,065 million)	3,639 ($1,005 million)	-217 ($60 million)

- = outflow

No figures available for 1950–1953.

Source: *Annual Reports of the Nederlandsche Bank.*

similar pattern holds true for the Netherlands, total outlays by Dutch multinational enterprises abroad would be in the order of $ 8.6 billion during 1954 to 1967.[26] Over the same period private short term capital outflows of around $ 1.0 billion were only slightly higher than inflows (Table 53). As a rule short term capital is also used to finance direct investments, but to what extent this has been the case cannot be ascertained for the years 1954-65. The Netherlands Central bank in its latest annual report has, however, given data on long and short term credits within multinational organizations for the past few years. These credits are from now on to be included in the definition of direct investments, as are purchases of land and buildings.[27] Table 54 contains the data on capital flows connected with direct investments for 1966-1968, using the broader definition; the category 'equity participations' is identical to the 'capital flows connected with direct investments' of table 53; no such reconciliation was possible for the 'private short term capital movements'. It can be seen from these figures that Dutch equity participations abroad are an important instrument in the financing of overseas investments, whereas foreign investors in the Netherlands appear to rely more on short and long term credits.

Yet another indication of the growth of Dutch investments abroad is the steadily rising stream of interest, dividend and other investment incomes received from abroad. This indicator is unfortunately not very precise as far as direct investments are concerned, because the remittances relate to both portfolio and direct investments. Payments on investments by foreigners, again covering portfolio as well as direct, are also increasing (Table 55).

A recent survey published by the Europa Instituut of the University of Leiden gives an insight into the Dutch direct investments in member EEC countries by 1966. A total of 490 companies with either industrial and/or commercial establishments in Common Market member countries were contacted. The big Dutch multinational companies were *excluded* from the survey.[28] From the total of 490 companies, 265 cooperated in the survey, and these companies had a total of 853 establishments in the EEC countries; in 1958 the 265 cooperating companies had only 325 subsidiaries, a growth of around 160 percent. Of the 853 establishments only 209 were in manufacturing, the other 644 being sales or service outlets. The industrial subsidiaries are concentrated in food, beverages and tobacco (124 establishments), chemicals (111), metal, machinery and electronics (91) and textile industries (57). No information is provided concerning value of the investment, sales, or scale of operation.

For the year 1968 we have an estimate of the Netherlands direct investments in West Germany.[29] The table on page 129 (Table 56) gives the total

Table 54. *Private capital movements connected with direct investments: the Netherlands 1966–1968 (in millions of guilders) (1 Hfl = .28 U.S. dollar)*

Netherlands investments abroad	1966	1967	1968p
Equity participations	–493	–756	–785
Credits within the multinational organization	–436	–323	–469
(of which short term)	(–107)	(53)	(–332)
Total outflows	–929	–1,079	–1,254
Foreign investments in the Netherlands			
Equity participations	214	162	479
Credits within the multinational organization	357	694	616
(of which short term)	(–10)	(98)	(234)
Total inflows	571	856	1,095
Balance	–358	–223	–159

p = preliminary
– = outflow
Source: 1968 Annual Report of the Nederlandsche Bank, adapted from Table 27, pp. 76–77.

Table 55. *Interest, dividends and other investment income, payments and receipts: the Netherlands, 1954–1968 (in millions of guilders) (1 Hfl = .28 U.S. dollar)*

Year	Interest, dividend and other investment income		
	Receipts	Payments	Balance
1954	676	380	296
1955	733	415	318
1956	700	455	245
1957	846	606	240
1958	908	582	326
1959	1,220	650	570
1960	1,217	769	448
1961	1,463	848	615
1962	1,397	1,015	382
1963	1,683	1,038	645
1964	1,864	1,126	738
1965	2,033	1,613	420
1966	1,998	1,415	583
1967	2,520	1,623	897
1968p	2,639	1,926	713

p = preliminary
Data from 1950–1953 not available.
Source: Annual Reports of the Nederlandsche Bank (Dutch Central Bank).

Table 56. Value of foreign direct investments in West Germany – end of 1968 (in millions of DM)

Industry	Value	
	Total	Netherlands
Petroleum	2,625.1	545.2
Food	1,187.5	467.0
Smelting	939.4	260.9
Electronics, electrical instruments	2,029.9	316.0
Chemicals	1,801.6	198.1
Other industries	5,913.0	230.3
Trade	1,497.9	162.4
Services	708.8	103.3
Finance, banks, insurance	729.2	26.1
	18,023.1 ($ 4,506 million)	2,409.3 ($ 602 million)
Percentage share	100	13.4

share of the United States: 43.6
Switzerland : 12.6
United Kingdom: 10.0 ; all others below 10 percent.

Source: Adapted from *Monthly Report of the Deutsche Bundesbank*, May 1969, 'Foreign Ownership in German Enterprises', p. 30.

foreign direct investment and the value of the Dutch participations. After the United States, the Netherlands is the biggest foreign investor in West Germany, with direct investments estimated at DM 2,409 ($ 602 million) or 13.4 percent of the total value of DM 18,023 million ($ 4,506 million).[30] The industrial concentration is closely tied to the activities of the multi-national companies in the Netherlands; Royal Dutch in petroleum, Unilever in food products, Hoogovens in smelting, the Philips Lamp Company in electronics and in chemicals AKU and Koninklijke Zout-Organon. In the other sectors the Dutch participation is rather modest, with the exception of trade and services.[31]

Bertin and Gervais analysed foreign investments in France.[32] Dutch direct investment is again represented by the familiar companies, Shell and Philips both with two subsidiaries, and Unilever with three establishments. There is also a subsidiary in machinery and tools (Stokvis & Sons). All these companies appear on the list of the 500 largest industrials in France in 1960, as published by Bertin.[33] He estimates the total value of the investments at 1,404 million francs ($ 284 million) with sales of 6,381 million francs ($ 1,292 million). Another figure is calculated by Gervais, who ranks the Netherlands as the third biggest investor in France, behind the US and the UK. The value of *all* Dutch direct investments in France by 1961 is put at $ 400 million, against $ 2 billion from the US and $ 500 million from the UK.[34]

A recent French government publication deals with the flow of foreign capital from 1962 to 1966.[35] It shows that (1) these foreign investments are but a small percentage of total French capital formation, and that (2) most of the investment originates in the United States, Switzerland and the Common Market countries. A breakdown among the latter indicates that Belgium and Luxembourg (BLEU) are the main investors, followed by Germany and the Netherlands. Unfortunately, the publication does not provide information on the accumulated direct investments in France.

The most complete information concerning Dutch direct investments is available for the United States, as published by the US Department of Commerce. Early estimates of the value of these investments were presented in Part 1 of this chapter. From 1950 to 1968 the Netherlands direct investments in the United States increased from 334 million dollars to $ 1,750 million, a growth of around 420 percent over 18 years. Total foreign investments in the US increased by roughly half this percentage, 220 percent from $ 3,391 million in 1950 to $ 10,815 million in 1968; the annual compound growth rate amounts to slightly over 4%, as against almost 8% for the Netherlands. Table 57 shows that the Netherlands investments are concentrated in the petroleum sector, with manufacturing a distant second. This pattern is remarkably similar to that of American investments in the Netherlands. As we have seen in Chapter 2, manufacturing investments were much lower than those in the petroleum sector up to 1964, when the trend was reversed. Such a reversal does not seem likely for Dutch investments in the United States.

The regular publication of the Department of Commerce, *The Survey of Current Business*, contains but little information on the direct investments by foreigners. The value of these investments for each country is given, as well as an over-all breakdown per activity (not on a country-by-country basis). In addition, some information on capital flows and earnings is available. In 1959 a detailed survey was made of all foreign investments, the results of which were published in 1962. Almost all specific information concerning the Dutch direct investments in America were found in the latter publication.[36]

One of the first points of interest is that the establishments from before 1941 account for almost 90 percent of the accumulated book value. Although the *number* of establishments in the periods 1941–1949 and 1950–1959 is about the same as for the years up to 1941, the value of these

Table 57. Value of Netherlands direct investments in the United States – by activity 1950–1968 (in millions of dollars)

Year	Total value	Annual increase	Value by activity			
			Petroleum	Manufacturing	Finance & insurance	All other
1950	334	–	226	44	34	30
1951	376	42	257	54	34	31
1952	423	47	289	68	34	32
1953	480	57	333	80	35	32
1954	533	53	364	98	36	35
1955	613	80	411	127	37	38
1956	681	68	461	142	38	40
1957	747	66	512	155	39	41
1958	816	69	553	176	41	46
1959	892	76	607	197	42	46
1960	947	55	639	213	42	53
1961	1,023	76	693	231	43	56
1962	1,082	59	–	–	–	–
1963	1,134	52	–	–	–	–
1964	1,231	97	842	296	39	54
1965	1,304	73	–	–	–	–
1966	1,402	98	–	–	–	–
1967	1,508	106	1,021	388	41	57
1968p	1,750	242	1,215	426	54	55

p = preliminary.
No data per activity available for the Netherlands in the years 1962–63; 1965–66.
Source: us Department of Commerce, *Balance of Payments: Statistical Supplement*, 1962.
us Department of Commerce, *Pocket Data Book, U.S.A.*, 1967.
us Department of Commerce, *Survey of Current Business*, September, October issues.

investments is very small (Table 58). This evidence bears out that the important Dutch subsidiaries were established before the Second World War. We have seen in the Introduction that this pattern is rather typical of *all* foreign investments in the United States (Table 51).

With regard to the financing of Dutch direct investments Table 59 is illustrative in that it shows the importance of reinvested earnings as a source of funds. Capital flows have, on the whole, financed only a minor share of the annual increase in bookvalues, except in 1968 when Royal Dutch exercised its option to purchase 69 percent of the new share issue of Shell Oil. The figures in Table 59 do not, however, indicate the financing pattern of annual investment outlays, which are undoubtedly some multiple of the increase in bookvalues. Depreciation and depletion allowances, as well as local capital will certainly have been used as additional

Table 58. *Number and value of Netherlands direct investments in the United States in 1959: all industries – by period of establishment*

	Number of establishments		Value (in millions of dollars)	
Up to 1941	26	(529)	778	(5,170)
1941 – 1949	21	(174)	56	(464)
1949 – 1959	24	(467)	59	(971)
Total by 1959	71	(1,170)	892	(6,604)
	6 percent of the total number of foreign establishments		13.5 percent of the total value of all foreign investments	

(Figures in parentheses refer to total foreign investments).
No breakdown per class of industry is available.
Source: US Department of Commerce, *Foreign Business Investments in the United States,* 1962.

Table 59. *Netherlands direct investments in the United States; annual increase in value, capital flows, net income and undistributed profits: 1950–1968 (in millions of dollars)*

Year	Annual increase in value	Capital flows	Net income of the in- vestment	Netherlands share of undistributed profits
1950	–	3	90	55
1951	32	4	89	38
1952	47	7	78	40
1953	57	6	71	51
1954	53	8	75	45
1955	80	18	83	62
1956	68	8	86	60
1957	66	4	88	61
1958	69	9	91	60
1959	76	6	104	72
1960	55	4	94	51
1961	76	2	101	74
1962	59	–19	–	–
1963	52	–35	–	–
1964	97	–6	121	102
1965	73	–33	147	120
1966	98	20	153	78
1967	106	12	177	93
1968p	242	141	192	102

p = preliminary.
Income and profit figures not available for 1962, 1963.
Source: US Department of Commerce, *Balance of Payments: Statistical Supplement,* 1962. US Department of Commerce, *Survey of Current Business,* annual September/October issues.

132

sources of funds. Unfortunately there are no data available on these aspects of foreign investments in the United States.

The sales and net income figures for 1959 (available only for that year), when related to the value of the investment, reveal some rather interesting aspects.[37] The comparison of the Netherlands with all areas shows that with 14 percent of all investments, the Dutch subsidiaries had 36 percent of total sales and earned 62 percent of total net income. The favorable relation of investment, sales and income holds true for petroleum manufacturing and all other sectors.[38] At least for 1959 the profitability of the Dutch direct investments in the US appears much better than for all areas together, 25 percent against 6 percent for total industries. For the petroleum and manufacturing sectors, the percentages are 30 and 20 for the Netherlands and 17 and 7 for all areas. These figures must be regarded with some suspicion, however, as other data on net income for the same year in the same publication are quite different. The figures in Table 60 presumably relate to the *whole* enterprise, whereas other data on net income refer to the *foreign* share of total net income (Table 61).[39] A comparison of the foreign share of net income, related to the value of the investment, also shows that Dutch investments are more profitable than all other investments together. No industry breakdown of earnings figures per country is available.

Finally, the 1959 publication contains evidence on the control aspect of Dutch foreign investments in the United States. It has been emphasized that control is the distinguishing characteristic of direct investments, and this holds true also for the Netherlands. By 1959, when the total Dutch investment was valued at $ 892 million, the percentage ownership was as follows: 95 percent or more, $ 224 million; 50 to 95 percent, $ 667 million; and 25 to 50 percent, only one million dollars.[40] Thus, for all practical purposes, the whole Dutch investment in the United States has a majority control by the Netherlands parent organization.

The following section deals with the American subsidiaries of the big four Dutch multinational enterprises, Royal Dutch, AKU, Philips and Unilever.[41] Many other companies have direct investments in the United States, but their scale is much smaller.[42]

2. THE BIG FOUR ON THE AMERICAN SCENE

The 1968 *Fortune* directory shows seven Dutch enterprises among the 200 largest industrials outside the United States, but if we include a 1969 merger, the total is six.[43] Two of these companies, Royal Dutch/Shell and

Table 60. Foreign direct investments in the United States: value of the investment, net sales* and net income for the year 1959 – the Netherlands and all areas, by industry (in millions of dollars)

	The Netherlands			All areas		
	Value of investment	Net sales	Net income	Value of investment	Net sales	Net income
Petroleum	607	2,102	181	1,184	2,356	197
	(51)	(89)	(92)			
Manufacturing	197	775	39	2,471	5,131	163
	(8)	(15)	(24)			
Other	88	42	6	2,949	575	5
	(3)	(7)	(120)			
Total	892	2,919	225	6,604	8,062	365
	(14)	(36)	(62)			

* Net sales or revenues.
(Figures in parentheses are the percentage share taken from the total figures under 'all areas').
Source: US Department of Commerce, *Foreign Business Investments in the United States,* 1962, tables 1, 13.

Table 61. Foreign direct investments in the United States: the foreign share in net income (or earnings) and the value of the direct investment – the Netherlands and all areas, selected years (in millions of dollars)

Year	The Netherlands			All areas		
	Value investment	Net income	Net income as percentage as investment value	Value investment	Net income	Net income as percentage as investment value
1950	334	90	27	3,391	344	11
1955	613	83	13	5,076	329	6
1959	892	104	12	6,604	415	6
1960	947	94	10	6,910	385	6
1964	1,231	121	10	8,363	596	7
1965	1,304	147	11	8,797	642	7
1966	1,402	153	11	9,054	695	8
1967	1,508	177	12	9,923	804	8
1968p	1,750	192	11	10,815	868	8

p = preliminary.
Source: US Department of Commerce, *Foreign Business Investments in the United States,* 1962, for 1950–1960.
US Department of Commerce, *Survey of Current Business,* September, 1966 for 1964; September, 1967 for 1965; October, 1968 for 1966, and October 1969 for 1967 and 1968.

Table 62. Netherlands industrial enterprises included in the 200 largest industrial companies outside the United States: 1967 and 1968

	Fortune rank	Sales	Assets	Employees
		(In millions of dollars)		
Royal Dutch/Shell	1	9,216	14,303	171,000
	(1)	(8,376)	(12,870)	(172,000)
Unilever N.V.	2	5,534	3,432	312,000
	(2)	(5,560)	(3,271)	(304,000)
Philips N.V.	6	2,685	3,407	265,000
	(6)	(2,402)	(3,064)	(241,000)
AKU	58	917	1,136	66,700
	(72)	(733)	(1,019)	(54,150)
Koninklijke	117	514	522	24,600
Zout-Organon	(117)	(463)	(444)	(22,800)
Hoogovens	153	391	827	20,280
	(161)	(342)	(740)	(19,600)
DSM	171	350	453	21,700
Staatsmijnen	(181)	(300)	(421)	(25,400)

(Figures in parentheses are the 1967 data)
Source: Fortune Directory, 'The 200 Largest Industrial Companies Outside the US', August 15, 1969 for 1968; September 1, 1968 for 1967.

Unilever, are Netherlands-British held; the others are 100 percent Dutch. Royal Dutch/Shell was formed by a merger of the Dutch Royal Petroleum and the British Shell Transport and Trading Companies; two new companies were formed, one Dutch, one British, and both were owned 60 percent by Royal Dutch and 40 percent by Shell Transport and Trading. Because of the majority holding by the Dutch the enterprise is considered to be under control of the Netherlands parent company. The other firm with a double nationality, the Unilever group, is divided along geographical lines into a British and a Dutch branch. The latter – Unilever N.V. – is the parent company of the group's United States subsidiaries.

Of the seven Dutch companies on the list of the 200 largest industrials outside the US in 1968 (Table 62), only Hoogovens N.V. does not, as far as I know, have subsidiaries in the United States, although it does engage in direct investments in other countries, most notably in West Germany. The American subsidiaries of Koninklijke Zout-Organon and DSM-Staatsmijnen are of relatively recent date, and little information about them is available. Consequently, the discussion will be limited to the direct investments of the four remaining companies, Royal Dutch/Shell, Unilever, Philips and AKU; the five subsidiaries of these companies easily made the list of the 500 largest US corporations (Table 62). Shell Oil is by far the

Table 63. Netherlands direct investment enterprises in the United States – 1967 and 1968

US subsidiary	Dutch parent company	Fortune rank	Sales (In millions of dollars)	Assets (In millions of dollars)	Employees
Shell Oil	Royal Dutch/ Shell	16 (14)	3,317 (3,073)	4,230 (3,421)	39,080 (38,330)
Lever Bros.	Unilever N.V.	214 (195)	453 (440)	238 (227)	7,660 (7,650)
North American Philips	Philips N.V.	195 (260)	501 (316)	382 (244)	18,000 (14,600)
American Enka	AKU	343 (380)	239 (186)	217 (197)	10,609 (9,328)
Thomas Lipton	Unilever N.V.	357 (343)	229 (211)	118 (110)	3,563 (3,456)

(Figures in parentheses are the 1967 data)
Source: Fortune Directory, 'The 500 Largest US Corporations', May 15, 1969 for 1968; June 15, 1968 for 1967.

largest of the Dutch subsidiaries, followed by the Unilever investments, Philips and AKU. The companies will be discussed in this order.

a. Shell Oil Company

The British Shell Transport and Trading Company acquired an interest in Texas oil production before 1900.[44] In 1903 Shell and Royal Dutch founded the Asiatic Petroleum Company, a move that was followed in 1907 by the merger of the two companies on a 40–60 basis. Expansion in the US was concentrated on the oil fields in Oklahoma and California, and the company grew spectacularly. Assets were valued at $ 17.7 million in 1914, at $38.5 at the end of the war, and at $ 205 million in 1922.

In 1922 a merger with the Union Oil Company of Delaware led to the foundation of the Shell Union Oil Corporation, with 32 percent of the new capital in the hands of Royal Dutch. The development of the company in the US took place mainly through three subsidiaries, the Shell Oil Company in California, the Shell Petroleum Corporation in the Midwest and the Shell Eastern Petroleum Products, a sales organization in the East. In 1938 the Shell Union produced roughly 26 percent of the total unrefined oil production of the Royal Dutch/Shell Company. Just before the Second World War, the company operated nine refineries, 5,000 miles of pipelines, 4,000 tankwagons and storage facilities for 57 million barrels. By that time the company was also engaged in the production of chemicals in the

Shell Chemical Corporation and the Shell Development Company, although the Shell Chemical Corporation was not established until 1929. Since 1946 sales have increased from $ 443 million to $ 3,317 million by the end of 1968, with assets of $ 4,230 million. The Shell Oil Company is not only a major oil producer but also an important chemical enterprise.

The American subsidiary is 69 percent owned by the Royal Dutch/Shell Company; in a recent increase of the share capital, Royal Dutch exercised its right to purchase 69 percent of the new issue, which resulted in a capital inflow into the US of $ 210 million.[45] Shell Oil is the largest foreign subsidiary in the United States and in 1968 it ranked as no. 16 on the *Fortune* list of the 500 largest American industrial corporations.

b. Lever Brothers and Thomas Lipton

These two subsidiaries, now under direct management of the Dutch Unilever branch, were established by the British Lever Brothers, Ltd.[46] In 1930 the latter firm merged with the Dutch 'Margarine Unie' to form Unilever; a reorganization in 1937 made the English branch responsible for all investments in the British Empire, with the rest of the world going to the Dutch Unilever N.V. Thus, the Dutch indirectly acquired a direct investment in the United States.

The Lever Bros. investments date from 1897 when a 60 percent interest was acquired in the Curtis Davis Company of Cambridge, Massachusetts. The company was renamed Lever Brothers in 1899 and specialized in the soap and fats industry; by this time the firm was 100 percent British owned. The beginning years were not successful, but by 1913 the trend was on the upswing. Sales increased from around $ 1 million in 1913 to $ 12 million in 1920, from $ 45 million in 1930 to $ 90 million in 1939. In 1939 the company operated five plants and produced soaps and edible fats. Some of these product names have a very familiar ring – Lifebuoy, Lux toilet soap and the vegetable shortening, Spry.

After the Second World War, the company continued to expand, although in the sixties growth has been slow relative to other corporations. Thus Lever Brothers slipped from a *Fortune* sales rank of 119 in 1957 (the first year it appeared on the list; before that time, sales had not been reported separately) to 122 in 1960 and 214 in 1968. The volume of sales increased from $ 346 million in 1957 to $ 453 million in 1968, a rise of only $ 107 million in eleven years. Assets were valued at $ 227 million in 1967 and slightly higher at $ 238 million in 1968.

Another Unilever subsidiary in the US is Thomas J. Lipton, operating since 1937, of which the parent owns 99 percent of the equity capital. This company, selling teas, soups, ready dinners, canned foods (Morton House Kitchens, Inc.), salad dressing and ice cream (Good Humor Corp.), ranked as number 357 on the *Fortune Directory* in 1968 (343 in 1967). Sales amounted to $ 229 million with $ 118 million in assets; for 1967 the figures were $ 211 million and $110 million respectively. If one views its sales ranking, the company has maintained its position among the 500 largest industrials, as its sales rank in 1955 was number 342.

c. North American Philips Company

It was not possible to collect much information concerning the Philips direct investments in the United States. The company's annual reports are superbly consolidated; all new investments are immediately written off and the information regarding foreign investments is negligible. Consequently, it was impossible to determine when the direct investment was made.

The continental edition of *Who Owns Whom* enables one to get an insight in the structure of the Philips' investments in the United States. The United States Philips Trust is a subsidiary of the parent company in Eindhoven (Netherlands), the Philips Gloeilampenfabrieken N.V. (Note that 'subsidiary' indicates an ownership of more than 50 percent by the parent company.) The US Philips Trust in turn is parent to two companies, a subsidiary, the North American Philips Co., and an affiliate, Consolidated Electronics Industries. ('Affiliate' denotes an ownership of between 10 and 50 percent of equity.) Matters were quite complicated, because the North American Philips Co. has, in its turn, an affiliate named Consolidated Electronics Industries (Conelco). A recent note in a weekly publication by a Dutch commercial bank, however, throws some light on the situation. According to this source the American interests of the Philips company are being combined by an exchange of stocks between North American Philips and Conelco.[47] North American Philips was a wholly-owned subsidiary, whereas the interest in Conelco amounted to around 35 percent. As a result of this stock exchange the Philips interest in Conelco will increase to 66 percent; the name will be changed into North American Philips.[48]

Conelco first made the *Fortune* list in 1959, ranking number 432 with sales of $ 87.3 million and assets of $ 77 million. In the subsequent years the company has grown impressively, partly as a result of mergers, and ranked no. 195 in terms of sales by 1968 (no. 260 in 1967); sales have increased to $ 501 million with assets of $ 382 million.

Through the years Conelco has acquired many other companies producing a wide variety of instruments and devices, as well as record albums and

138

plastic components. One of the subsidiaries is the Philips Electronics and Pharmaceutical Industries Corporation, which is 66.7 percent owned by Conelco. This company also manufactures instruments and electronic components as well as pharmaceuticals, fine chemicals, and agricultural and industrial chemicals, activities that are in part carried out by ten subsidiaries and associated companies. In addition, Conelco has an 80 percent interest in a clock company, a minority investment in a computer firm, and four other subsidiaries abroad.

Thus until recently, the structure of the Philips' direct investment was rather complicated, possibly because of US anti-trust laws; its activities are widespread and its sales volume is growing impressively.

d. American Enka

This subsidiary of the Algemene Kunstzijde Unie (AKU) was established in 1928 and is 55 percent owned by the Dutch parent company.[49] After the First World War, a number of European countries, among them the Netherlands, exported artificial fibers and silk to the United States. American import tariffs subsequently forced these European exporters into production in the United States if they wished to retain their markets.[50] The initial investment of $ 16 million had increased to $ 217 million in assets by 1968 ($ 197 million in 1967), a growth that has been largely financed with internally generated funds. Sales of nylon, polyester rayon, filament yarn and rayon staple fibers reached a level of $ 186 million in 1967, rising to $ 239 million in 1968. The company has grown quite well, advancing from sales rank 411 in 1955 with $ 71 million sales to rank 343 in 1968.

As sales of artificial fibers fluctuate a great deal, the company has made a determined effort to diversify the product line. It now operates four plants, two of which produce chemical fibers, the two others manufacturing insulated wire and cable products. In 1966 a joint venture with General Electric resulted in the establishment of the G. E.-Enka Fibers Corporation, with an initial Amerenka investment of $ 700,000. It is expected that the diversification will improve the company's future growth.

CONCLUSION

The broad survey presented in this chapter shows quite clearly that direct investments have a rather long history, which in the case of the Netherlands vis-à-vis the United States starts off with the famous purchase of Manhattan Island. In the history of investments by foreigners in the US the Dutch businessman and investor has played an active role. Of many ventures undertaken four very large direct investment operations remain, each part of multinational companies of truly international stature. These subsidiaries have attained a strong position in the American market, which is reflected in their sales-rankings in the *Fortune Directory*. Two companies in particular, Shell and North American Philips have done remarkably well.

Mainly because of these subsidiaries of the Dutch 'Big Four' the total Netherlands direct investment in the United States is the third highest, behind the United Kingdom and Canada. These Dutch investments provide a healthy balance against the United States business operations in the Netherlands.

NOTES

1. Cleona Lewis, *America's Stake in International Investments* (Washington, D.C.: The Brookings Institution, 1938).

2. *Ibid.*, pp. 117–29.

3. *Ibid.*, p. 130.

4. *Ibid.*, pp. 140–43. Figure for 1941 from US Department of Commerce, *Foreign Business Investments in the United States*, 1962.

5. The main difference in *total* foreign investments between the United States and the rest of the world lies in the preference for *direct* investments on the part of US investors, as against *portfolio* investments for the rest of the world. (See also Chapter 2.)

6. *Foreign Investors Tax Act of 1966* (Public Law 89–809), United States Statutes at Large: 89th Congress, 2d session, 1966, Vol. 80, part 1, pp. 1539–87.

7. 'Luring Foreign Cash: US Seeks to Promote European Investment in American Factories', *Wall Street Journal*, October 4, 1967.

8. For a discussion of the obstacles to foreign private investment in the United States, see *Obstacles and Incentives to Private Foreign Investment: 1962–1964* (the experiences of the investors of twelve nations in eighty-eight countries), (New York: National Industrial Conference Board, 1965), *Studies in Business Policy*, No. 115, pp. 125–26.

9. 'Amerikaanse Investeringen in Europa', *Orbis Economicus*, 11e Jaargang No. 3, oktober 1967, p. 24, from the discussion by A. W. J. Caron.

10. *Ibid.*, p. 25.

11. It would depend among other things on whether the companies in question were a large factor in the market. The point is that there are *no* such considerations in Europe.

12. 'Luring Foreign Cash: US Seeks to Promote European Investment in American Factories', *Wall Street Journal*, October 4, 1967. One example given in the article concerns the Volkswagen-Werk A.G. which bought a factory in New Jersey and planned to build cars there. It was dissuaded both by labor costs and by the difficulty of getting US companies to supply parts in metric sizes. The plant was sold and the company continues to import fully assembled cars from Germany.

13. There are some signs that US direct investments may be slowing down, with the reverse development taking place for European and Japanese investments in the United

States. See e.g. SIDNEY E. ROLFE: 'The International Corporation in Perspective', *The Atlantic Community Quarterly*, Summer 1969, pp. 255-261.

14. CLEONA LEWIS, *Debtor and Creditor Countries: 1938-1944* (Washington, D.C.: The Brookings Institution, 1945), p. 9.

15. VIOLET BARBOUR, *Capitalism in Amsterdam in the 17th Century* (Ann Arbor, Mich.: University of Michigan Press, 1963), pp. 35-36. For a more extensive coverage of the Dutch direct investments and trading in munitions and ordnance, see CARLO M. CIPOLLA, *Guns and Sails in the Early Phase of European Expansion, 1400-1700* (London: Collins, 1965).

16. BARBOUR, *op. cit.*, p. 119.

17. *Ibid.*, p. 121.

18. *Ibid.*, p. 118.

19. K. D. BOSCH, *De Nederlandse Beleggingen in de Verenigde Staten* (The Netherlands Investments in the United States), (Amsterdam-Brussel: Uitgeversmaatschappij Elsevier, 1948), covering the period 1782-1940.

20. *Ibid.*, pp. 41, 154-64, 213-15.

21. LEWIS, *America's Stake in International Investments*, Chap. V, 'Foreign Controlled Enterprises in the United States', pp. 78-113. Also BOSCH, *op. cit.*, pp. 123-207.

22. LEWIS, *Debtor and Creditor Countries*, p. 10.

23. In a doctoral dissertation of 1945, C. D. A. VAN LYNDEN devoted a chapter to the Dutch investments in Indonesia because 'the major part of the Netherlands investments in the Netherlands-Indies falls in the category of direct investments.' (*Directe Investeeringen in het Buitenland* (Direct Investments Abroad), ('s-Gravenhage: L. J. C. Boucher, 1945), p. 116.) The Dutch share in the total value of all investments in Indonesia was estimated at around 75 percent.

24. LEWIS, *op. cit.*, p. 10.

25. US Department of Commerce, *Foreign Business Investments in the United States*, 1962, p. 34, Table 1.

26. Calculation: $\frac{1,725}{20} \times 100 = \$ 8,625$ million, where 1,725 represents the total Dutch capital outflow during 1954-1967.

27. Nederlandsche Bank, *Annual Report 1968*, p. 78. It should perhaps be pointed out that investments out of reinvested earnings are not incorporated in the balance of payments tabulations.

28. H.W. DE JONG and E.A. ALKEMA, *Communication du Côté de l' "Europa Instituut" de l'Université de Leyde*, 13.530/iv/67-F. The authors do not make explicit the year in which the survey was conducted. I have assumed this to be 1966. The reason for excluding the Dutch multinational companies lies in the rather special place they take in the national economy.

29. The April 1966 *Monthly Report* of the Deutsche Bundesbank, 'Patent and License Transactions with Foreign Countries in 1964 and 1965', pp. 31-37, discusses yet another aspect of direct investments. Patents and licensing agreements are not covered in my study, but it is interesting to note that the Netherlands has a credit position vis-à-vis Germany. Net payments are particularly large in the electrical goods industry, followed by food and beverages, metal working and producing, and chemicals. It could well be that receipts from patents and licenses are positively correlated with the direct investment position.

30. The relative position of the Netherlands as a direct investor has fallen since 1964, when the Dutch share amounted to 17.4 percent of total $ 2,785 million foreign invest-

ments in Germany. *Monthly Report* of the Deutsche Bundesbank, 'Foreign Ownership in German Enterprises', May 1965, p. 59.

31. *Monthly Report* of the Deutsche Bundesbank, May 1969, 'Foreign Ownership in German Enterprises', pp. 22-30. Earlier articles on foreign direct investments appeared in the Monthly Reports of May 1965 (pp. 50-59) and of October 1966 (pp. 15-24).

32. G.-Y. BERTIN, *L'Investissements des Firmes Etrangères en France* (Paris: Presses Universitaires de France, 1963), p. 284. See also J. GERVAIS, *La France Face aux Investissements Etrangers* (Paris: Editions de L'Entreprise Moderne, 1963), p. 217.

33. BERTIN, *op. cit.*, pp. 307-08.

34. GERVAIS, *op. cit.*, pp. 54-55.

35. 'Evolution des mouvements de Capitaux Privés entre la France et l'Etranger de 1962 à 1966', Ministère de l'Economie et des Finances, Déc. 1967 (in millions of francs)

Year	Total direct investment	Investment by individual countries					
		US	Switzerland	EEC	BLEU	Germany	Netherlands
1962	2,474	681	931	484	172	127	105
1963	2,512	516	971	601	250	194	90
1964	3,426	838	1,116	928	534	224	105
1965	3,399	848	1,035	888	423	244	135
1966	3,099	1,007	784	846	398	205	167

Adapted from tables II, VI and VII.

36. US Department of Commerce, Office of Business Economics, *Foreign Business Investments in the United States* (Washington, D.C.: 1962).

Note: A foreign direct investment was defined as a 25 percent or higher ownership in the voting stock of an American corporation (pp. 26-27). Since October, 1968, the ownership percentage has been lowered to 10 percent – see: *Survey of Current Business*, October, 1968, p. 21.

37. For other years the data refer to the *foreign* share in net income, rather than total net income (see Table 61).

38. One rather obvious reason for these favorable ratios could lie in undervaluation of the direct investment. This factor would also affect other investments, but as such a large part of the Dutch investments dates from before 1939 the undervaluation could be of a greater magnitude.

39. *Foreign Business Investments in the United States*, p. 58. Foreign share in net income = net income minus branch profits, preferred dividends and the US share. Out of total net income for 1959 of $ 474 million, the US share amounted to $ 56 million and the foreign share was $ 328 million.

40. US Department of Commerce, *Foreign Business Investments in the United States*, p. 39, Table 5.

41. Royal Dutch Petroleum is owned 60 percent by the Dutch and 40 percent by the English. Unilever N.V. is part of the Unilever Company, together with Unilever Ltd. (a 50-50 share of Dutch and English). But the Dutch company runs the American direct investment, although the subsidiary was established by the predecessor of the English company.

42. A good impression of the number and industrial activity of all Dutch direct investments, including in the United States, can be found in the continental edition of *Who Owns Whom*, compiled and published by O.W. Roskill and Co. (Reports) Ltd. (London: 1968).

43. *Fortune*, 'The 200 Largest Industrials Outside the US', August 15, 1969. In mid-1969 the merger of AKU and Koninklijke Zout-Organon was announced; the resulting company would rank no. 30 on the 1968 Fortune list, with sales of $ 1,432 million.

44. Information concerning the early history of the American Shell Oil Company can be found in C. GERRETSON, *Geschiedenis der 'Koninklijke' (History of the 'Royal')*, (3 vols.; Haarlem: 1941). The data presented here were found in K. D. BOSCH, *De Nederlandse Beleggingen in de Verenigde Staten* (Amsterdam: 1948). Bosch used the work by Gerretson as information source.
See also: K. BEATON, *Enterprise in Oil: a History of Shell in the United States* (New York: Appleton, Century, Crofts, 1957).

45. *Survey of Current Business*, June, 1968, p. 26.

46. A very informative study of the Unilever Company is: CHARLES WILSON, *The History of Unilever – A Study in Economic Growth and Social Change*, Vol. I: *Lever Brothers;* Vol. II: *Jurgens' and van den Bergh's* (London: Cassel and Co., Ltd., 1954).

47. Algemene Bank Nederland N.V., *Beursweek*, 24 okt. 1968, No. 199, p. 2.

48. The other equity is owned by third parties.

49. Algemene Bank Nederland, *Beursweek*, No. 219, 20 maart 1969.

50. BOSCH, *op. cit.*, p. 432. This is a good example of a 'defensive' direct investment.

6. The characteristics of direct investment

I. CHARACTERISTICS DEFINED

The analysis now turns to the aspects of direct investment abroad that are considered characteristic of the phenomenon.[1] In essence, these are hypotheses derived from the theory of direct investments as presented in Chapter 1. The theory can be briefly summarized as follows: Multinational corporations try to maximize their sales, subject to a profit constraint. In the pursuit of these goals foreign markets are included and the establishment of an operation abroad by a multinational company will be called a direct investment.[2] These direct investments can be classified as either 'positive' or 'defensive', depending on the circumstances that led to the establishment of the foreign operation. If the investment was made in response to higher sales and/or profit opportunities, it is called a positive direct investment. On the other hand, a defensive direct investment is undertaken in order to protect existing rates of return and / or sales volume of the whole enterprise. Oligopolistic interactions between producers in the home market with respect to operations abroad are included in the category of defensive direct investments. On the basis of this theory the following characteristics of direct investments can be formulated:

a. Control

'Foreign direct investments are characterized by high degrees of control of their equity capital by the parent company.'

This characteristic would seem to be a truism in view of the statistical definition of direct investments, namely a ten percent or higher equity ownership in a foreign enterprise. The statement, however, refers to the fact that foreign ownership is typically closer to a 100 rather than a ten percent share of the equity capital.[3]

Through the ownership of the equity capital the company controls pricing and product policies of the foreign based subsidiary.[4] Reasons for control may lie in the desire to capitalize fully on the advantages of the company over local competition. Exploitation as well as the protection of special knowledge would naturally lead to the exclusion of local investors. In cases where the company establishes itself through acquisition, competition is removed and a possibility may exist to reap monopoly profits. It is in the company's interest, especially as a foreigner, to cover up such exploitation as much as possible. Other reasons for a high degree of control may lie in profit distribution, choice of supplier (often another subsidiary of the same company) and geographical range of exports. One important problem that can be avoided with wholly-owned subsidiaries pertains to the share that equity holders will contribute to any expansion of the investment. Typically this would involve valuation, in money terms, of technological or other intangible contributions of the partners.

b. Capital flows

'Capital flows connected with direct investments are mainly used to obtain (or to maintain) control over the foreign enterprise. Expansions are financed to a large degree with locally raised funds, reinvested earnings, or depreciation and depletion allowances'.

There is some evidence to suggest that growth of established direct investments does not take place through new capital inflows but rather through other forms of financing. That the phenomenon is not restricted to direct investment subsidiaries is clear from the following quotation:

But a preference for expansion through retained earnings is becoming increasingly characteristic of the modern corporation, and of particular interest from the point of view of foreign investment is the situation, especially favored by American firms, in which the parent company holds all, or nearly all, of the equity and permits the subsidiary to expand with its own earnings.[5]

The fact that foreign capital is mainly used for purposes of equity ownership, and the operation or expansion of overseas subsidiaries largely financed with other sources of funds has a number of important implications, some of which were discussed in Part 3 of Chapter 1. For one thing, a relatively small equity investment can grow through reinvested earnings into a very large holding, where the remitted dividends stand in no relation to the initial capital inflow. This can create a serious foreign exchange problem, especially for underdeveloped countries. Another aspect is that of local borrowing, where the foreign company competes with domestic entrepreneurs. In countries where new capital is desperately needed (again the underdeveloped ones) this competition does not add to the supply of savings, and may actually deprive domestic companies access to their only source of funds.

c. Production functions

'Positive direct investments will exhibit more efficient production functions than those of domestic enterprises. Through time the whole industry in which the direct investment took place may be operating more efficiently'.

In Chapter 1 it was shown that positive direct investments are usually based on advantages held by the multinational corporation over domestic entrepreneurs. In so far as these advantages are based on better production techniques, superior management, marketing and organization, a more efficient combination of factors of production will result. However, the presence of the foreign owned enterprise will certainly spur domestic producers on and force them to become more efficient as well. Thus the whole manufacturing sector will become more productive.

d. Size

1. 'Companies engaging in direct investments abroad not only tend to be large in their industry, but also large relative to the whole manufacturing sector.'
2. 'Their foreign direct investments also tend to be large not so much in relation to the parent, but also relative to the foreign economy where they are established.'

With respect to size one can distinguish between the *unit of decision* (the multinational corporation) and the *unit of production* (the factory or plant). Characteristic (1) pertains to the size of the decision unit. Its importance derives from the ability of the large enterprise to conduct research and development, to launch new products, and to open up new markets. And as Schumpeter has pointed out, this ability will be matched by a willingness to engage in the process of 'creative destruction' so typical of the large corporation in a capitalistic society. Furthermore, to finance these activities the large company can either generate funds internally, or have relatively easy access to capital markets as opposed to small enterprises. One may safely assume that the ability to engage in direct investments abroad is related to the financial strength of the decision unit.

The size of the production unit (characteristic (2)) enables an enterprise to reap fully the benefits of economies of scale in production. With direct investments abroad one would expect that multinational corporations take advantage of these scale benefits, just as they do in their investments at home. This seems to be particularly true for American investments, where the us technology favors the large scale production unit.[6] This is done, for example, by letting each foreign subsidiary specialize in certain products, and have them trade among themselves, each buying from the other affiliates the products (either final or intermediary goods) that it does not produce itself.

e. Research and Development

'Multinational companies, especially those undertaking positive direct investments, engage in extensive research and development efforts. Those R & D programs will be concentrated in the home country of the investing company'.

We have already touched upon the role of R & D to establish, and afterwards to maintain, technological abilities and advantages. The relationship between expenditures on research and technological innovations requires detailed analysis. It is, however, increasingly realized that *without* R & D there is no hope whatsoever of obtaining technological breakthroughs, except for licensing agreements, or when the new technology has not been protected with a patent. The latter would seem to occur only incidentally and cannot be relied upon to furnish new technological know-how. As far as licensing agreements are concerned, Hymer has pointed out that with imperfect market structures it may be impossible to secure a satisfactory return. In those cases the company would engage in direct investments abroad to fully appropriate the returns on the advantage.[7]

f. Competition

'Direct investments will result in higher degrees of industrial concentration and change the nature of competition into oligopolistic or monopolistic directions'.

The effects of direct investment on competition, national and international, have not been adequately analyzed and the discussion here will consequently be rather general.[8]

Acquisition as a form of establishing a foreign subsidiary cuts down the number of independent competitors (horizontal integration). The effect on international competition would seem to depend on the number of remaining independent competitors, as well as on the actual possibility of trade between the two locations. Tariffs and freight rates, for instance, may have effectively prevented any trade and thus international competition would not be reduced if those two points of production would come under the same ownership. Vertical integration (from raw material source to final product) may enable a company to realize monopoly profits, when its subsidiary is the only producer and the parent company the only buyer. These instances would seem to be restricted to mining and agricultural direct investments.[9]

If we ignore the way in which the direct investment is established there still remains the continuing effect of the mere presence of the foreign firm on the national market structure. The size of the actual investment, as well as that of the parent company may well work towards concentration among the independent domestic producers. Such a development has been apparent in Western Europe, specifically in the Common Market countries.[10] Lastly, it should be recognized that subsidiaries of the same multinational corporation in different countries do not as a rule engage in direct competition with each other, whereas independent companies might have competed.

These aspects of direct investments are, in my opinion, characteristic. Most of them have not been analyzed thoroughly and much supporting evidence has yet to be collected. In the following sections I will return to these characteristics and look at the evidence available through the survey of US direct investments in the Netherlands; other information will be presented as well.

2. CHARACTERISTICS REVISITED

In the following discussion the evidence collected in the survey of US affiliated companies in the Netherlands will be used in a partial test of the characteristics (or hypotheses) of foreign direct investments.

a. Control

'Direct investments are characterized by high degrees of control of the equity capital by the parent company.'

In Table 64 some control figures for the Netherlands, Australia and the United Kingdom have been presented. The data suggest that around 60 percent of the firms in those countries are wholly US owned. These companies employ a high percentage of the total number of persons working in US controlled enterprises, a percentage that varies from close to 80 percent for Australia to 60 and 50 percentage points for the Nether-

Table 64. Number of U.S. affiliated companies and employment: by percentage of U.S. equity ownership: Australia – the Netherlands – the United Kingdom

Percentage of US shareholding	Australia[1] – mid 1962				The Netherlands[2] – end 1966			
	Number of companies		Employment		Number of companies		Employment	
Less than 25	n.a.		n.a.		3	(1)	1,706	(6)
25 – 49	28	(13)	7,606	(8)	7	(7)	1,353	(5)
50 – 74	50	(24)	13,401	(14)	27	(25)	6,555	(24)
75 – 99	5	(2)	665	(.7)	9	(8)	2,840	(10)
Wholly-owned	125	(60)	74,821	(77)	62	(57)	15,139	(55)
Total	208		96,493		108		27,593	

Source: 1. DONALD T. BRASH, *American Investment in Australian Industry*, pp. 60 and 65.
2. Survey results of 108 US companies in the Netherlands, see Chapter 4.

Percentage of US shareholding	United Kingdom[3] – Dec 1953			
	Number of companies		Employment	
Less than 25	n.a.		n.a.	
25 – 40	3	(1.5)	2,100	(1)
41 – 60	19	(9.5)	69,600	(28)
61 – 80	21	(10.5)	53,100	(22)
81 – 99	11	(5.5)	7,600	(3)
Wholly-owned	146	(73)	112,500	(46)
Total	200		244,900	

Source: 3. JOHN H. DUNNING, *American Investment in British Manufacturing Industry*
(Figures in parentheses are percentage shares.)
n.a. = not available.

lands and the UK respectively. When the whole class of majority control is considered (from 50 to 100 percent of the equity) close to 90 percent of the American direct investments in these three countries fall into that category. Although Dunning uses a slightly different breakdown, his figures regarding US investments in Great Britain also show a high American equity ownership.

Table 65 contains control data for US subsidiaries in the Netherlands, broken down by industrial activity. Very slight variations in the degree of control exist between industries, and these do not appear to be significant. Bonin has presented control figures for US investments in Canada; the degree of equity ownership is very high, regardless of the sector of industry.[11]

Control figures for foreign investments in the United States were presen-

Table 65. U.S. Subsidiaries in the Netherlands: degree of control and industrial activity: 1966

		\multicolumn{6}{c}{Degree of control}					
		100	75–99	51–74	50	25–49	25
Food, tobacco	I	5	1	1	–	–	–
	II	1,642	850	1,978	–	–	–
Textiles, wearing apparel	I	3	1	2	5	1	–
	II	416	20	231	954	200	–
Chemicals	I	15	1	–	11	1	1
	II	1,647	30	–	2,251	130	40
Petroleum	I	4	–	–	–	–	–
	II	3,320	–	–	–	–	–
Metal	I	8	3	–	4	1	–
	II	888	154	–	141	600	–
Machinery, except electrical	I	15	1	2	1	2	–
	II	4,012	186	30	400	221	–
Electrical equipment	I	54	–	–	1	1	1
	II	1,498	–	–	570	30	110
Scientific equipment	I	6	1	–	–	–	–
	II	1,006	250	–	–	–	–
Miscellaneous	I	2	1	–	–	1	1
	II	710	1,350	–	–	172	1,556
	I	62	9	5	22	7	3
	II	15,139	2,840	2,239	4,316	1,353	1,706

I = firms
II = employment
Source: Questionnaires of 108 US companies in the Netherlands.

ted in Chapter 5; much more evidence is available, all of it pointing to high degrees of control.[12] Consequently one can accept that foreign direct investments are characterized by high degrees of equity control by the multinational enterprise.

b. Capital flows

'Capital flows connected with direct investments are mainly used to obtain (or to maintain) control over the foreign enterprise. Expansions are financed to a large degree with locally raised funds, reinvested earnings, or depreciation and depletion allowances'.

This characteristic has already been discussed on a number of occasions, most notably in Part 1 of Chapter 1 [where the inconsistencies between portfolio and direct investments were analyzed], in Part 3 of that same chapter and also in Chapter 5, dealing with foreign direct investments in the United States. All that evidence appears to confirm the characteristic formulated above, although it is impossible to determine the actual extent of capital flows in the financing of expansions.

c. Production functions

'Positive direct investments will exhibit more efficient production functions than those of domestic enterprises. Through time the whole industry in which the direct investment took place may be operating more efficiently'.

With regard to the 'efficiency of production' characteristic, no information was collected through the survey. Anyway, it would be very difficult to obtain reliable quantitative data to test the hypothesis properly. On the qualitative side one can find a confirmation of the 'efficiency' presumption in the studies by Dunning and Brash on American direct investments in the UK and Australia respectively.[13] In the discussion of the magnitude of American investments in the Netherlands, some statements were quoted to the effect that Dutch industry, and the subcontracting sector in particular, had become more efficient as a result of the US presence. Thus, on the basis of this qualitative support, one can accept the hypothesis. A reliable test will have to await the availability of quantitative data.

d. Size

'Companies engaging in direct investments abroad not only tend to be large in their industry but also large relative to the whole manufacturing sector. Their foreign direct investments similarly tend to be large, not so much in relation to the parent but relative to the foreign economy where they are established'.

Two aspects of size are interesting, namely that of the *enterprise* (the unit of decision making) and that of the *plant* (the unit of production). With respect to the former, the evidence for the Netherlands shows 86 out of 210 American parent companies with subsidiaries in the Netherlands appeared on the 1966 *Fortune* list of the 500 largest US industrial enterprises.[14] Similarly, among the parents of trading, service and banking investments, one can find many of the largest American companies, while the majority are of a smaller size. The Dutch investments abroad are also characterized by a preponderance of medium-sized parent companies. To be sure, the big Dutch internationals (AKZO, Philips, Royal Dutch and Unilever) have many direct investments; but the majority of Dutch companies with foreign subsidiaries operate on a smaller scale. These results are confirmed in a paper published by the Europa Instituut of the University of Leyden, which deals with the Dutch direct investments in the EEC countries. The four internationals were excluded because of their special position; the survey covered 490 enterprises. The 265 cooperating companies operated a total of 853 establishments by the end of 1966.[15]

What does seem to be true, on the whole, is that the subsidiaries of the large multinational enterprises are large relative to the local economies. The American investments of the Dutch internationals, for example, all appear on the *Fortune* list of the 500 largest industrials, while the subsidiaries of these companies in Germany, France and Italy show up on the Chase Manhattan list of the 100 largest industrial enterprises in the Common Market.[16] However, the survey of American subsidiaries in the Netherlands showed that these US enterprises were of a scale similar to that of the Netherlands manufacturing industry; these figures were presented in Chapter 4.

With respect to the scale of the *unit of production*, I again refer to Chapter 4, where the results of the survey in the Netherlands were published. The size distribution of Dutch industry was compared to that of 109 US companies in the Netherlands, operating 142 plants. The conclusion of that analysis is that American operations in the Netherlands, when measured in terms of employees, are of larger scale than Dutch industry as a whole. Similar evidence is available for the United Kingdom, namely that collected by John Dunning.[17]

The foregoing discussion does not lead to a firm conclusion with respect to the size of foreign direct investment enterprises. Regarding the production units, however, there exists strong evidence that, at least for the Netherlands, the US establishments are of much larger size than their Dutch counterparts in the various industry classes.

e. Research and development

'Multinational companies, especially those undertaking positive direct investments, engage in extensive research and development efforts. Those R & D programs will be concentrated in the home country of the investing company'.

It is not feasible to analyze the R & D programs of all US companies with direct investments. Instead one should perhaps be satisfied with a recent OECD study which shows that US expenditures on research are the highest of all countries studied, and is estimated at 3.1 percent of GNP in 1962.[18] A good 71 percent of these massive research outlays are spent directly in the US business sector, against 65 percent in Belgium, 63 percent in the

UK and much lower figures for other European countries. Another OECD study reports on the relationship between R & D and the size of the business enterprise (Table 66). These figures show that while firms of the smallest size hardly engage in research, almost all companies in the largest size category do. The bulk of total R & D is carried out by those companies.[19] The reason behind this relationship is presumably due to a 'threshold' level below which an R & D program as dictated by the technology of the industry is simply not possible.[20]

The evidence on research and development of US companies collected through the survey of American subsidiaries in the Netherlands is presented in detail in Chapter 3. I have noted that the question relating to research programs of the parent companies elicited rather ambiguous answers. It is clear however that almost all US multinational companies have R & D programs. As far as the geographical distribution of these research efforts is concerned, in the majority of cases no R & D programs took place either in the Netherlands or in Western Europe as a whole.[21]

Table 66. The relation between R & D expenditures and business size in the U.S. and the U.K.

	USA (1958)			UK (1959)		
	Size in terms of employment					
	5,000 +	1,000 to 4,999	less than 1,000	2,000 +	300 to 1,999	less than 300
% of enterprises doing research	89	50	4	90	58	18
% of total R & D expenditures	85	8	7	93	16	1

Source: OECD, *Science, Economic Growth and Government Policy* (Paris, 1963), p. 87.

The few cases where a high proportion of total research expenditures did take place in the Netherlands were invariably linked to participations of existing companies where the American parent was not very large.

f. Competition

'Direct investments will result in higher degrees of industrial concentration and change the nature of competition into oligopolistic or monopolistic directions'.

Industrial concentration can be related to both the unit of production (plant) and the unit of decision (enterprise). As Bain states, 'The *degree of plant concentration* in any industry ... reveals the *existing technical basis* of the *going degree of concentration of control* of an industry by firms or other control units. The degree of plant concentration in an industry suggests a *feasible minimum* for firm concentration' [my emphasis].[22] Professor Bain has shown quite clearly that plant concentration in other countries is rather low as compared to the United States. A similar result was found to apply to firm concentration.[23] Changes in the degree of plant concentration would seem to be of a long run nature, whereas firm concentration can be changed almost overnight through mergers or through acquisitions.[24] It is this phenomenon which affects the nature of competition by reducing the number of independent companies.

In the discussion of the *size*-characteristic, we found the plant concentration of US subsidiaries in the Netherlands to be higher than the Dutch manufacturing sector. Although the comparison of the size of the enterprise did not reveal any significant differences (except in the very high employee classes, where the Dutch enterprise is larger) an American subsidiary abroad is really an overseas representation of the whole multinational corporation. In this sense the size of the US controlled sector is almost always larger than that of the domestic industry; consequently, the mere presence of US affiliates affects the degree of concentration. Now it is a fact that concentration affects competition, but the ultimate result depends on many other factors as well. One has, for instance, to distinguish between the number of independent companies and their behavior in the market. It is conceivable that even though the degree of concentration goes up (the number of independent companies is reduced) the degree of competition increases as well. This may be due to the fact that e.g. two weak companies merge into one strong enterprise which will now be better able to compete. In general, one would have to examine every sector of industry to determine the effect of concentration on competition.

Affiliates of US companies abroad are being established either by starting a new operation, or by acquisition of an existing company. The latter mode of entry into a foreign market may well remove competition, although this is not necessarily so. It would depend on the fact whether or not competition between the two producers was at all possible. Tariffs and/or freight charges may well have kept the two markets separated. Often an acquisition serves to broaden the productline of the company, and in this case competition would not be directly affected.[25]

The survey of US affiliates in the Netherlands showed that 29 companies were already in operation as independent Dutch enterprises. The other

82 subsidiaries have been newly established, and are either wholly US owned or operate on a joint-venture basis with a Dutch corporation. The Dutch survey also provides an example of both horizontal and vertical integration in the food industry. The American multinational enterprise acquired two independent units, which were competing in some products. The acquisition thus reduced competition and led to horizontal integration. One of the companies, however, processes the raw material and sells the semi-finished base product to other firms, among which is the other acquired Dutch company. Consequently, the acquisition also resulted in a vertical integration.

Evidence on acquisitions is available for other countries as well, but it is very hard to determine the intention behind such moves or to measure the effect on the degree of competition.[26] It is especially difficult to assess the impact of takeovers on the degree of competition since many new establishments are created as well. Also, acquisitions are by no means the most important instrument of establishing direct investments abroad.[27]

Finally the effect of foreign operations of multinational corporations on *international* competition should be mentioned. Acquisition of existing independent enterprises again may affect international competition in much the same way as it does nationally. Subsidiaries producing similar products in various countries obviously do not compete with each other. In addition, an international vertical integration of activities within a multinational corporation may eliminate competition. Thus raw materials, half products and semi-finished manufactures are supplied to subsidiaries by other affiliates or subsidiaries of the *same multinational corporation*. For instance, American agricultural or mining enterprises abroad find a ready outlet for their products in the United States.[28] With respect to exports from the US to foreign affiliates, evidence exists that a very large share of these exports are channeled through the foreign affiliates of US companies abroad. Around 30 percent of those exports consist of products to be processed or assembled further in the foreign subsidiaries of American enterprises.[29] As to the direction of exports of US subsidiaries, little is being sold to the United States itself, which is what one would expect.

The evidence for US direct investments in the Netherlands was presented at length in Chapters 3 and 4 and the conclusions will be briefly restated here. Imports by US affiliates of raw materials and semi-finished products from either the American parent or from other affiliated companies were sizeable; it was noted however that such imports are rather typical for all Dutch manufacturing industry. The imports of finished products for resale varied considerably for each industry, and no particular pattern could be discerned. Both finished and semi-finished products, as well as raw materials, however, were purchased from members of the same multinational company. As to exports, it was noted that the over-all export performance of the American sector was better than that of Dutch manufacturing industry as a whole. The direction of those export sales closely parallelled the pattern for the Netherlands, with the exception of sales to the United States.

To sum up the discussion, it is difficult to arrive at any firm conclusion on the basis of the evidence presented above. The presumption is that competition has been reduced as a result of especially US direct investments. No hard evidence is available however to prove that contention and sales information for other, non-American, direct investments does not exist at all.

CONCLUSION

In the foregoing analysis a number of characteristics of direct investments, considered significant, were first stated and subsequently tested with the empirical evidence available. The data collected in the survey of US direct investments in the Netherlands, and the information from a number of publications leads one to conclude that all of these characteristics can, at least partially, be supported by the evidence. For the characteristics of control, capital flows, size and R & D programs some quantitative information is available. But regarding the other hypotheses of production functions and competition that appear to be of very considerable importance, only scattered qualitative statements can be found. Consequently, much additional information, especially of a quantitative nature, has to be collected before the characteristics can be refuted or accepted unconditionally. That information should pertain to the direct investments of all countries, not only those undertaken by the American multinational corporations.

NOTES

1. KINDLEBERGER discusses a number of aspects of direct investment, such as: capital movements, control, growth of the firm, monopolistic competition, economies of scale and efficiency. There is however no attempt in his lecture to separate theory and characteristics of direct investment. See: *American Business Abroad*, lecture 1, pp. 1–36.

2. For a precise definition the reader is referred to pp. 1–2.

3. One has to take into consideration that until October, 1968, the statistical definition of direct investments referred to foreign equity ownership levels of 25 percent and higher. Even so, however, the characteristic is no truism, because foreign ownership remains closer to 100 percent rather than 25 percent.

4. There are also political implications that arise from the control aspect, when for instance, a government tries to influence the foreign operations of its multinational corporations. As an example one can think of purchasing policies of raw materials and/or semi-finished products. Similarly, some governments do not treat foreign owned establishments in the same way as the domestic enterprises. See also: KINDLEBERGER, *op. cit.*, pp. 5-6; pp. 38-45.

Yet another political implication is the way in which the operations of multinational corporations affect the foreign policy of a country. The well-known examples in this respect are the interactions between the United Fruit Company and us foreign policy vis-à-vis the Latin American 'Banana Republics'. But it would be naïve to presume that only the us can be guilty of such behaviour: earlier examples can be found involving English and Dutch (to name but two countries) commercial imperialism. See also, KINDLEBERGER, *op. cit.*, pp. 70-73.

5. EDITH T. PENROSE, 'Foreign Investment and the Growth of the Firm', *The Economic Journal*, Vol. LXVII, No. 262, June, 1956, pp. 227-228.

6. In addition, the organizational and managerial requirements for setting up a foreign production unit will work towards larger scale operations to make the operation worth the effort.

7. HYMER, *Dissertation*, p. 24.

8. KINDLEBERGER, *op. cit.*, also discusses the effects on competition, pp. 11-14, 62-67.

9. Vertical integration across countries also allows the company to let profits accrue at the location that is most favorable in view of e.g. tax purposes. A good example here are the pricing practices of petroleum companies, where the profits accrue in the production, rather than the consumption areas.

10. In the EEC the formation of the larger market without trade barriers also played a very important role. Unfortunately, the tremendous influx of American direct investment occurred at around the same time, which would make independent assessment of these two effects rather difficult.

11. BERNARD BONIN, *L'Investissement Etranger à Long Terme au Canada: Ses Caractères et ses Effets sur L'Economie Canadienne* (Université de Paris, Thèse, 1966), p. 247.

12. References to the control aspect of foreign direct investments: BONIN, *op. cit.*, p. 247.

us Department of Commerce, *U.S. Business Investments in Foreign Countries*, 1960, Tables 13-14, pp. 101-02.

us Department of Commerce, *Foreign Business Investments in the United States*, 1962, Table 5, pp. 38-39.

H.W. DE JONG and E.A. ALKEMA, 'Communication du Côté de l' "Europa Instituut" de l'Université de Leyde', 1967, p. 4 and Annexes I and II.

G.-Y. BERTIN, *L'Investissement des Firmes Etrangères en France* (Paris: Presses Universitaires de France, 1963), Chap. X, pp. 150-65.

13. JOHN H. DUNNING, *American Investment in British Manufacturing Industry* (London: George Allen & Unwin Ltd., 1958), Chapters VI-IX, pp. 154-284.

DONALD T. BRASH, *American Investment in Australian Industry* (Canberra: Australian National University, 1966), Chapters VI, VII and VIII, pp. 136-202.

14. *Fortune Directory*, 'The 500 Largest us Industrial Corporations', June 15, 1967.

15. DE JONG and ALKEMA, *op. cit.*, p. 3.

16. Chase Manhattan Bank, *Report on Western Europe*, No. 37, August-September, 1965.

17. DUNNING, *op. cit.*, pp. 90-93.

18. OECD, *The Research and Development Effort in Western Europe, North America and the Soviet Union* (Paris: 1965), p. 71.

19. OECD, *Science, Economic Growth and Government Policy* (Paris: 1963), p. 87.

20. D. SWANN and D. L. MCLACHLAN, *Concentration or Competition: A European Dilemma* (London: The Chatham House/P.E.P., 1967), European Series No. 1. They present some figures for the electronics industry; minimum amounts of R & D in those sectors vary from 40,000 to 70,000 for radio communication receivers to between two and eight million for communications satellites (p. 21).

21. Similar evidence was presented by BRASH (*op. cit.*, p. 151): '... relatively few American affiliated companies do conduct research in Australia ...' See also ALLAN JOHNSTONE, *United States Direct Investment in France* (Cambridge: The MIT Press, 1966), pp. 63–72, and D. SWANN and D. L. MCLACHLAN, *op. cit.*, p. 26. The latter state that '... there is good evidence that where US enterprise has subsidiary firms manufacturing in the United Kingdom, the research intensity there is much lower than in the United States and in some cases there is no British-based research at all.'

22. JOE S. BAIN, *International Differences in Industrial Structure: Eight Countries in the 1950's* (New Haven and London: Yale University Press, 1966), p. 25.

23. BAIN, *op. cit.*, Chaps. 1 and 2.

24. In the countries of the European Economic Community, these mergers are actively stimulated by the Commission. Aside from the American presence, one finds here the stimulus of a much larger market, without internal tariff barriers.

25. Competition may be affected as a result of the much stronger position of the former independent firm vis-à-vis its competitors. As an entity of the multinational corporation the firm would have access to the resources of the whole corporation (see the definition of the multinational corporation by VERNON on page 6 of Chapter 1).

26. G.-Y. BERTIN, *op. cit.*, p. 152 (for France); BONIN, *op. cit.*, p. 242 (for Canada). Data on US direct investments in general are published by the US Department of Commerce in its *Survey of Current Business*.

27. For data on new establishments in Western Europe, Chase Manhattan Bank, *Report on Western Europe*, No. 34, February-March, 1965.

28. Support for this statement is found in figures published by the US Department of Commerce, which show that a high percentage of total sales of mining and smelting companies goes to the United States. *Survey of Current Business*, November, 1966, p. 10.

29. *Survey of Current Business*, December, 1965, pp. 14–16.

7. Concluding remarks

Many aspects of direct investments have been discussed in the foregoing chapter, and a summary of the main findings may be useful.

The basic contribution of the dissertation lies in the new data collected through a survey of American manufacturing enterprises, operating in the Netherlands by the end of 1966. This information is used to evaluate the magnitude and impact of US direct investments in the Netherlands. In addition, the data serve in a test of characteristics of direct investments. It was necessary, however, to develop the theory of direct investments and in so doing obtain a clearer understanding of the phenomenon that has lately attracted so much attention. The attempt to formalize the theory of direct investments constitutes the second contribution of this study. As was pointed out the theory of international capital movements is not able to explain direct investments, although it continues to be an adequate framework of analysis for portfolio investments.

The theory of direct investments formulated in this dissertation uses the concept of a multinational corporation, which is assumed to be guided in its actions by the objective of sales maximization, subject to a profit constraint. Within this framework of analysis two types of direct investment can be distinguished, 'positive' and 'defensive'. As the terms indicate, a positive direct investment is an action in response to higher sales and/or profit opportunities abroad, whereas a defensive move results from exogeneous threats to the existing sales and profits position of the multinational corporation. It is expected that this classification will facilitate the analysis of direct investments and clarify the motivations that guide business companies in their foreign operations. Special attention is given to the case where oligopolistic interdependencies in the home market force oligopoly members into a follow-the-leader pattern abroad.

The explicit formulation of the theory of direct investments permits one to derive a number of characteristics of these investments that are significant. These characteristics (or hypotheses) relate to aspects of overseas operations such as the degree of control, the use of foreign capital, the effect on competition, and the conduct of research and development programs. The evidence collected through the survey of US enterprises in the Netherlands is subsequently used to test these hypotheses. Information from other studies is presented as well. The main conclusion derived from this meeting of hypotheses and facts is that indeed these characteristics are typical of foreign direct investments, but that more quantitative data is required for an enhaustive test.

An important part of the study deals with the effects of direct investments on the domestic economy, as well as on the host country. It is first shown that the conventional arguments in the 'home versus foreign investment' controversy do not apply to direct investments, but rather to portfolio investments. The conclusion of the 'conventional' analysis is that too much capital is invested abroad, because of a divergence between private and social cost-benefit calculation; governments are advised to take measures that will eliminate this divergence. My discussion subsequently deals with effects of direct investments on host countries, where the emphasis lies on the underdeveloped economies. In that context a number of recommendations are made; by implementing these recommendations in agreements concerning direct investments, governments may be able to significantly reduce the cost of the direct investment to their countries, and at the same time increase the benefits associated with these investments.

The survey of US direct investment enterprises in the Netherlands constitutes the core of the dissertation. Because of the highly gratifying cooperation by the American subsidiaries much new information could be collected. This data is used extensively in the analysis of the magnitude of US direct investments in the Netherlands. The criteria used to measure the importance of the American investments are (1) the value of property, plant and equipment, (2) the annual investment expenditures, (3) employment, and (4) production, imports and exports. On all these counts the US controlled sector is found to contribute significantly to the economic growth and prosperity in the Netherlands. This conclusion augurs well for other developed countries with American direct investment, although it would be difficult to extend the result to underdeveloped countries. Nor is there only reason for optimism; it seems clear that a further strengthening of the Dutch ability to continue to compete effectively in the future is necessary, which could be achieved best by improvement in education and a greater emphasis on applied research and development.

Subsequently the Netherlands direct investments in the United States are discussed. One reason for this presentation is the fact that Dutch direct investments in the US are greater than the value of American controlled enterprises in the Netherlands. Another reason is the number of very large Dutch multinational corporations that are in many respects the equals of the top US corporations. One can thus expect to find a number of similarities in the patterns of foreign operations. Although these similarities do indeed exist, the differences are more pronounced. All of the Dutch companies, for example, had established their US subsidiaries many years before the outbreak of World War II and the growth in investments after the war was rather slow. This is in contrast to the American investments in the Netherlands.

The final observation is that the analysis of both American and Dutch direct investments has shown that disadvantages commonly associated by host countries only with US direct investments apply equally to other foreign overseas ventures. The sheer size of the American investments however tends to magnify these points of friction.

Appendices

I. The inconsistencies between portfolio and direct investments

Following is a discussion of some of the inconsistencies that arise when the framework of international capital movements is applied to portfolio and direct investments. These inconsistencies point to the need for a distinct theory of direct investments, as developed in Chapter I, Part 2.

The existence of cross-movements
After the Second World War portfolio investment flowed to the United States, mostly from Western Europe, whereas the US direct investments were concentrated mainly in Western Europe and Canada. At the same time, however, direct investments by Europeans in the United States continued to grow, although at a modest rate. Similarly, US portfolio investments in Europe increased from year to year. In Table 67 the existence of these cross-movements between portfolio and direct investments is illustrated for Western Europe and the United States.

Table 67. *Long-term investments in some post-war years: the United States and Western Europe (in millions of dollars)*

	1946	1950	1958	1963	1966	1967	1968 P
US long-term private holdings in Western Europe – total	2,258	3,091	6,905	15,343	20,723	22,618	24,687
of which: direct	1,041	1,720	4,573	10,340	16,209	17,926	19,386
other long	1,217	1,371	2,332	5,003	4,514	4,692	5,301
Western European long-term holdings in the United States – total	4,775	5,127	10,399	16,237	17,853	20,248	26,037
of which: direct	1,737	2,056	3,080	5,491	6,273	7,004	7,750
other long	3,038	3,071	7,319	10,746	11,580	13,244	18,287

p = preliminary
Source: US Department of Commerce, *Survey of Current Business*, September/October issues.

Table 68. List of cross-direct investments by foreign companies in the United States

Industry	Name of company	Country
Business Machines	Moore Business Machines	UK
	Olivetti*	Italy
Chemicals	American Enka	Netherlands
	Shell Oil	Neth/UK
	Unilever	UK/Neth
Electronics	North American Philips	Netherlands
Farm machinery	Massey, Harris, Ferguson	Canada
Food products	Nestle's	Switzerland
	Orange Crush	UK
	Unilever	UK/Neth
	Weston's	UK
Paper products	Bowater Paper	UK
Petroleum	American Petrofina	Belgium
	Shell Oil	Neth/UK
Sewing machines	Necchi Sewing Machine	Italy
Tires and tubes	Dunlop Tire and Rubber	UK

* The Olivetti investment has been terminated in 1968.

Although the figures are for the post-war period, similar cross-movements existed in the 1920's and 1930's.[1]

The existence of cross-direct investments

Interestingly enough, in almost all sectors of industry where American corporations have undertaken direct investments abroad, foreign companies have also established themselves in the United States. The list of companies in Table 68 is certainly not complete, but suggests that the cross-movement is of a general nature, and not due to chance occurrences.

The type of investor

Direct investments are concentrated in petroleum and manufacturing sectors (Table 69) and the main investors are business enterprises in those industries. If interest rates were the prime mover of capital, as the theory of international capital movements contends, then one would expect financial companies to do the moving. This is not the case with direct investments.

1. See CLEONA LEWIS, *America's Stake in International Investments* (Washington, D.C.: The Brookings Institution, 1938).

Table 69. Industry sector shares of total U.S. direct investments abroad: some selected years (in millions of dollars)

	1950	1957	1966
All industries	11,708	25,262	54,562
Manufacturing	3,831	8,009	22,050
	(32)	(31)	(40)
Petroleum	3,390	9,005	16,262
	(29)	(35)	(30)
Mining and smelting	1,129	2,361	4,135
	(10)	(10)	(8)
Banking and finance	170	423	n.a.
	(1.5)	(1.5)	
Trade and others	3,188	5,464	n.a.
	(27)	(21)	

(Figures in parentheses are percentages).
Source: US Department of Commerce, *Survey of Current Business*, September/October issues.

Table 70. Total and foreign sales of some U.S. companies in 1965 or 1966

Company	Total sales (in millions of dollars)	Percentage of foreign business to total	
American Home Products	910	14	
Pfifer (Chas.)	622	48	
Caterpillar Tractor	1,524	43	(1965)
International Harvester	2,583	27	(1965)
Union Carbide	2,224	34	
IBM	4,248	31	
Corn Products	1,048	44	(1965)
Colgate-Palmolive	932	54	(1965)
National Biscuit	720	21	
Bendix	1,052	41	
Eastman Kodak	1,742	33	
General Motors	20,209	14	
Singer	1,049	51	

Source: 1965 data: RAYMOND VERNON, *Manager in the International Economy* (Englewood Cliffs, N.J.: Prentice-Hall, 1968), p. 170.
1966 data: *Investor's Reader*, MERRILL, LYNCH, PIERCE, FENNER and SMITH (New York, January, 1968).

The relation of foreign to domestic activities

Direct investments abroad are connected to the domestic activities of the multinational companies. Especially for American firms these foreign operations are assuming an increasingly important share of the total activities. In Table 70

Table 71. Expenditures on plant and equipment by U.S. companies allocated in the United States and abroad: selected manufacturing industries (in millions of dollars)

	1960		1963		1966	
	Total expenditures	Foreign % of total	Total expenditures	Foreign % of total	Total expenditures	Foreign % of total
Mining and petroleum	5,523	34	6,247	37	9,463	38
Food	1,017	10	1,102	12	1,645	13
Paper	828	9	854	16	1,731	16
Chemical	1,837	13	2,064	21	4,119	28
Rubber	298	23	338	29	618	30
Metals	1,143	12	1,304	16	2,265	20
Machinery	1,232	11	1,570	21	3,755	20
Electrical machinery	784	13	854	19	1,395	19
Transportation	1,646	20	2,120	25	4,109	27
Total selected industries	8,705	13	10,108	20	19,637	23

Source: US Department of Commerce, *Survey of Current Business*, September issues, 1966 data preliminary.

Table 72. Financing of U.S. direct investments abroad sources of funds: all areas, selected years (in millions of dollars)

	1957	1960	1963	1964	1965
Total sources	7,292	4,985	7,636	8,721	11,247
Capital from the US	2,033	1,046	1,393	1,422	2,490
	(28)	(21)	(18)	(16)	(22)
Retained earnings*	1,758	995	1,501	1,390	1,471
	(24)	(20)	(20)	(16)	(13)
Depreciation and	1,626	1,927	2,590	3,012	3,390
depletion allowances	(22)	(39)	(34)	(35)	(30)
Locally raised capital	1,718	1,017	2,056	2,743	3,578
	(24)	(20)	(27)	(31)	(32)
Other	167	n.a.	96	154	318
	(2)		(1)	(2)	(3)
* Net income	3,649	3,255	4,262	4,645	4,985
Paid out	1,819	2,260	2,761	3,255	3,514
Retained	1,758	995	1,501	1,390	1,471

(Figures in parentheses are percentage shares.)
Source: US Department of Commerce, *Survey of Current Business*, September issues. No data available for 1966 or 1967 yet.

Table 73. Area distribution of balance sheet items: Standard Oil of New Jersey and Royal Dutch Petroleum Companies

Standard Oil of New Jersey (millions of dollars)

	United States		Other countries		Total	
	50	*66*	*50*	*66*	*50*	*66*
Total assets	4,880	6,144	4,598	7,709	9,478	13,853
Total liabilities	979	1,370	2,042	3,501	3,021	4,871
Net assets	3,901	4,744	2,556	4,208	6,457	8,982

Royal Dutch Petroleum (millions of pounds)

	Europe plus Eastern Hemisphere		United States		Other		Total	
	58	*66*	*58*	*66*	*58*	*66*	*58*	*66*
Long term assets	660	1,717	347	735	490	561	1,497	3,031
Current assets – current liabilities	553	498	113	173	67	109	773	780
Long term liabilities	116	373	205	502	108	79	429	918
Net assets (1 + 2 — 3)	1,097	1,878	255	406	499	591	1,801	2,875

Source: Annual Reports for 1958 and 1966.

figures are presented for some of the better known US companies on total and foreign sales. (A complete list can be found in the cited publications.) Yet another indication of the importance of the foreign operations of US companies are the plant and equipment expenditures of these companies in the United States and abroad. Table 71 contains data for some selected years. The percentage of foreign to domestic investments increased from 13 percent in 1960 to almost 23 percent in 1966 for selected manufacturing industries.

Thus one can conclude that the foreign activities of American-based companies are of increasing importance: furthermore, these foreign activities are a direct outgrowth of, or closely related to their domestic operations.

The financing of the direct investment

US Department of Commerce data indicate that roughly one-fifth of total investments abroad by American companies is being financed by capital flows from the United States. The remainder comes from retained earnings abroad, depreciation and depletion allowances of foreign subsidiaries, and locally raised capital. The breakdown in sources of funds in Table 72 is illustrative. If one regards the retained earnings also as new capital from the United States the share of US capital in total funds has been around 35 percent. Local borrowing is becoming increasingly important, and financed roughly 32 percent of total outlays in 1965.

Direct investments by foreign based companies in the United States is financed almost completely by reinvested earnings, depreciation and depletion allowances, and by capital raised in the United States itself. Occasionally rather large capital inflows from abroad supplement these sources.

If interest rates indeed would determine capital flows connected with direct investments one would certainly not expect that in addition to US capital, locally raised funds were used to finance the investments. In this connection the balance sheet items of two big petroleum companies both actively engaged in direct investments are illustrative (Table 73). These two companies borrow considerably wherever they have undertaken direct investments.

One can conclude from these observations that direct and portfolio investments are two different types of international investment, and that a separate treatment of direct investments is therefore justified.

II. Data collection

Following is the questionnaire form sent to US direct investment enterprises in the Netherlands, operating by the end of 1966.

Survey of US Affiliated or Associated
Companies in Manufacturing Industries
(operating in the Netherlands by the end of 1966)

Confidential: Information requested in this survey is to be used exclusively for the preparation of statistics and the testing of theoretical propositions. Reports of individual companies will be treated in strict confidence and only aggregated industry figures will be published.

If, for any reason, not all the requested information can be supplied, I would appreciate receiving the partially completed survey anyway.

1. Name of the reporting company: ....

2. Please describe briefly the type and nature of business of your company in the Netherlands, including principal products manufactured and services rendered.

....
....
....
....
....

3a. Does the US company, with which your firm is affiliated or associated, engage in a program of research and development?

1 [   ] Yes   2 [   ] No

IF YES: ↓

> 3b. Is any of the US company's research and development effort farmed out to the Netherlands or other Western European countries?
> Could you indicate what percentage of the total research and development takes place in the Netherlands and the rest of Western Europe respectively?
>
> | | % of Total R & D |
> |---|---|
> | 1 [   ] The Netherlands . . . . | |
> | 2 [   ] Other Western Europe. . . . . . | |

172

4. The information from the following section is to be used for a comparison of the scale of operation of US affiliated or associated and Dutch companies in the same industry.

> 4a. Please indicate the approximate amount of the total investment of your company in plant, machinery, land and buildings in the Netherlands by the end of 1966.
>
> .... Approximate amount in Dutch guilders
>
> Could you specify whether you are using:
>
> 1 ☐ Market value (present prices)
>
> 2 ☐ Historical value (actually paid prices)
>
> 4b. How many factories (or plants) did your company have in the Netherlands at the end of 1966?
>
> .... Number of factories at the end of 1966
>
> 4c. How many employees did your company have in the Netherlands in 1966? Please give the information for the end of September or the beginning of October to enable a meaningful comparison with Dutch statistics.
>
> .... Number of employees by end September or beginning October
>
> 4d. Does your company also sell finished products that are *not* produced by the company in the Netherlands, but, e.g., imported from the US company?
>
> 1 ☐ Yes   2 ☐ No
>
> IF YES: ↓
>
> > 4e. Approximately how many employees of the total given in question 4c are working in this line of activity?
> >
> > .... Number of employees working on storage and sale of imported finished products
>
> 4f. Please indicate below the size of your factories in the Netherlands in terms of the number of employees, measured around the end of September or the beginning of October of 1966. Please be sure to show the number of factories in each category.
>
> | Size by number of employees | Number of factories in each category | Size by number of employees | Number of factories in each category |
> |---|---|---|---|
> | 1– 10 . . . . | | 351– 500 . . . | |
> | 11– 20 . . . . | | 501– 750 . . . | |
> | 21– 50 . . . . | | 751–1000 . . . | |
> | 51–100 . . . . | | 1001–1500 . . . | |
> | 101–200 . . . . | | 1501 and up . . | |
> | 201–350 . . . . | | | |

5. The information requested below will be used for an analysis of the effects of American direct investment abroad on international trade flows.

5a.	How much were the total sales of your company in the Netherlands in 1966? (in guilders)	Hfl.
5b.	How much of this total consisted of finished products imported from:	
	1. The US company with which your firm is associated or affiliated (in guilders)	Hfl.
	2. Other affiliates or subsidiaries of the same US company that are operating in or outside of the United States (in guilders).	Hfl.
5c.	Approximately how much of your total sales was exported (in guilders or percentages).	
5d.	Could you indicate how much of the total exports in 1966 went to:	
	1. The United States (in guilders or percentages) . .	
	2. The Common Market (in guilders or percentages)	

5e. Did your company import, in 1966, any raw materials or semi-finished products from:

	Yes	No
1. The US company with which your firm is associated	☐	☐
2. Other affiliates or subsidiaries of the same American company	☐	☐

IF YOUR ANSWER WAS 'YES' TO EITHER PART 1 OR 2 FROM QUESTION 5e ABOVE, PLEASE ANSWER QUESTION 5f. IF 'NO,' PLEASE GO ON TO THE NEXT PAGE.

If you answered 'yes' to question 5e:

5f. What percentage are the imports from the US company or one of its other affiliates or subsidiaries of the total production in the Netherlands in the year 1966?

(Total production = the value of all finished goods and services produced in the Netherlands)

Please check one box for the approximate percentage of imports

1	☐	Less than 5%	6	☐	30–40%
2	☐	5–10%	7	☐	40–50%
3	☐	10–15%	8	☐	50–60%
4	☐	15–20%	9	☐	60–75%
5	☐	20–30%	10	☐	More than 75%

6. Please list below the individual product or products that together made up 80%
   or more of your total sales in the Netherlands for the year 1966.
   If possible, could you also indicate in the column to the right the share of each
   product in the total sales?

Products that together accounted for 80% or more of total sales in 1966		Percentage share of each product
1.	. . . .	....
2.	. . . .	....
3.	. . . .	....
4.	. . . .	....
5.	. . . .	....

7. Were the products that are now manufactured by your company in the Netherlands
   previously imported from

	Yes	No
1. The US company with which your firm is affiliated/ associated	☐	☐
2. Another affiliate or subsidiary of the same American company.	☐	☐

8a. Before becoming affiliated to or associated with the US company, was your firm
    already in operation or was a new firm established?

    1 ☐ Already in operation   2 ☐ New firm established

    IF YOUR COMPANY WAS ALREADY IN OPERATION:

    > 8b. What motives led to the decision to start an affiliation or association with
    > the American company?
    >
    > ....
    > ....
    > ....
    > ....

9. What was the degree of US ownership in your company's share capital at the end
   of 1966?

1 ☐	100%		4 ☐	50%	
2 ☐	75–99%		5 ☐	25–49%	
3 ☐	51–74%		6 ☐	Less than 25%	

A possibility exists that the survey will be followed up by personal interviews in the
Netherlands. In case this possibility materializes, I would like to know the name of the
person who can be contacted concerning these data.

 .... Name of the person to be contacted

III. Presentation of the data

Following is detailed information collected in the survey of US direct investment enterprises in the Netherlands in 1966.
a. 95 fully completed questionnaires (Table 74).
b. 16 partially completed questionnaires (Table 75).
c. Motivation of existing Dutch companies to associate or affiliate with an American enterprise (answers to question 8b of the questionnaire).

Table 74. Detailed results of complete questionnaires: by industry group – 1966

Industrial sector	No. of firms	Value of the investment (dollars)		No. of plants	Employees		
		Total	us share		Total	On imports*	On production
Food, beverages, tobacco	5	31,892	26,490	14	3,220	–	3,220
Textiles	9	13,702	9,305	9	1,008	–	1,008
Wearing apparel	2	2,044	1,395	6	723	10	713
Printing, publishing	1	2,127	787	1	172	–	172
Rubber	1	16,989	2,888	1	1,556	–	1,556
Chemicals	24	134,162	102,588	28	2,899	142	2,757
Petroleum	4	308,756	308,756	5	3,320	5	3,315
Metal products	13	7,823	6,022	14	1,452	20	1,432
Machinery, except electrical	21	18,864	17,826	31	4,849	443	4,406
Electrical equipment	6	9,127	7,970	8	1,638	46	1,592
Transportation	2	6,133	5,479	2	1,650	200	1,450
Control, scientific instruments	6	5,088	5,038	7	1,241	73	1,168
Photography	1	4,972	4,972	1	410	26	384
Total	95	561,679	499,516	127	24,138	965	23,173

* handling imported finished products for resale.
† imported finished products.
Source: 95 completed questionnaires.

Total sales	Imports †			Exports		
	Total	From parent	From other affiliate	Total	To EEC	To US
54,964	1,137	–	1,137	29,437	8,035	2,052
30,764	663	–	663	24,753	20,606	–
4,356	1,362	9	1,354	1,434	1,064	–
3,978	–	–	–	2,785	1,170	–
17,182	–	–	–	5,746	3,149	–
156,788	39,069	31,664	7,405	116,106	45,924	757
333,094	45,028	–	45,028	125,000	49,647	3,347
19,114	4,162	1,448	2,714	5,987	3,736	180
48,289	6,433	3,836	2,597	31,247	14,428	1,182
25,885	9,176	433	8,743	7,251	4,506	162
108,425	70,994	552	70,442	21,354	21,354	–
22,604	1,809	1,806	–	15,920	11,572	75
1,713	939	939	–	1,541	1,156	77
827,154	180,773	40,688	140,085	382,562	186,347	7,833

Table 75. Detailed information of partially completed questionnaires (16 companies)

Industrial sector	No. of firms	Value of the investment (000 dollars)		No. of plants	Employees		
		Total	us share		Total	On imports	On production
Food, beverages, tobacco	2	n.a.	n.a.	3	1,250	–	1,250
Textiles	1	n.a.	n.a.	1	90	–	90
Chemicals	5	34,669	16,254	5	1,199	–	1,199
Glass*	1	n.a.	n.a.	1	200	–	200
Metal products	4	1,547†	975**	4	619	–	619
Electrical equipment	2	n.a.	n.a.	1	570	220	350
Control, scientific instruments	1	9	9	1	15	–	15

	Sales (000 dollars)						
	Imports			Exports			
tal es	Total	From parent	From other affiliatie	Total	To EEC	To US	Notes
,000	–	–	–	4,678	3,255	930	Only 1 company provided sales data.
359	–	–	–	20	4	14	
a.	n.a.	n.a.	n.a.	Ranging from 70 to 90% of total sales	Ranging from 33 to 63% of exports	Ranging from 0 to 5% of exports	4 companies provided investment data as well as export percentages
a.	n.a.	n.a.	n.a.	n.a.	n.a.	n.a.	
a.	n.a.	n.a.	n.a.	Ranging from 15 to 60% of total sales	Ranging from 40 to 90% of total exports	Ranging from 0 to 10% of total exports	3 companies provided investment as well as export data.
000	290	290		Ranging from 70 to 90% of total sales	Ranging from 60 to 80% of total exports	–	Only 1 company gave data on employment factories and sales. Both gave export data.
a.	n.a.	n.a.	n.a.	94%	25%	–	

This company was willing to cooperate but in process of reorganization.

3 companies.

2 companies.

ource: 16 partially completed questionnaires.

c. Motivation of existing Dutch companies to associate or affiliate with an American enterprise. (Answers to question 8b of the questionnaire, translated when necessary.)

1. a) Feeling that association with a large US based international company would enhance growth.

b) Impending retirement of head of owning family and desire to withdraw from active business [Food sector].

2. Reinforcement of our financial situation in order to materialize necessary expansions [Tobacco].

3. To get an entry into the EEC and enable the parent to penetrate further into European markets [Food].

4. The owners sold the stock [Food].

5. American company was interested to join the Common Market [Textiles].

6. Strengthening of technological and financial position in increasing competition [Chemical].

7. Technological know-how and investment problems [Chemical].

8. Combining know-how and R & D [Chemical].

9. Developed from long term representation [Chemical].

10. Dutch trading company merged with the present American parent in 1925 to provide the US company with permanent sales organization in Europe and to secure continuous supply (of raw materials) for the Dutch company. In 1960's local production started to take the best possible advantage from the Common Market [Chemical].

11. Association was sought in order to establish a broader basis for business and to ensure continuity for the enterprise [Chemical].

12. In the family-owned company there was no capable member of family available to take over management in case of death or retirement. Also, wish to have support of bigger company for research and development [Chemical].

13. Need for capital, acquisition of technical know-how [Chemical].

14. The American company, in partnership with an international concern, acquired the existing company. Market potential which has proved successful in the United States [Chemical].

15. In 1891 the company was established by a broker's firm in Rotterdam, which up till then had been importing the product from the parent company. In the course of spreading its interests the US company increased its ownership, becoming a majority share holder during World War I and a 100% owner after World War II [Petroleum].

16. Need for technological know-how [Glass].

17. Better growth and development [Metal Products].

18. Dutch company completely passive – initiative by US firm [Metal Products].

19. Personal motives of single owner [Metal Products].

20. Because our Canadian mother company was bought up we automatically became a daughter of the us company [Metal Products].

21. Expansion of operations [Metal Products].

22. To face the competition and to keep a grip on the markets in Western Europe [Metal Products].

23. In order to put up a new production line, which until the association was not an end product of the Dutch company [Metal Products].

24. Enlarging penetration in the market resulting in faster growth and expansion of business [Machinery].

25. Not profitable, was owned by one family [Machinery].

26. We are operating in the public sector and liked to enter a market of durable consumer goods [Machinery].

27. Operation was purchased from other foreign company [Transportation].

28. Before affiliation to the us company the existing firm has been representing the us firm as sole agent for almost 8 years. Due to growing volume of business for the American firm, there was a need to start manufacturing in Europe. Negotiations then started with the existing (Dutch) firm with the result that the firm is now 100% affiliated to the American company [Scientific and Control Instruments].

29. Two us investment funds bought 60% of the shares, then made offer to various us firms from which present 'mother' was mutually agreed the best fit with own line for future [Scientific and Control Instruments].

30. Before affiliation production was restricted to bulk division – the wish to add package division [Other Industries].

Bibliography

BOOKS

ADLER, JOHN H. (ed.), *Capital Movements and Economic Development* [Proceedings of a Conference held by the International Economic Association] (St. Martin's Press: New York, 1967).

BAIN, JOE S., *International Differences in Industrial Structure: Eight Countries in the 1950's* (New Haven and London: Yale University Press, 1966).

BARBOUR, VIOLET, *Capitalism in Amsterdam in the 17th Century* (Ann Arbor, Michigan: University of Michigan Press, 1963).

BAUMOL, WILLIAM J., *Business Behavior, Value and Growth* (New York: Harcourt, Brace and World, Inc., 1967), Revised Edition.

BEHRMAN, JACK N., *Manufacturing Investment and the Balance of Payments* (New York: National Foreign Trade Council, 1969).

BELL, PHILLIP W., 'Private Capital Movements and the Balance of Payments Position', *Factors Affecting the U.S. Balance of Payments* (US Congress, Joint Economic Committee, 87th Congress, 2nd session, 1962).

BERTIN, GILLES-Y., *Les Investissements des Firmes Etrangères en France* (Paris: Presses Universitaires de France, 1963).

BONIN, BERNARD, *L'Investissement Etranger à Long Terme au Canada: Ses Caractères et ses Effets sur l'Economie Canadienne* (Paris: Thèse, Université de Paris, 1966). This dissertation has been published under the same title by the 'Presses de l'Ecole des Hautes Etudes Commerciales de Montreal'.

BOSCH, K. D., *De Nederlandse Beleggingen in de Verenigde Staten* (Amsterdam, Brussels: Uitgeversmaatschappij Elsevier, 1949).

BRASH, DONALD T., *American Investment in Australian Industry* (Canberra: Australian National University Press, 1966).

BRECHER, I. AND REISMANN, S. S., *Canada – United States Economic Relations* (Ottawa: Royal Commission on Canada's Economic Prospects, 1957).

BURENSTAM-LINDEN, S., *An Essay on Trade and Transformation* (New York: Wiley, 1961).

CAIRNCROSS, A. K., *Home and Foreign Investment: 1870–1913* [Studies in Capital Accumulation] (Cambridge: At the University Press, 1953).

CASSEL, GUSTAV, et al., *Foreign Investments* [Lectures on the Harris Foundation] (Chicago, Ill.: The University of Chicago Press, 1928).

CHRISTEN, RUDOLF MATTHIAS, *Die Amerikanischen Auslands-Investitionen in der Nachkriegszeit* [Ihre Motive und Wirkungen] (Winterthur: Verlag P. G. Keller, 1966).

CIPOLLA, CARLO M., *Guns and Sails in the Early Phase of European Expansion, 1400–1700* (London: Collins, 1965).

DUNN, ROBERT W., *American Foreign Investments* (New York: B. W. Huebsch and the Viking Press, 1926).

DUNNING, JOHN H., *American Investment in British Manufacturing Industry* (London: George Allen and Unwin Limited, 1958).

FANNO, MARCO, *Normal and Abnormal International Capital Transfers* (London: H. Milford, Oxford University Press, 1939).

FRANKS, H. GEORGE, *Holland's Industries Stride Ahead – The New Netherlands of the 1960's* (Federation of Netherlands Industries, 1961).

GALBRAITH, JOHN K., *The New Industrial State* (Boston: Houghton-Mifflin Company, 1967).

GARVAN, F. P., *Hot Money vs. Frozen Funds* (New York: Chemical Foundation Inc., 1937).

GATES, T. R. and LINDEN, F., *Costs and Competition: American Experience Abroad* (New York: National Industrial Conference Board, 1961).

GERVAIS, JACQUES, *La France Face aux Investissements Etrangers* (Paris: Editions de l'Entreprise Moderne, 1963).

HARTMAN, HEINZ, *Amerikanische Firmen in Deutschland* (Köln und Opladen: Westdeutscher Verlag, 1963).

HELLMANN, RAINER, *Amerika auf dem Europamarkt* (Baden-Baden: Nomosverlagsgesellschaft, 1966).

HIRSCHMAN, ALBERT O., *The Strategy of Economic Development* (New Haven: Yale University Press, 1958).

HOLLANDER, JACQUES, *Les Investissements Américains en Belgique* (Bruxelles: Les Editions du Centre Paul Hymans, 1963).

HOMAN, A. GERLOF, *Some Measures and Interpretations of the Effects of the Operations of U.S. Foreign Enterprises on the U.S. Balance of Payments* (Menlo Park: Stanford Research Institute, 1962).

HUFBAUER, G. C. and ADLER, F. M., *Overseas Manufacturing Investment and the Balance of Payments* (Washington, D.C.: US Treasury Department, 1968).

HYMER, STEPHEN H., *The International Operations of National Firms: A Study of Direct Investment* (Cambridge: MIT Ph. D. Dissertation, 1965).

HYMER, STEPHEN H., 'Direct Foreign Investment and the National Economic Interest', in: PETER RUSSEL (ed.), *Nationalism in Canada* (Toronto: McGraw-Hill, 1966), pp. 191–202.

IVERSEN, CARL, *Aspects of the Theory of International Capital Movements* (Copenhagen: Levin and Munksgaard, 1935).

JOHNSON, HARRY G., *The Canadian Quandary* (Toronto: McGraw-Hill, 1963).

JOHNSTONE, ALLAN W., *United States Direct Investment in France: An Investigation of the French Charges* (Cambridge: The MIT Press, 1966).

KINDLEBERGER, CHARLES P., *International Economics*, Revised 3rd Edition (Homewood, Illinois: R.D. Irwin, 1963).

KINDLEBERGER, CHARLES P., *Foreign Trade and the National Economy* (New Haven: Yale University Press, 1962).

KINDLEBERGER, CHARLES P., *Europe's Post War Growth: the Role of Labor Supply* (Cambridge, Mass.: Harvard University Press, 1967).

KINDLEBERGER, CHARLES P., *American Business Abroad: Six Lectures on Direct Investment* (New Haven: Yale University Press, 1969).

KLOPSTOCK, FRED H., *The Euro-Dollar Market: Some Unresolved Issues*, Essays in International Finance (Princeton, N.J.: Princeton University Press, March, 1968).

KOHLER, MARC, *The Common Market and Investments* (New York: Vantage Press, 1960).

KRAUSE, L. B. and DAM, K. W., *Federal Tax Treatment of Foreign Income* (Washington, D.C.: The Brookings Institution, 1964).

KREININ, M. E., *Alternative Commercial Policies – Their Effect on the American Economy* (East Lansing: Michigan State University, 1967).

KUBY, HEINZ F., *Provokation Europa* (Köln: Kiepenheuer und Witsch, 1965).

LAMFALUSSY, A., *Investment and Growth in Mature Economics* (Oxford: Blackwell, 1961).

LANDAU, HENRI, et al., *Doing Business Abroad* (New York: Practising Law Institute, 1962).

LAYTON, CHRISTOPHER, *Trans-Atlantic Investments* (Boulogne-sur-Seine: The Atlantic Institute, 1966).

LETICHE, JOHN M., *Balance of Payments and Economic Growth* (New York: Harper, 1959); Revised Edition (New York: Augustus M. Kelly, 1967).

LETICHE, JOHN M., 'US Direct Investment and the Balance of Payments', in *Industrial Policy of an Integrated Europe and the Supply of Foreign Capital* (Paris, 1968).

LEWIS, CLEONA, *America's Stake in International Investments* (Washington, D.C.: The Brookings Institution, 1938).

LEWIS, CLEONA, *Debtor and Creditor Countries: 1938–1944* (Washington, D.C.: The Brookings Institution, 1945).

LEWIS, CLEONA, *The U.S. and Foreign Investment Problems* (Washington, D.C.: The Brookings Institution, 1948).

LUCRON, C. P., *Croissance Economique et Investissement International* (Paris: Presses Universitaires de France, 1961).

LUND, HARALD, *Svenska Företags Investeringar i Utlandet* (Katrineholm: Sörmlands Grafiska AB, 1967).

LYNDEN, C. D. A. VAN, *Directe Investeeringen in het Buitenland* ('s-Gravenhage: Fa. L. J. C. Boucher, 1945).

McCREARY, EDWARD A., *The Americanisation of Europe: The Impact of Americans and American Business on the Uncommon Market* (Garden City, N.Y.: Doubleday, 1964).

MARTYN, HOWE, *International Business, Principles and Problems* (London: Collier-MacMillan Ltd., 1964).

MIKESELL, RAYMOND F., ed., *U.S. Private and Government Investment Abroad* (Eugene: University of Oregon Press, 1962).

MURLEY, S. A., *American Corporate Investment Abroad Since 1919* (University of California at Berkeley, Ph. D. Dissertation, 1965).

MULDAU, BERND, *U.S. Investitionen in der E.W.G.* (Hamburg: Verlag Weltarchiv, 1966).

NICB, *Obstacles and Incentives to Private Foreign Investment: 1962–1964* [The experience of the investors of twelve nations in eighty-eight countries] (New York: National Industrial Conference Board, 1965).

NURKSE, RAGNAR, *Internationale Kapitalbewegungen* (Wien: Springer Verlag, 1935).

NURKSE, RAGNAR, *Equilibrium and Growth in the World Economy* [Economic Essays by Ragnar Nurkse, ed. by GOTTFRIED HABERLER and ROBERT M. STERN] (Cambridge, Mass.: Harvard University Press, 1961).

OHLIN, BERTIL, *Interregional and International Trade*, Revised Edition (Cambridge, Mass.: Harvard University Press, 1967).

PEARSON, LESTER B. (Chairman), *Report of the Commission on International Development* (Washington, New York: Praeger, 1969).

PENROSE, EDITH T., *The large international firm in developing countries: the International Petroleum Industry* (London: Allen and Unwin, 1968).

POLK, JUDD, MEISTER, IRENE W. and VEIT, LAWRENCE A., *U.S. Production Abroad and the Balance of Payments* [A Survey of Corporate Investment Experience] (New York: The National Industrial Conference Board, 1966).

REDDAWAY, W. B. (with others), *Effects of U.K. Direct Investment Overseas – An Interim Report* (Cambridge: University of Cambridge Press, paper # 12, 1967).

REDDAWAY, W. B., et al., *Effects of U.K. Direct Investment Overseas – Final Report* (Cambridge: At the University Press, 1968).

ROBINSON, JOAN, *The New Mercantilism: An Inaugural Lecture* (Cambridge: At the University Press, 1966).

SAFARIAN, A. E., *Foreign Ownership of Canadian Industry* (Toronto: McGraw-Hill Co., 1966).

SALANT, WALTER S., et al., *The United States Balance of Payments in 1968* (Washington, D.C.: The Brookings Institution, 1963).

SCHUMPETER, JOSEPH A., *Capitalism, Socialism and Democracy*, 3rd Edition (New York: Harper and Brothers Publishers, 1950).

SERVAN-SCHREIBER, JEAN-JACQUES, *Le Défi Américain* (Paris: Denoel, 1967). American edition, *The American Challenge* (New York: Atheneum, 1967).

SODERSTEN, BO, *A Study of Economic Growth and International Trade* (Stockholm: Almqvist and Wiksell, 1964).

SOUTHARD, FRANK A., *American Industry in Europe* (Boston and New York: Houghton-Mifflin Company 1931).

STANDKE, K. H., *Betriebswirtschaftliche Aspekte Amerikanischer Investitionspolitik in der E.W.G.* (Berlin: R.K.W. Frankfurt, 1965).

STEVENS, GUY V. G., *Fixed Investments Expenditures of Foreign Manufacturing Affiliates of U.S. Firms: Theoretical Models and Empirical Evidence* (Yale University, Ph. D. Dissertation, 1967).

STONEHILL, ARTHUR I., *Foreign Ownership in Norwegian Enterprise* (Oslo: Central Bureau of Statistics, 1965).

SWANN, D. and MCLACHLAN, D. L., *Concentration or Competition: A European Dilemma* (London: The Chatham House/P.E.P. Despatch Department, 1967).

SWOBODA, ALEXANDER, *The Euro-Dollar Market: An Interpretation* [Essays in International Finance] (Princeton: Princeton University Press, February, 1968).

TRIFFIN, ROBERT, *The Balance of Payments and the Foreign Investment Position of the*

United States [Essays in International Finance] (Princeton: Princeton University Press, September, 1966).

VERNON, RAYMOND, *Manager in the International Economy* (Englewood Cliffs, N.J.: Prentice-Hall, Inc., 1968).

VINER, JACOB, *International Economics: Studies by Jacob Viner* (Glencoe, Illinois: The Free Press, 1951).

WELLS, S. J., *British Export Performance: A Comparative Study* (Cambridge: At the University Press, 1964).

ARTICLES

ALBREGTS, PROF. DR. A. H. M., 'De Omvang en Betekenis van de Nederlandse Directe Investeringen in het Buitenland', *De Economist*, Jaargang 110, No. 12, December, 1962, pp. 813–827.

ARNDT, H. W., 'A Suggestion for Simplifying the Theory of International Capital Movements', *Economia Internazionale*, Vol. VII, August, 1954, pp. 469–81.

ARNDT, H. W., 'Overseas Borrowing – The New Model', *The Economic Record*, Vol. 33, August, 1957, pp. 247–260.

BALOGH, T. and STREETEN, P. P., 'Domestic Versus Foreign Investment', *Bulletin of the Oxford University Institute of Statistics*, Vol. 22, August, 1960, No. 3, pp. 213–224.

BOTZEN, DR. F. W., 'De Positie van Nederland in de Stroom van Amerikaans Investeringskapitaal voor West-Europa', *Economisch-Statistische Berichten*, 1 mei 1968, 53e Jaargang, No. 2642, pp. 423–26.

BOTZEN, DR. F. W., 'Investeringen in Vaste Activa (Investments in Fixed Assets)', *Economische Voorlichting*, No. 7, 12 februari 1964, pp. 4–6.

BOTZEN, DR. F. W., 'De Amerikaanse Investeringen in Nederland', *Economisch-Statistische Berichten*, 28 augustus 1968, 53e jaargang, No. 2659, pp. 794–795.

BOURRINET, JACQUES, 'Note sur l'Afflux des Investissements Directs Américains dans la CEE', *Revue Economique*, juillet, 1966, No. 4, Vol. 17, pp. 537–559.

CHAKRAVARTY, S., 'A Structural Study of International Capital Movements', *Economia Internazionale*, August, 1961, Vol. 14, No. 3, pp. 377–403.

CLARK, JOHN M., 'Towards a Concept of Workable Competition', *American Economic Review*, June, 1940. Reproduced in: *Readings in the Social Control of Industry* (Philadelphia: The Blakiston Company, 1949), pp. 452–475.

CORDEN, W. M., 'Protection and Foreign Investment', *The Economic Record*, Vol. 43, June, 1967, pp. 209–232.

CORDEN, W. M., 'Australian Economic Policy Discussion in the Post-War Period: A Survey', *American Economic Review*, Supplement, Part 2, Vol. LVIII, No. 3, June, 1968, pp. 89–138.

DAVIES, GETHYN, 'Direct Investments in Sterling Area Export Markets', *The Banker's Magazine*, July 1969, pp. 17–21.

DISCHAMPS, J.-C., 'L'Intégration Communautaire et l'Evolution des Investissements dans la CEE', *Revue Economique*, janvier, 1967, Vol. 18, No. 1.

DUNNING, JOHN H., 'UK Capital Exports and Canadian Economic Development', *Moorgate and Wallstreet*, Spring, 1962, pp. 3–38.

DUNNING, John H., 'The Foreign Investment Controversy', series of three articles in *The Bankers Magazine*, I-'The Return on Foreign Investment', May 1969, pp. 307–312; II-'The Effects of Foreign Investment on Resources', June 1969, pp. 354–360; III-'The Cost of Foreign Investment to the Investing Country', July 1969, pp. 21–25.

DUNNING, JOHN H. and ROWAN, D. C., 'British Direct Investment in Western Europe', *Banca Nazionale del Lavorno*, June, 1962.

EMERY, ROBERT F., 'The Relation of Exports and Economic Growth', *Kyklos*, Vol. XX, Fasc. 2, 1967, pp. 470–484.

FRANKEL, MARVIN, 'Home Versus Foreign Investments: A Case Against Capital Exports', *Kyklos*, Vol. XVIII, Fasc. 3, 1965, pp. 411–433.

GRAY, PETER H. and MAKINEN, GAIL E., 'The Balance-of-Payments Contributions of Multinational Corporations', *The Journal of Business*, Vol. 40, No. 3, July, 1967, pp. 339–343.

GRUBER, W., MEHTA, D. and VERNON, R., 'The R & D Factor in International Trade and International Investment of United States Industries', *Journal of Political Economy*, February, 1967, Vol. 75, No. 1, pp. 20–37.

HAMADA, JOICHI, 'Economic Growth and Long Term International Capital Movements', *Yale Economic Essays*, Spring, 1966.

JASAY, A. E., 'The Social Choice Between Home and Overseas Investment', *The Economic Journal*, March, 1960, Vol. LXX, No. 277, pp. 105–113.

JOHNS, B. L., 'Private Overseas Investment in Australia – Profitability and Motivation', *The Economic Record*, June, 1967, Vol. 43, pp. 233–61.

JONG, H. W. DE, and ALKEMA, E. A., *Communication du Côté de l' 'Europa Instituut' de l'Université de Leyde*, No. 13.530/IV/67-F.

JORGENSON, DALE W., 'Capital Theory and Investment Behavior', *American Economic Review*, Vol. 53, No. 2, May, 1963, pp. 247–259. See pp. 248–251 for summary of theory.

KARSTEN, C. F., 'Should Europe Restrict US Investments?', *Harvard Business Review*, September-October, 1965, pp. 53–59.

KEESING, D. B., 'The Impact of R and D on US Trade', *Journal of Political Economy*, Vol. 75, No. 1, February, 1967, pp. 38–48.

KEMP, M. C., 'Foreign Investments and the National Interest', *The Economic Record*, Vol. 38, No. 81, March, 1962, pp. 56–62.

KEYNES, JOHN M., 'Foreign Investment and the National Advantage', *The Nation and the Atheneum*, August, 1924.

KOO, ANTHONY Y. C., 'A Short-Run Measure of the Relative Economic Contribution of Direct Foreign Investment', *The Review of Economics and Statistics*, Vol. XLIII, No. 3, August, 1961, pp. 269–276.

LETICHE, JOHN M., 'US Direct Investment and the Balance of Payments', in: *Industrial Policy of an Integrated Europe and the Supply of Foreign Capital*, Paris, 1968.

LETICHE, JOHN M., 'European Integration: An American View', *Lloyds Bank Review*, January, 1965, pp. 1–22.

MACDOUGALL, G. D. A., 'The Benefits and Costs of Private Investment from Abroad – A Theoretical Approach', *The Economic Record*, Vol. 36, No. 73, March, 1960, pp. 13–35.

MAIN, JEREMY, 'The European Who Thinks the US Has All the Answers', *Fortune*, September 1, 1968, pp. 165–166. (Review of 'The American Challenge' by Jean-Jacques Servan-Schreiber.)

MAY, RONALD S., 'Direct Investments in the Less-Developed Countries, British and American Investments, 1958–1964', *The Journal of Development Studies*, Vol. 4, No. 3, April, 1968, pp. 386–423.

MOFFATT, G. G., 'The Foreign Ownership and Balance-of-Payments Effects of Direct Investments from Abroad', *Australian Economic Papers*, Vol. 6, No. 8, June, 1967, pp. 1–24.

MURPHY, J. CARTER, 'International Investment and the National Interest', *The Southern Economic Journal*, Vol. XXVII, No. 1, March, 1960, pp. 11–17.

NURKSE, RAGNAR, 'International Investment Today in the Light of 19th Century Experience', *The Economic Journal*, Vol. 64, December, 1954, pp. 744–58.

PENROSE, EDITH T., 'Foreign Investment and the Growth of the Firm', *The Economic Journal*, Vol. LXVII, No. 262, June, 1956, pp. 220–236.

PERKINS, J. O. N., 'Some Fallacies About Overseas Borrowing', *The Australian Quarterly*, June, 1960, pp. 74–88.

PHILLIPS, E. A., 'American Direct Investments in West-German Manufacturing Industries, 1945–1959', *Current Economic Comment*, Vol. 22, No. 2, 1960, pp. 29–44.

RHOMBERG, RUDOLF R. and BOISSONNEAULT, LORETTE, 'Effects of Income and Price Changes on the US Balance of Payments', *I.M.F. Staff Papers*, Vol. XI, March, 1964, pp. 59–124.

ROLFE, SIDNEY E., 'The International Corporation in Perspective', *The Atlantic Community Quarterly*, Summer 1969, pp. 255–261.

SCAPERLANDA, ANTHONY E. and MAURER, LAURENCE J., 'The Determinants of US Direct Investment in the EEC', *American Economic Review*, September 1969, pp. 558–568.

SINGER, H. W., 'The Distribution of Gains between Investing and Borrowing Countries', *American Economic Review*, Vol. XL, No. 2, May, 1950, pp. 473–485.

SMIDT, M. DE, 'Foreign Industrial Establishments Located in the Netherlands', *Tijdschrift voor Economische en Sociale Geografie*, 57ste jaargang, No. 1, januari/februari 1968, pp. 1–19.

SOLOW, HERBERT, 'The Dutch Get Private Dollars', *Fortune*, September, 1954, pp. 120–131.

STUBENITSKY, FRANK, 'Annual American Investment Outlays in the Netherlands – A Comment', *Economisch-Statistische Berichten*, 21 augustus 1968, No. 2658, pp. 771–774.

STUBENITSKY, FRANK, 'Amerikaanse Ondernemingen in Nederland in 1966', *Economisch-Statistische Berichten*, 3 September 1969, pp. 839–846.

TROWBRIDGE, ALEXANDER B., 'The Facts about the Gap', *The Atlantic Community Quarterly*, Vol. 5, No. 3, Fall, 1967, pp. 392–401.

VERNON, RAYMOND, 'Saints and Sinners in Foreign Investment', *Harvard Business Review*, May-June, 1963, pp. 146–161.

VERNON, RAYMOND, 'International Investment and International Trade in the Product Cycle', *Quarterly Journal of Economics*, Vol. 80, May, 1966, pp. 190–207.

VERNON, RAYMOND, 'The Multinational Corporation', *The Atlantic Community Quarterly*, Vol. 5, No. 4, Winter, 1967–68, pp. 533–539.

WEINER, JOHN M., 'Developing a European Capital Market', *Lloyds Bank Review*, July, 1967, pp. 16–28.